S T A T E S

S0-BRX-686

S. Antonio

Laredo

LEGEND

- - - - Route Traveled by Author

onterrey Matamoros

Gulf of Mexico

TAMAULIPAS

Potosí

Tampico

POTOSÍ

ato

Tuxpan

a

Progreso

Mérida

Valladolid

Tula

Muna

Ticul

Tecax

Campeche

YUCATAN

TLAXCALA

oluca Mexico City

Veracruz

QUINTANA ROO

Cuernavaca

Puebla

MORELOS

VERACRUZ

CAMPECHE

TABASCO

o

Chilapa

OAXACA

Tlaxiaco

CHIAPAS

Chilpancingo

Acapulco

Tehuantepec

Salina Cruz

Tapachula

S. Benito

G U A T E M A L A

Crockett
Seven Mile Ford
Dec. 1860

GRINGO REBEL

(MEXICO 1913-1914)

PLATE I

The Author.
Mexico City, September 1914.

GRINGO REBEL

(MEXICO 1913-1914)

I. Thord-Gray

G.C.A., K.C.S., K.C.R., K.C.V., Ph.D., F.G.S., F.R.G.S.

Member Royal Academy of Arts and Sciences of Uppsala

University of Miami Press

Coral Gables, Florida, U. S. A.

To

my wife Winnifred
who urged me to write this book

also

to the memory of my compañeros,
General Miguel M. Acosta, and Indian
scouts Pedro, Tekwe, Jesus, Lopez,
Francisco — warriors all.

PREFACE

Ever since reading of Montezuma and his Aztec warriors when I was a boy I longed to visit Mexico, but this desire was not realized until 1913 when the country was in the grip of a Civil War. About forty-five years have elapsed since I left Mexico in 1914 to rejoin the British Army for World War I. During this period I have steadfastly declined to write about the revolution, although requested to do so by friends in Mexico and the United States, not to mention brothers and a raft of nephews, nieces and those in the fourth generation.

The purpose of writing at this time is to try and satisfy the seemingly increasing enthusiasm about Mexico among the younger generation and to encourage further knowledge of that country. The reader should remember, however, that my notes were written as I saw it, not yesterday, but half a century ago.

The material used comes from my personal field notes and letters sent home during the conflict. There are, however, several interesting episodes which can hardly be made public, incidents caused by the ambiguous struggle for advancement, often with fatal consequences.

These happenings have deliberately been erased from the original notes as their publication may cause embarrassment to some of my old friends or their surviving families. Besides, it wouldn't be cricket, as we are dealing with some young lieutenant or captain now perhaps a general, senator, governor, or president. Not less than six members of our revolutionary army of 1913-1914 became presidents of Mexico.

Geographically, Mexico is the third largest of the Latin American Republics with an area of about 767,000 square miles. In 1910 the population was a little over 15 million, but it had increased to about 27 million by 1959. The population of Mexico City in 1910 was 471,000, but I am to understand it jumped to over 3 million in 1959.

Generally speaking, northern Mexico was a desert-like region for about two hundred miles south from the American Border. It was comparatively sparsely populated, but the inhabitants were of strong and sturdy stock—the remnants of warrior and hunting tribes brought up to find a living the hard way. Farther south again, the vegetation becomes more luxurious and everything one plants grows as the climate is balmy, sometimes hot.

The inhabitants of Mexico are, one might say, made up of a conglomeration of various Indian tribes comprising about 30 per cent of the population and speaking some fifty different languages and dialects. Many of these preferred to converse in their own tribal tongue rather than Spanish: in fact most tribes in the remote regions spoke Spanish very badly in 1914, some not at all. About 60 per cent are White-Indian mestizos. With the exception of the upper class the White-Indians are, as a rule, more Indian than White in thought, culture and blood. About 10 per cent may be called pure White, but this includes most of the White foreigners.

The Mexicans are very proud of their ancestry whether Aztec, Tlaxcalan, Maya, Zapotec, Mixtec, Yaqui, Tarahumara, or other Indian, a mixture of White and Indian, or descending from a Spanish caballero or conquistador. In many families the accent is placed on the Indian kinship rather than the Spanish and some seem to wish to forget all Spanish connections. There are others, of course, who cling with pride to their Spanish descent.

The tourists never, and a very few educated Mexicans ever, see the wonderful panorama of the great sierras in Mexico. Here we find intensely picturesque and almost frightening scenery of uncommon beauty. In some places the precipitous defiles, known as *barrancas,* drop perpendicularly through solid rock for thousands of feet. When looking down into these, one stands in awe of the tremendous abyss, and indeed feels relatively very small and unimportant. One seems to be in another world, and in the twilight, with darkness below, a shiver may go through the spine for it reminds one of Dante's Inferno.

I. Thord-Gray

6800 Riviera Drive
Coral Gables 46, Florida, U.S.A.
September 3, 1960

CONTENTS

ILLUSTRATIONS

INTRODUCTION

This book is an historical perspective as seen by the non-Mexican writer while serving in the Rebel Cavalry through the turbulent Mexican Revolution of 1913-1914, which freed the Peons and Indians from the whipping-post and peonage slavery. However, it does not deal with all the faces, or all the fronts, of the revolution. It is confined as nearly as possible to the relatively narrow horizon of the cavalry, to where I was and what I saw. Certain insertions have, nevertheless, been made to obtain a more coherent picture of the whole.

The old and difficult peonage-cycle with its numerous insurrections exhausted itself with the flight of President Diaz or rather, perhaps, when General Huerta followed him into exile two years later in 1914. From that time began a new and better period for the working people in Mexico, although the great change did not take place until a few years later when the thunder of war had passed, and the greed of some of the leaders had been satisfied.

When we think of Mexico and wonder at its many perplexing social problems, or try to compare it with

17

other countries, we should in fairness to the Mexicans look back in time and try to understand the fundamental or underlying reasons for these conditions. To further our conception of Mexico's past, two appendices have been added. These contain some drastically contracted notes on the cause of revolution and the aftermath thereof.

This is done in the hope of clarifying, at least a little, the reasons for the hate against the White Man. If it does, it should, nevertheless, be remembered that abbreviated notes, like an incomplete map, cannot present a complete picture, nor can it show every bend in the road.

The social problems of Mexico in 1913-1914 became the great problem of Russia, in fact of the whole world, a short time thereafter. They are still pressing heavily upon the minds of deep thinking people, as revolution may be the cause, but not the reason of true liberty. Further, the Mexican revolution of which we speak cannot be brushed aside as an ordinary Latin American Insurrection or a *cuartelaso* (barrack revolt) for it was development—the inevitable process of political evolution.

A tremendous moral force seems to have been created by the tragedies endured by the people over the centuries, and was brought to life and action by the unethical methods of the *cientificos* (SEE INDEX). One might say that 1913 was the beginning of a New Age of internal strife, wholesale political retrogression, Revolutions and World Wars — the Epoch in which we now live.

I

The reason why to Mexico—With Pancho Villa—Pedro joins my staff—The battle of Tierra Blanca—A very young soldier—Gun-running—The story of Pancho Villa

The bar at the German Club in Shanghai was crowded with people when I entered to join an American friend for a gin-and-bitters before tiffin one day in October, 1913. Here were heated arguments, a bedlam of opinions, over the Mexican revolution now in full swing.

The Times of Malaya and other newspapers in the Far East had for some time released scattered items referring to the revolution, such as Madera's murder and the war against Huerta. Reports and rumors were telling of wholesale plunder, confiscation and murder by the revolutionaries.

The American, whom I will call Bradstock because he reminded me of an old friend in Cape Mounted Riflemen, hinted on several occasions that he was a free-lance newspaperman also interested in gathering material for a book. But he acted more like an agent

19

of some government nosing around for information. About ten months after this Shanghai meeting, I found him with the federal army in Jalisco, Mexico.

Baron von Trotta, a German international prototype, asserted in his forceful Junker manner, "All rebels should be strung up by the neck or shot as they are a danger to the peace of the world." My friend, Bradstock, surprised me by agreeing with the German when he lashed out at the methods used by the rebels to gain their ends in Mexico.

Mr. Alcantara, a nice looking Venezuelan, stood up for the revolution. He declared bluntly that those present did not know the facts nor the underlying reasons for the revolt, and added with some feeling, "My beloved country will also have a revolution some day to overthrow the dictatorship of Gomez."

Since all this news from Mexico seemed one-sided, and having nothing better to do, I decided to have a look for myself. Bradstock made a bet that the revolution would be over and lost before I could get there. The challenge was accepted and a passage to the United States was booked immediately. Then I called on the Mexican Consul and he kindly gave me a special permit to travel throughout Mexico for six months on archaeological and anthropological work. Thus prepared I landed in beautiful San Francisco in the early part of November 1913.

The following morning the newspapers mentioned a few words of a large Mexican federal force marching on Juarez to put down the revolution. As it was necessary to move quickly before the revolution petered out, I boarded the first train for El Paso, and put up at Hotel Paso del Norte. When settled in the hotel, I went out to gather information, particularly on Pancho Villa and Carranza, and found that the Carranzistas and Villistas were called bandits by the federals. The rebels returned the compliment with a name they considered worse and called the federals *cientificos* (SEE INDEX).

It was considered by everybody in El Paso that Villa was the undisputed rebel leader in northern Mexico, and all were surprised at Villa recognizing Carranza as First Chief (*Primer Jefe*) with headquarters far away in the State of Sonora. Americans, in the know, said this arrangement would not last for Villa was difficult to subordinate. Besides, his high strung temperament made him uncertain, capricious, almost freakish and he willfully did terrible things.

In spite of this information I was looking forward with some eagerness to meeting Pancho Villa, because he had done wonders, almost the impossible, as a cavalry leader, which was interesting to me, a cavalryman.

With Pancho Villa

No vehicles were allowed to cross over the International bridge into Mexico without special permit. I had to proceed on foot, but was detained by the U. S. Border Guard. They advised me to remain on the American side, as the Mexicans hated all foreigners and would soon dispatch me to the Happy Hunting Grounds. It took some time to convince them of my firm intention to go over and I was allowed to do so after showing the Mexican Consular permit from Shanghai. Once over the Rio Grande, it did not take

21

long to reach General Villa's headquarters, but many people seemed to follow my movements with suspicion and by their scowls it was evident that foreigners were not particularly trusted or wanted in this land.

After announcing myself, and waiting for half an hour, I was ushered into a large room and stood before Villa. My first impression of Pancho Villa, the reputed outlaw, bandit, murderer of hundreds, and general extraordinary, was not very bad in spite of his unsavory reputation, and his unshaven and somewhat unkept appearance. He was powerfully built, forceful looking, robustious, with a roundish large head and slightly bloated face. The lips were large and strong but sensuous . The upper lip was covered with a heavy stumpy mustache. The eyes were bloodshot as if in need of sleep. The hair was out of sight under a sombrero which was tilted back. He wore soft leather leggings reaching above the knee. His face was dirty looking but a gorilla-grin, not at all unkindly, illuminated his countenance which otherwise seemed hard and coarse.

As the great Villa did not condescend to look my way, there was time to observe that the unventilated room stank with noxious human exhalations, stale sweat-soaked clothing and cigarette smoke. A bunch of pretty hothouse flowers stood in front of Villa, stuck in an expensive blue Chinese jar from the Ming period, a beautiful museum piece.

Eventually Villa looked but when he saw me his face turned into a scowl, almost of anger, associated, it seemed to me, with arrogance or contempt. His whole attitude was a challenge, startling though not altogether objectionable. But, for the moment, it reminded one of a bull-ape beating his chest in the

African or Malayan jungle. I couldn't help feeling this was a pose or a show put on for the benefit of his staff to cover up some idiosyncrasies or, perhaps, not unlikely, to scare me.

When introduced by a staff officer, I saluted and presented my credentials from the Mexican Consul in Shanghai. General Villa did not return the salute nor did he in any way acknowledge my presence. In fact, he seemed completely oblivious of my existence which nettled me perhaps a little. He took the document from the officer and read it carefully, upside down, and then I realized Villa could not read. After "reading" the permit he passed it to an aide with a remark ,which in Mexico, I found later, is equivalent to son-of-bitch, or worse.

The staff officer, a thin, undersized, sallow-faced, half-breed Indian, looked at the letter and asked in good English, "Where did you obtain this permit to enter Mexico? Why are you here?" When I explained that my trip across the Pacific was for the purpose of archaeological research work in Mexico, but that I wished to join the revolutionary army, he looked incredulous and unconvinced but told his chief.

Evidently Villa did not believe my answer either, as he appeared enraged once more and the words, *"Gringo* spy," came from his almost frothing mouth. It was evident that this hard man's nerves were on edge. He was caught off his guard and looked repulsive. I seemed to have met baboons in South Africa better looking than Villa at this moment. He turned to me with blazing bloodshot eyes, shouting orders for me to get out of Mexico.

When requesting the return of my permit, Villa tore it up with some more juicy insults and accused me of being an American agent, sent to spy on him for Huerta in Mexico City.

There was nothing more for me to do. Not wishing to lose my temper, I walked out without saluting, to return to El Paso. It was obvious my long trip from China had been in vain, but I had not lost my bet with Bradstock which consoled me a little, perhaps. There was, of course, the Mexican Federal Army to be considered, but I dismissed the evil thought. Then it flashed through my mind to return to China and more friendly people.

On my way back through Villa's camp, however, I noticed two field guns by which stood a handsome but dejected looking officer, obviously not a Mexican. Having been through a course in Horse Artillery in the C.M.R. while in Pondoland, I became interested naturally and wanted to see what kind of guns they had in Mexico, and stopped.

I found the man to be an American, keen to pour out his trouble to someone, not a Mexican. He had been a sergeant in the U. S. Infantry, and got into trouble over a woman by hitting an officer and had skipped into Mexico rather than face a court-martial. He offered his services to Villa who, possessing no artillery officer, made him captain of his artillery, taking for granted that the American sergeant would know something about guns.

The captain informed me he was in trouble as he knew very little about artillery, but thought the guns had been tampered with by the federal gunners before they abandoned them. I examined the breech-blocks, found that the firing pins had been broken, and suggested he make new ones. The possibilities of making temporary pins astounded the man, and he admitted he didn't know how. Personally, I wasn't sure either, but was willing to try and offered to do so, at which he brightened up but was horrified when told I needed to take one of the blocks to El Paso.

At this point, the officer straightened up like a ramrod and ordered me to move on. But, it was too late as Villa with a few men was striding towards us. When he spotted me he roared out an order at which four men, armed with guns, machetes and long knives, closed in and grabbed me. I was under arrest. There was a tall swarthy looking man standing close to Villa who constantly kept his eyes on me in an unfriendly manner. Afterwards I found out it was the much feared Rodolfo Fierro, better known as *El Carnicero* (The Butcher), because of his unscrupulous killings.

The officer intervened and spoke to Villa explaining that this foreigner, pointing to me, was an expert on artillery. I had never said anything of the kind, but it worked wonders. My arrest was suspended for the moment. Villa's stern and angry face became relaxed and transformed into an open-mouthed grin and he looked me over with some interest. When the conversation led to the necessity of taking a breechblock out of Mexico he flared up in anger but calmed down and asked, "Why can't you fix them in Juarez?" The outcome was obvious, he needed the guns desperately, and I could not fix them without one of the blocks and a good machine-shop, so he gave in. But, while this conversation was going on, misgivings had entered my mind as to the possibility of the breech-block being confiscated by the United States on the bridge into El Paso. It was heavy and it would take two men to carry it between them on a pole, in a gunny-sack, and therefore difficult to smuggle past the boundary guard on the other side of the Rio Grande. Besides, Villa had stipulated that the block must be back in Mexico within two days, so there was no time to maneuver around farther up or down the river.

It was therefore necessary to dismantle the block in Juarez. A machine-shop was found to which the gun was moved. It was not an easy operation. Luck was with us though for the firing-pin was, in fact, merely broken at the point; consequently, fairly easy to copy on a lathe. With this pin in my pocket I began to walk toward the bridge when the captain impressed upon me that he would be imprisoned or sent back to the States if the pin was not back within the specified time. I then went over the bridge to El Paso.

Due to my newly acquired relationship with the revolutionaries, I thought it prudent to keep my own counsel and began looking for a trustworthy owner of a machine-shop, and to get further information about the trouble in Mexico. I moved about and listened to conversations in bars where usually one obtains most valuable information.

To my surprise there was a decided mixed feeling for and against the revolution. Some were downright hostile, others felt sorry for the peons' desperate struggle for freedom and wished them luck. No one seemed to like Pancho Villa, his reckless shooting of prisoners and confiscation of cattle, especially cattle and horses. He was severely censured yet many admired his ability.

Eventually a machine-shop was found with an owner in sympathy with the peons. This man wished them luck but did not think they had a chance to win because the United States and Great Britain were against the rebels, and besides, there was a large well trained Mexican army moving northward against them.

I returned to work at the machine-shop the following morning and after several tries we had two fairly good looking firing-pins cut on a lathe, and with these I again crossed the bridge into Mexico on the afternoon of the second day. My appearance was a great relief to my new friend, the captain in charge of the guns. He almost pulled me to the shop to see if the pins fitted. They did.

With my firing-pin mission completed, I wished the captain good-bye and luck with his guns. As I was about to leave, an officer marched up with four armed men and informed me that General Villa had commanded my detention until further orders as he wanted the presence of the *gringo* at the gun trials the following day. I protested vigorously as I had an appointment in El Paso that night, but to no avail. The order had come from Villa himself.

Thus I was under arrest once more. I was allowed to walk around, but four armed soldiers were detailed to see that no harm came to me in their words. Resigned to my fate, I took this opportunity to inquire into the artillery pieces which had caused so much trouble. They were Montregon guns so named for a Mexican artillery general who served several years in the French Army. When asked about the gun-sights and instruments, my new friend simply remarked, "There are none."

Early next morning Villa turned up with his staff and off we went galloping along a very dusty road for the gun trials. As speed was required, the so-called gunners were all mounted. On a low ridge a

27

few miles south of Juarez, Villa pulled up his horse and pointed to a small bush-covered ridge standing out clear, thus making a good target, and ordered the guns to be trained on it.

I calculated the distance to be some 12,000 yards and informed him it was too far. Villa seemed embarrassed but gave a new target, a little shack, and called out, "Hit that house." He appeared extremely impatient and annoyed, but it was my unpleasant task to enlighten this bandit general that it was difficult, if not impossible, to hit the house, or even come anywhere near it, without a range-finder or a gun-sight of some kind. Having become a little irritated myself at his attitude, and at being forcibly detained the day before, I reminded him that I had only promised to try to fix the firing-pins and that this had been done.

I fully expected Villa to fly off the handle but was agreeably surprised when he looked at me hard for a few seconds, dismounted, and came to the unlimbered guns. He petted them in a gentle caressing manner with both his big hands and asked almost humbly, as in a prayer, "Is there no way in which these cannons can be used against that usurper Huerta in this our fight for land and freedom?"

There was something so pathetic about this hard, flea-bitten rough-neck showing such deep sentiment that I felt sympathy for him. Then I told him they could be fired without sights or instruments by guessing the elevation, but only as a temporary measure, as the shots would be erratic and ineffective. The guns might act as a surprise to the enemy, however, and I suggested that we fire one shot per gun to make sure the firing-pins worked.

When the interpreter had explained these points, which I could not express intelligently enough in Spanish, Villa frowned, shook his head doubtfully but remained silent. This gave me the opportunity to study the man and I came to the conclusion that he considered the suggestion of range-finders and other instruments silly and superfluous, or a subterfuge on my part. Then again he might be pondering what to do with this *gringo* who had told him, Pancho Villa, what he could or could not do.

Suddenly, Villa straightened up and called out, "All right, let us try the firing-pins, but hit that house!" Pancho Villa was himself again, ignoring everything said about sights. Without any further comment I guessed the range to be about 5,000 yards, and gave the order, "Fire!"

The gun went off, thank goodness, but the shell was over one thousand yards short and to the left kicking up sand and dirt. The shell from the second gun did not hit any nearer. It went high. To everybody's surprise, four men were seen running from the house and disappearing over the ridge beyond. Then came the unexpected. Villa walked up to me and, to my amazement, gave me a Mexican embrace (*abrazo*). Words shot from his lips like bullets from a gatling-gun; I had suddenly become his friend (*amigo*) and companion (*compañero*).

A few minutes later he proclaimed me as his "Chief of Artillery" with the rank of first captain (*capitan primero*). My command consisted of two 75 mm field guns, no officers, no non-coms. There were a few half-wild Apache gunners who knew nothing about guns and some could not speak but their own language, except a little pigeon-Spanish.

Now I was faced with a poser. To join the revolutionary cavalry was one thing, the artillery another. But I felt this was not an opportune time to express personal views and kept my own counsel. Two days later, however, I had the opportunity to talk to Villa in this regard but he said, "I have practically nothing but cavalry. You remain with the guns." Then he added, "My cavalry is the best in the world and with them I will destroy Huerta and his regular army!" At Villa's side stood, as always, Rodolfo Fierro who grinned sneeringly at me when Villa spoke.

It so happened that his cavalry had been under my close surveillance for several days and it obviously needed organization, discipline and some instruction in cavalry tactics. There was no question, however, that Villa's cavalry had become notorious if not downright famous in his successes against highly trained government forces.

As a natural cavalry leader he had applied the hit and run tactics of guerrilla warfare, at which he was supreme, and made monkeys out of the federal cavalry. Cleverly and with great cunning he spread false information among the enemy and picked his own time and place for the attack. Because of the Indian in him, and his childhood and bandit training, he moved secretly and silently during the darkness of night, and always and only when he outnumbered the enemy. When his small but powerful guerrilla bands were pursued, they retreated into the vast and inaccessible terrain of Sierra Madre. But now this no longer could be done as each of his guerrilla bands had grown into large units of regiment and brigade strength.

I was smarting a little, perhaps, from the insults

hurled at me by Villa only a few days before and took this opportunity to hit back at his ego by acquainting him with my impressions of the "best cavalry in the world" and what was needed to lick his men into shape. My answer was naturally and obviously not pleasing to his ears. He was resentful when I told him his troops lacked training and above all discipline. He gave me a flinty but puzzled kind of look, blustered a little as if embarrassed, but waved a hand for me to sit down and said, "We have little time. Outline your ideas, but be brief." At my request an interpreter was sent for as I knew the subject would be too complicated for my pigeon-Spanish.

Bluntly, but respectfully, I told Pancho Villa the truth about his cavalry. His phenomenal self-control and eagerness to listen and learn conveyed the thought that the status of his troops was not quite to his liking either, but he did not seem to detect what was wrong or what action to take. After an hour it became evident that he could not or would not be able to grasp the perplexing details of army organization problems.

This otherwise capable man did not seem to see or calculate more than a few days ahead. His self-confidence was great, but he did not realize his handicaps such as lack of training and mode of living. His old bandit associations were embodied in his army. All made discipline difficult. He knew something was lacking, especially among the officers, but he himself refused point blank to receive any instructions in military strategy. The successful bandit was, I thought, too proud.

When I suggested the creation of an officer's school to teach cavalry tactics, strategy and discipline,

31

he asked, startlingly, "What is the difference between strategy and tactics?" Villa had obviously become a little interested.

Villa's request pushed aside the original idea of the meeting, the training of cavalry. He appeared most interested when mentioning battles of the past, won and lost, by good or bad strategy. When I mentioned Napoleon's dictum, "The secrets of war lie in the communications," Villa banged his fist on the table and remarked, "President Madero told me about that *hombre* (man). I have always tried to destroy the communications of an enemy."

When Villa was informed that not all stratagems of war are aimed at the hostile force, for some are aimed at the hostile commander, he smiled and assented. When he came to the point that a fight may be considered a conflict between the brains and grit of two commanders, in which an accident or carelessness of one may be the turning point in the battle, he remarked, "Why wait for accidents? Attack!"

During this extemporaneous talk I had tried several times to impress on Villa the necessity of reserves, and never going into a fight without keeping a substantial mobile force on hand in case of need, for the unexpected often happens. He had been sitting listening with some eagerness, and I thought some progress had been made. When I stopped talking he remained silent and immovable. Then he spoke with some emotion, "I have won many battles against the trained federal army with my, what you call, undisciplined cavalry. You have stressed the importance of artillery support, and what I need is the aid from the guns. Put them in order. We will need them soon."

I got up, saluted and left, as his words were final.

When I reached the doorway, he called out with a gorilla-like voice but friendly grin, "Be ready to move out with the guns at three o'clock tomorrow morning. We are marching south and will probably contact the federals in the afternoon."

What a man! Here I was with two field guns, ten untrained half wild Apache-speaking gunners, no trained officer, no gun-sights of any kind, no range-finder, and the limbers more than two-thirds empty. Yet, he gave orders to prepare for action.

Villa was without doubt a bundle of energy and strength willing to take grave risks to gain his objective, and he did so, fearlessly. I was beginning to like this Attila of northern Mexico. I did wonder, nevertheless why the haste for the troops were not ready, but I would not have been surprised had I known that the enemy was advancing against us on a broad front and only a day's march away. The newcomer, although commanding the guns, was a *gringo* —no need to inform him.

Pedro Joins my Staff

That same evening, two proud and fine looking Indians reported for duty as dispatch runners and scouts between General Villa and the guns. They were full-blooded Indians from the large Tarahumara tribe, living high in the Sierra Madre in the western part of the State of Chihuahua, who enjoyed a great reputation of being long distance runners.

During the necessary briefing given these men that evening, I found one of them a shaman-doctor named Pedro. After about an hour's talk, I became so interested that my notebook came out and my first

33

observations on the Tarahumara tribe began. These notes grew with the years and were compiled into a Tarahumara-English, English-Tarahumara Dictionary printed by the University of Miami Press in 1955.

Pedro and his friend were dressed in white loose fitting trousers which seemed to be pinched or tied at the ankles. Over this garment was a triangular looking piece of woven material tied around the waist. Each man wore a short kind of shirt over which a leather bag hung from the shoulders, containing important articles: a knife, tobacco, flint-lighter, punk, a stick with heavy bark on it, probably some medicine, and a piece of *peyote* (mescal button). In the bag carried by Pedro were also two reed-like tubes about four inches long. Later I found these to be the "sucking-tubes" of the shaman-doctor, the instrument of his profession, so necessary when "curing" the sick.

Their long black hair was held in place by a hair ribbon around the head about the middle of the forehead. These were woven in four colors, white, black, red and green. They wore no hats that evening but the following morning Pedro sported a native sombrero made of bear-grass. They wore sandals made of leather and each carried a folded blanket hanging over his shoulder. No weapons could be seen except a knife and a sling (*pabaraka*) which had leather straps about three feet long fastened to a leather pouch for the stone. I have had the pleasure of seeing the Tarahumara use their slings, and it is a deadly weapon in their hands. They kill animals and sitting birds with astonishing ease with the sling, as well as by throwing stones by hand.

Pedro and I became close friends, that is friends

in the Indian meaning of blood-brothers. They distrust all strangers. They are natually clannish, normally reticent and of an unsocial taciturn disposition which is hard for a city man to understand. This mistrust may in time become less tense and be replaced by a silent and affectionate understanding as was the case with Pedro, who risked his life many times for me. It may, on the other hand, have been based on the Tarahumara word *norawa* (friend; my friend) a word used by Pedro several times when introducing some of his countrymen. When two of this tribe have consummated an important trade or contract, such as the sale of a few goats, they will touch each other's shoulder with one hand and thus become socially related. A friendship has been created, and they call each other *norawa*.

This man, Pedro, had an unbelievable knowledge of tribal history, legends, plants, animals, medicinal herbs, and cures. He came from near the village of Urique but had been all over the Sierra Madre as a scout for Villa and his guerrillas. He had also worked for some American mining men near Zapuri, could speak fairly good Spanish, and some English which was invaluable to me during the campaign ahead. The other scout who came with Pedro was recalled for duty elsewhere before midnight. By the time I had finished with Pedro, it was very late and, as we had to rise within the hour, I turned in fully dressed.

Just before the arrival of the two Indians, a staff officer informed me that Villa had telegraphed General Carranza in Sonora that he had a foreigner who could fix broken field-guns. This was bad news for I had decided not to continue indefinitely in the artillery. I said nothing but couldn't help wondering why the telegram had been sent. A few days later it was disclosed that Villa knew nothing about the telegram. It had been sent by his friend Fierro who resented the *gringo* commanding the guns.

The Battle of Tierra Blanca

When General Mercado heard of the debacle at the city of Juarez on November 16, 1913, which is mentioned later, he sent a new force against Villa, endeavoring desperately to cope with the revolutionaries and regain some of his losses.

On November 21, 1913, these federal troops numbering some 5,000 men were joined with about 2,000 others who had managed to escape Villa's clutches in Juarez. With this well equipped force, the federals took up position at Tierra Blanca some twenty-five miles south of Juarez.

Long before dawn on November 23, the morning following my extended conference with Villa, all troops were aroused noiselessly in their billets, that is, in the open behind walls of houses, the Church, the Plaza pavilion, or whatever shelter had been found against the bitterly cold wind. Except for a few senior officers, no one seemed to know what it was all about. The men were told to eat and be ready to march at dawn in full marching order, and "without women." Rumors soon began to spread of a large enemy force marching against us and not far distant. The men accepted the news with calm and austere fortitude, but some did show elation in their stoic Indian manner.

PLATE II

Gen. Venustiano Carranza.
Hermosillo 1913.

Just before sunrise this ill-equipped little rebel force of about 5,500 men, with bandoleers three-quarters empty, moved out of Juarez. The column was most unusual and colorful, but I was moved by a strange sympathetic sadness toward these brave little peons and Indians. Their cause seemed so helpless against such great odds. Some of them didn't even have a gun, but proudly carried their machetes and vicious looking long knives, many of them bowie-knives. It may here be mentioned that scalping was not entirely out of fashion, for, say what they will, some scalps were taken and highly valued, especially by some of the Apache braves, during these early days of the revolution.

The women camp-followers had orders to remain behind, but hundreds of them, hanging on to the stirrups, followed their men along the road for a while. Some other women carrying carbines, bandoleers and mounted, managed to slip into the ranks and came with us. These took their places in the firing line and stood all hardships and machine-gun fire as well as the men. They were a praiseworthy lot. It was a richly picturesque sight, but the complete silence, the stoic and yet anxious faces of the women was depressing, as it gave the impression that all were going to a tremendous funeral, or their doom.

The silence had been perfect, no trumpets or drums, no one shouting orders. The only noise came from the rattling of bits, jangling of heavy spurs and the neighing of horses. The secrecy was in order to avert suspicion among the numerous federal secret agents in El Paso, for they were suspected of being in cahoots with some U. S. officials. Although Villa did not show it, he was afraid, very much afraid, of what America might do.

Being warned, Villa anticipated the possibility of the Mexican federals deliberately shelling El Paso so as to provoke intervention, which would mean the probable surrender of his force to the American Army or facing the federal firing-squads. Even if there were no intervention, Villa, used to the open range, was too astute a guerrilla leader to be hemmed in at Juarez.

The troops moved in units, but in a Gypsy kind of formation. Only one regiment, Villa's own, and perhaps one more, marched in anything resembling military order. With but a few exceptions, the rank and file did not wear uniforms, but carried their carbines and bandoleers over their shabby clothing with as much pride of bearing as members of any Imperial Guards.

Many newspaper men in the United States criticized as a "filthy-looking lot" these home-loving, patriotic Peon-Indians who were soldiers fighting for an idea, freedom, land, and a place in the sun. The same thing was said of the American revolutionaries by the officers of George III.

It would be interesting indeed to see what some of these critics would look like after spending a few years in a Mexican revolution. They must, of course, start in a Mexican white cotton shirt and pants without a single change of clothing, no razor, no money, no soap. Yes, there was soap in the shape of amole dug up by hand, the bark of some plant, or perhaps ashes from certain bushes.

We halted about noon and prepared to bivouac for the remainder of the day and night. We had covered only a few miles and the progress had been slow as the different units had to be instructed as to their position in the general plan, en route. As we halted I noticed a number of young boys among the group, one little fellow in particular, for he was not over ten years old. When he came walking by me he looked hungry and tired, so I offered him a tortilla and some water which he gulped down. He told me he came from Lake Guzman in northern Chihuahua and didn't know if his father or mother were alive, but thought his father had been shot by the federals because he refused to be drafted into the army. As he left I told him to look me up when the fight was over and with a *gracias señor,* he was gone. Then I noticed his right arm was bandaged and hung as if useless by his side. I called to him but something else came up and I dropped the matter as the guns had to be placed.

The following day, November 24, scouts reported eleven long trains packed with enemy infantry and having several cavalry screens covering their advance toward us. We broke camp immediately and moved southward against them on a broad front with the railroad track in our center. About twenty miles south of Juarez, we contacted the federals who, after a few severe skirmishes, withdrew for about five miles, and we followed them.

Close to Tierra Blanca they took up what appeared to be a prepared position on both sides of the railroad on a low ridge, a natural bulwark made by nature, in the dunes overlooking the flat country toward us and Juarez. Their field guns could be seen clearly for the federals made no secret of their presence. In fact, it appeared as if they were deliberately parading the guns in our faces to impress or frighten us. They also thought we had no artillery as the guns captured by Villa had been made useless.

General Villa, to my astonishment and dismay, extended his entire force to the east and west without keeping any men, not even a corporal's guard, in reserve. Also, he was well within the effective range of the enemy guns when we halted, but they were silent. Our center dismounted and moved forward into position but the extreme ends of both flanks remained with their horses, and again I wondered why the federals didn't use their artillery. Then I realized that Villa was gambling on his good luck.

The whole thing looked peculiar and I tried to find a suitable place for the guns. Villa should have warned me before reaching so far, but he was no doubt busy elsewhere. The guns had halted within the effective range of the enemy batteries, but as luck would have it, they were located in a dip behind a sand dune which kept us from view. The guns were manhandled up the slope and we dug in the best we could behind some bushes. This both amused and scared me for we were hardly 2,000 yards from the federal batteries.

I had expected to see and learn much from the great Pancho Villa this day, but apparently he was not himself for he lost the initiative from the outset. He gave the impression of being uncertain how to handle the different units, and relied, it seemed, too much on the various commanders to do the right thing without giving them definite orders. This was, however, his usual practice when leading his guerrilla bands.

Before our formations had occupied their points of vantage, the enemy cavalry made a long sweep and tried to get around our left flank. They tried vigorously time and time again but did not succeed. As we had no reserves to deal with the situation, their maneuver forced us to extend our line eastward, and naturally weakened not only our left flank but also our center. It was a shrewd, tactical move by the federal commander but, thank goodness, his guns were silent.

Before our left had repulsed the encircling movement, the federal general, who in the past had given Villa a great deal of trouble, was at him again. He began to shell our right wing in a softening-up process. Then he sent forward some infantry of about regimental strength and occupied a position behind a low ridge well within effective rifle range. Here, protected by some low sand-dunes, he massed quite a number of machine-guns and opened immediate fire on our flank. Our men, very short of ammunition, had orders to hold their fire.

Under the protecting umbrella of these bullet-spewing guns the federals moved forward in two waves on our right flank. They failed, but the machine-guns kept on their demoralizing work and played havoc in our lines. The commander of our right wing was eventually forced to ask for reinforcement, which he received from the center. This was quite a difficult maneuver for the men had to move laterally for almost a mile across the enemy front in full view and within range. Why the enemy did not open with shrapnel was beyond my comprehension, especially when eight of their guns had so far been silent. Two hours later another request for assistance came from the same quarter, which said, "If no reinforcement is received at once we must give ground." As this would have been fatal, some troops who had been riding and fighting continuously to prevent an encirclement, were sent from the left flank.

As my only chance to use the guns without instruments was to aim over and alongside the gun-barrel, one of them was pushed forward from the bushes to the top of the rise, where we could see the enemy infantry and two machine-guns. Our position was most precarious as we were in full view of the enemy batteries, but we had to give a hand before it was too late.

Setting the shrapnel fuse by a guess and elevating the gun by another guess, we fired. It wasn't such a bad shot, but did no damage as it was a dud. With a shortened time-fuse the second shell made a splendid show but burst too high. It did no damage but had some moral effect, as the federal lines halted, temporarily at least. Evidently they had brought their machine-guns and infantry into an exposed position thinking we had no artillery.

My satisfaction at halting their advance was short-lived, as an enemy battery began to rake our one-gun position unmercifully with shrapnel. With three men hit and shrapnel bursting in front of us about every ten seconds, I was forced to abandon the gun and moved the men back under cover of th low ridge. The Apache gunners behaved splendidly. They could have run but, instead, they picked up their wounded comrades and brought them along. While doing this a fourth man was badly wounded and passed away shortly afterwards. After a while the federals opened up with armor piercing shells with delayed action fuses. The last of the three shells hit some twenty feet in front of the gun, kicked up a tremendous amount of sand, stones and smoke. Apparently satisfied that the gun was out of commission the firing ceased.

There never should have been any doubt as to the outcome of this important battle for the control of the northern terminal of Mexican railways. The federals had the superiority in manpower, artillery, machine-guns, and a seemingly inexhaustible supply of ammunition. Had they opened up with the artillery and made a general assault, like that on our right, we would have been hopelessly lost. For some strange and unaccountable reason their center remained inactive and eight of the guns were silent all day. Their chance for a complete victory—yes, indeed, our annihilation—was forfeited. It was a grave tactical blunder by the federal general for we were completely at his mercy.

While watching the enemy, I was bewildered as well as pleased by the stupidity of the man for he must have seen our plight. First, I thought it an oversight. Then I wondered if Villa's fame had played tricks with his imagination and he had become overcautious or even scared. Then again he might also be waiting for something. The possibility of an encirclement came to my mind and Pedro was despatched to have a look. However, the longer the suspense lasted the more I became convinced that the federal commander either had lost his nerve, for he had deliberately thrust aside the overwhelming advantages already gained, or he could not see the tactical expedience of an attack.

We could not move because of the lack of ammunition. Our left flank was wavering for lack of men, the right was almost tottering and in confusion. Defeat was staring us in the face. Retreat was almost impossible without terrible losses. Besides, retreat to where? We had only one alternative as I could see it, run a bluff and attack.

Pedro had returned without seeing an enemy on our flank, and I sent him with a verbal message to Villa giving my unasked-for opinion on the enemy commander and to intimate my views. Under ordinary circumstances, the idea of offering advice to Pancho Villa would never have occurred to me. However, Pedro had seen him several times during the day, so I knew he was under some nervous strain and was acting uncertain. He might welcome an unbiased opinion. Pedro, looking like a wooden Indian, took a peep at the enemy, glanced toward the rear, then at me, and saying nothing raised his hand and went off at high speed

No sooner had Pedro gone when a miracle occurred. From out of nowhere appeared a body of mounted men, like a cohort of Roman cavalry, some 300 strong on the federal's left flank which was pushing our right to the limit. The commander of this regiment was a remarkably clear-headed and resourceful young man. He saw the extended order of the enemy, and his Mounted Infantry without the slightest hesitation charged without sabers. For us it was a perfect move, for him a very risky one, but he saved us from disaster.

This young lieutenant colonel, an uneducated half-breed Apache, was a cavalry leader to be admired. His unexpected charge had a startling effect on the enemy. Instead of turning the machine-guns on him, the federals broke formation and ran in haste

44

back to the main body on the ridge, leaving several machine-guns on the field.

The federals consolidated their position, but no further attempt was made on our lines except for spasmodic bursts of machine-gun and rifle fire on our advanced line. This firing continued through the 25th. We, with bandoleers almost empty, remained silent. The federals seemed to be peculiarly timid, however, for they did not come out to reap the fruits of victory, for which we were truly thankful.

About 2 a.m., November 26, our Indian scouts reported the almost unbelievable. The federals had moved in their flanks toward the center for a considerable distance. Further, they had not seen any flanking patrols or even a scout of the enemy. On receiving this information and apparently anticipating that something was going to happen, Villa, now desperate, made the best decision of his life. He ordered a general advance, a frontal attack, without ammunition, an hour before dawn. A cavalry regiment from each flank was ordered to withdraw silently and encircle the enemy flanks.

The flanking movement took longer than expected and we could not attack before daybreak which was too late. We tried but the federals held us at bay quite easily as we could not penetrate the deadly zone of machine-gun fire without artillery support. About noon, the enemy spotted the hitherto unseen cavalry deploying on and around their flanks, "the sweep of the Dragon's Wings." This by no means an easy operation was many hours late but executed to perfection.

At about 2 p.m., the enemy, fearing complete encirclement, lost their nerve and with their morale broken started to evacuate their positions. At this moment Pedro drew my attention to a battery of four guns right in front of us. They were training their guns eastward and had their back toward us, preparing, evidently, to give the encircling troops from our left wing a warm reception. Apparently our troops on that flank had turned inward, toward the enemy main position, too soon and would be greeted with grapeshot when within range.

The squadron which had been sent as my escort during the day now received orders to stand in readiness to move against the enemy guns. This was not as bad as it sounds for the guns could not see our movements until we were almost on top of them. This done, our two guns were trained the best I could without sights, on the back of the federal gunners who at that light were plainly seen. I sighted No. 1 gun by a guess and fired, then did the same with No. 2 gun. The shrapnel burst too high and did no damage. But as expected, it had a demoralizing effect. When he saw the other batteries leaving their position in flight this, the only decent federal artillery officer there, ordered his men to limber-up and they went off, southward. We fired six shrapnel per gun on the enemy position and I felt quite satisfied with the result. Then I countermanded the order to my cavalry escort.

Besides our flanking movement, a special dynamiting party under Rodolfo Fierro went out during the night to blow up the railroad tracks behind the enemy. Fierro, as an old railroad hand, was good at this kind of work and a thoroughly efficient dynamiter. As luck would have it, he managed to capture an incoming train during the confusion in the afternoon by blowing up the track. He detached the engine from the train and loaded it with dynamite and percussion caps all tied to the cow-catcher. The engine was sent at full speed toward the enemy trains standing on the tracks. The explosion was terrific but the demoralizing effect on the enemy was even worse.

My third opportunity to use the gun came when the federals began to remove their batteries and run for the trains. We fired a few rounds and the eighth shell hit a railroad car, which was not what I aimed at, but it blocked several trains behind it and then Fierro's dynamite trick did the rest.

About this time quite a number of federal soldiers came out toward us carrying a white flag and with their hands in the air. Since many of Villa's men had previously been shot while accepting such surrenders, these men were shot down to the last man. The rest of the enemy was now in a disgraceful retreat, abandoning guns and trains in their wild scramble to escape Villa's wrath. It was a rout.

It was deplorable that our horses had been without food and water for almost two days and we could not make a large scale pursuit. We tried to prevent the trains from leaving, not one of them should have escaped, but five did.

Late in the afternoon our mounted patrols scouted to the south trying to prevent scattered remnants of the enemy from rallying. About fifteen miles from our position and not far from Samalayuca, a patrol consisting of a corporal and four men discovered a train standing on the track. The corporal, who was made a sergeant next day, noticed the absence of life on the train and decided that it has been abanoned since it was standing there like a ghost with the locomotive still hot from use. The reason for abandoning this train is problematical and open to conjecture, as the locomotive was in perfect order with plenty of coal and had steam up.

It appears that the hope of the officers fell in consequence of the panic, and being in fear of certain death if captured, had pushed too fast and too far ahead of the men. The soldiers, likewise apprehensive, finding themselves alone, deserted and made for the open country.

That same evening, three or four miles south of the abandoned train, the scouts found over 300 good federal horses grazing peacefully —a very valuable asset as we needed remounts badly.

The booty was great and among the many things captured were: four good locomotives, four long trains with supplies, eight field-guns, and one five-inch siege gun mounted on a flat-car, seven machine-guns, 400 rifles, over 400,000 rounds of ammunition and 350 horses. The limbers of the guns were packed with shells besides the reserve ammunition found in the box-car. We also got 70,000 Mexican pesos which were negotiable in America where Villa's money was valueless.

General Mercado, the federal commander of northern Mexico, knew of Villa's ammunition predicament but forgot the man's versatility and thought his well equipped division was sufficient to crush this bandit. He did not even dream of the possibility of defeat. His field commander, as well as Villa, made the same unpardonable blunder. They did not keep a single man in reserve. Further, he could have won this battle within the first six hours if he had used his guns well. He also underestimated the sturdy quality of the peon-rebel leader. The surprise that Villa had artillery was much greater than expected, and he did not anticipate any tactical mistakes by his commander. The demoralizing, almost paralyzing, effect of Pancho Villa's name on his officers and men also seemed to have affected his general in command.

The ammunition captured put new hope and life into Villa and his troops. Some had only two or three rounds left per man. Many had none at all. This shortage was due principally to an American embargo on arms for the rebels.

In desperation Villa purchased 600,000 rounds secretly in the States but lost it all when he tried to smuggle this vast shipment into Mexico only a week or so before the battle of Tierra Blanca. Someone had double-crossed Villa in this shipment. The American government was tipped off and several mule-trains were intercepted and confiscated before they reached the Border.

When some of our troops came marching past, I noticed among them a number of young boys which made me think of the ten year old soldier of a few days before. I sent Pedro to find him and he, aided by another Indian, returned after a while carrying the boy between them. No sooner had they placed him on the ground when Pedro reverted to the type of a shaman-doctor and removed the bandages from the boy's arm. There staring us in the face was a severe and terrible looking wound, full of gangrene.

It appeared hopeless, but Pedro was determined to try to save the child's life. He looked at me and shook his head. He urinated on a rag and began to clean the wound, as we had no water. Then he

49

placed some herbs on the child's head to ease the burning fever. Before cutting some of the dead flesh from the arm, Pedro tried to take the old muzzle-loader from the boy, but this brave little soldier hung on to it for grim death with his free hand. The boy's action brought back wistful memories of how proud I had been when, at his age, my father let me have my first long rifle, an old muzzle-loader with a bayonet.

When Pedro had done everything that could be done, he informed me that the lad could hardly live another day, but that there was a small chance if the arm was amputated at once. Then he added, "He can't live anyhow." I had not known Pedro more than a few days, but he had already shown himself to be capable and trustworthy, and since the City of Juarez was far away, I asked him if he could operate. He admitted having done some surgical work in the field several times, but felt sure the boy didn't have a chance. I pulled out my emergency kit and gave the boy a shot of morphine. Pedro was skillful and made the most of his long and clumsy hunting-knife. The operation completed, he reiterated his prediction that the boy could not live long as the gangrene had taken hold of the upper part of the body.

Pedro and I were stripped to the waist as our shirts and undergarments had gone for bandages. Still without water, we used our own and the gunner's urine for washing the wound. When it was all over, I took another good look at the youngster, who was so proud to be a soldier and carry a gun, to see if we could possibly take him back to Juarez. When we were about to place him on a limber, he came to and his weak smile of recognition was a wonderful thing to see. His gun which had been placed by his side was there when he made an effort to find it and again that grateful smile, full of understanding. Then he took something out of his pocket, gave it to me, and said, "I got this from my mother a long time ago, will you please keep it for me?" It was a brightly polished American 25 cent piece.

As we could not remain in the field, I gave him my last dose of morphine and placed him on a limber with a man to hold him. When we started back for Juarez we were the last to leave, except for a few straggling wounded. The boy lost consciousness after coming out of the last morphine dose and died the next day. Pedro got two men with spades and we rode south for about a mile and buried him with his gun and his mother's silver coin in his pocket.

Villa and most of his troops loaded with the spoils of war returned to Juarez on November 28 to lick their wounds and celebrate, of course, the great victory of Tierra Blanca, with a befitting *fiesta*. More wounded were brought in. Men had crawled away from the firing line in the hope of dressing their wounds, but many had died from exposure and lack of medical aid.

The strength of the federal force at Tierra Blanca was estimated at 7,000 men as against our 5,500. Villa won this fight not from superior strategy or tactics but because of the miscarriage of a dispatch and an apparently scared federal commander.

The regiment which saved the day had been ordered to join us in Juarez the day before, but the order had gone astray and its commander did not receive it before the morning of the 26th. He rushed across the desert-like country from Mezquite or Sapelio, located some miles in a westerly direction, and thus surprised the enemy and us.

The rebels estimated the federals lost 1,000 killed, but 600 would probably be the more correct figure as we found only about 400 rifles left behind. One of the federal generals, Salazar, was badly wounded but escaped eastward with some men and eventually crossed the Rio Grande and surrendered to the American authorities. We lost about 200 dead including Colonel Talamantes, and a little over 300 wounded. Among these was General Rodriguez with a nasty machine-gun wound in the knee.

This was a victory but a bloody one, for almost all enemy wounded were killed. All officers of the federal army and the volunteer corps were shot as a matter of course.

A volunteer from northern Mexico serving with the federals recognized Villa as an old friend and called to him. Villa walked up to him smiling, embraced and patted the man on the back in a friendly manner, and then stepped aside. The man was shot a few seconds later. In another place eighty prisoners were slaughtered. One might assume this was a war of extermination of the educated class, but it wasn't so, for the federals, representing in a way the upper class, shot all of our officers and many thousands of peons and Indians for good measure.

The battle of Tierra Blanca was, of course, a great triumph for Pancho Villa and his name went far and wide throughout Mexico as the champion and leader of the downtrodden people. Villa was, at this time, the principal revolutionary leader in Mexico. This fact created jealousy as well as animosity against him among many generals in other states, for they considered themselves as champions of the Peon-Indian, but were not doing so much about it.

The long list of victories so justly scored up in honor and praise of Villa's generalship should not really include this so important, almost decisive, battle for he did everything wrong and yet came out as the conqueror. He rushed head on with his cavalry and mounted infantry without proper scouting and should have been captured with his entire force in the first few hours if the federal commander had known anything about cavalry and artillery. He had both. Villa went in without any reserves and very little ammunition which should have made him cautious. He kept his horses saddled needlessly without food or water for almost two days and nights. He lost the initiative and allowed himself to be immobilized from the start, floundering like a horse in quicksand. He struggled helplessly in confusion to extricate himself but didn't know how, a strange thing for Villa, indeed. He was apparently learning the hard way how to handle large numbers of men beyond a guerrilla band. This battle, which almost became his Waterloo, taught him, I hoped, the necessity of reserve troops.

Gun-running

On our return to Juarez it was discovered that President Woodrow Wilson had sent a note to all foreign governments, which in part read:

> "The policy of the government of the United States is to isolate General Huerta entirely; to cut him off from foreign sympathy, aid and form domestic credit, whether moral or material, and to force him out. It is hoped and believed that isolation will accomplish this end and shall awati the results without irritation or impatience. If General Huerta does not retire by force of circumstance it will become the duty of the United States to use less peaceful means to put him out. . . ."

Rumors said that the federals, so badly beaten at Tierra Blanca, were only a portion of the army south of Chihuahua City and that heavy troop reinforcements were being rushed forward toward the northern Border. These reports were false because General Mercado was actually abandoning the city of Chihuahua and preparing to move all federals, men, women and children, eastward over the desert to Ojinaga on the American Border opposite Presidio, Texas.

In spite of the federal espionage system, Mercado didn't know that Villa was unable to pursue him, not only because of the poor condition of his horses but also the need of ammunition which had to be smuggled over the Border from the States.

Early in the morning of November 29, General Villa sent me a message to report to him immediately. This, my last meeting with the great guerrilla leader, took less time than writing about it. When I entered his quarters, Villa was sitting in a chair with both his leather covered legs on the table, his hat tilted back and a very serious look on his face. Behind him stood his body-guard, friend, adviser and iniquitous companion, Rodolfo Fierro, and two other senior officers.

I was informed of an arms shipment which, for some strange and mysterious reason, had been mislaid and shipped to Arizona instead of Texas. Villa went on to explain that he wanted someone he could trust to proceed forthwith to Tucson, Arizona, where his agent would be at Santa Rita Hotel the following morning. This man would have pack-mules, horses and men in readiness at a certain railroad station for the loading of the guns and ammunition. This pack train would then move toward the Mexican Border at the greatest possible speed and cross it at a place not far from Nogales. Once over the Border another man would take over the pack animals and proceed by mountain trails into the State of Chihuahua. Then he asked, "Will you do this for me?"

I realized at once that this was the acid test, the work of that murderous Fierro standing there smirking and anticipating, no doubt, my falling into the hands of the U. S. Border Patrol, for *El Carnicero* hated all *gringos*. The request was extremely distasteful. Joining the rebel army was one thing, gun-running was another, but it was obvious these things go together. While I pondered his request for a second or two, Villa removed a leg from the table and pulled out a fat wad of notes from the drawer and asked me to count them. There were 250 one hundred American Dollar bills.

"Amigo," he continued, "I want you to take this money and give it to the station agent in Arizona in exchange for guns and ammunition packed in boxes suitable for mule packs and labeled Agricultural Machinery and Spare Parts. The first payment

has been made but the boxes will only be delivered against this amount in cash."

I did not wish to do this smuggling job, but as I knew his fast-growing army needed both guns and ammunition, I assented, at which he seemed quite relieved. Then he surprised me by saying, "When your mission is completed proceed to Hermosillo and report to Carranza, but do not mention this shipment as it would not do you any good."

When I asked the reason for the transfer, he waved his hand as if trying to find an answer, but said, "I understand the reason why you wish to leave here. Besides, Carranza has ordered the transfer of the man who repaired my guns as he has several that need your attention." He stopped and seemed depressed and as if in doubt about something, but he only said, "Good-bye comrade!" (*Adios compañero!*). As there seemed to be no object in my cross-examining a man who deliberately evaded my qustion, I saluted and left. I did, however, think he had taken an awful risk as I could have taken the guns to Carranza, or kept the money and not returned to Mexico at all.

The more I thought of it, the more I was convinced Villa had been hoodwinked by Fierro and that he actually believed I had asked for a transfer. But if so, why trust me with the important gun-running mission? I was debating on returning to find out the truth, but being an half-fatalist, I let the matter drop and continued on to my camp. This decision turned out for the best in the long run, although some of my new acquaintances on the Obregon side never let my association with Pancho Villa get out of my hair.

When I told Pedro of my mission, he did not like it at all, but begged my consent to come along. At the same time he asked permission to leave me in Nogales for a month as he wished to see someone in Tarahumaraland, but would rejoin me in Hermosilla or wherever I was. This arrangement suited me to perfection and within an hour we were on the train speeding westward and arrived in Tucson after a somewhat tedious run from El Paso.

I went to the Santa Rita Hotel, and there found an American waiting for me. He must have been well informed of our movements for everything was in readiness. The pack-mules, horses to ride, guns and ammunition packed in small boxes were at a station which I think he called Calabasas, some ten or twelve miles north of Nogales. We arrived there by train within the hour.

The money was given to the agent and the boxes of "Agricultural Machinery" were handed over. We loaded some 400 Winchester 30-30 carbines and about 40,000 rounds of ammunition and sent the pack-mules in small parties and in different directions under cover of darkness. The men were Mexican *charros* (cowboys) and Indians in sympathy with the revolution, but all had been professional smugglers for years.

I went with the twelve pack-horses making up the last pack-train. We moved along the desert-like land away from the road trying to shield ourselves from view, for we had been told of a U. S. Cavalry Patrol, constantly on the move up and down the Border. I had three Indian scouts; one in advance, and one on each flank. Pedro with two men came in the rear and I behind them all, for there could be no stragglers.

Everything went as per schedule up to about two miles from the Border when the left-wing scout came galloping hell-for-leather and told us he had run into the Border Patrol. When they spotted him he galloped north instead of coming direct and thus led them off our trail for awhile.

Hearing this, we abandoned all precautionary measures and increased our speed to a sharp trot. The packs were heavier than they should have been and the horses kept stumbling. I had moved up front and as we came on the sky line of a ridge, some bullets came zipping by but did no harm. At this point a cowboy told me he didn't wish to clash with the American troops and suggested we abandon some of the pack-animals and save ourselves by galloping to the Border. As the rest did not seem to mind the danger, we urged the animals to a greater speed.

We were moving at a good pace, but the U. S. cavalry, not hampered by any impedimenta, moved faster and were gaining on us. While I was seriously considering abandoning most of the pack-animals to save our own skin, the cavalry opened up a heavy fire which meant they had dismounted. One of my men got hit but was able to continue and we urged the animals into a gallop.

A minute or two later, I noticed the malcontented cowboy missing. He had disappeared in the dark, scared, I thought, into the desert, but who wasn't scared? Then there was a shot quite close which startled me for I thought we had been cut off. It was then Pedro told me the cowboy had dismounted in the hope of holding the Americans back with his cut-off Winchester which was always carried hidden under the flap of the saddle. The move was successful, but an hostile act against the United States. When I looked again, we were 200 yards from the Border which we crossed by the grace of God and a low ridge which concealed us from the patrol.

I didn't dare to stop our staggering animals when at the Border line as I wasn't sure what the U. S. Cavalry might do. A minute later, however, I halted when a Mexican patrol came between us and the pursuers who had pulled up by a pile of stones, probably a border beacon.

After giving the horses rest and taking care of the wounded man, we moved to the previously arranged meeting place in the southern outskirts of Nogales. I was surprised at not being questioned by the sergeant in charge of the Mexican patrol as he merely continued on as if this were a daily occurrence. All the mule-trains had arrived by ten o'clock without any trouble or interference on the American side.

Villa's agent arrived at eleven, took over everything and was ready to move over the mountain trails into Chihuahua which would take about two weeks, he said. He was afraid the Carranzistas would find the real contents of the boxes and proposed to move on without even feeding the animals. I opposed the move on account of the pack horses, but let him start at noon when Pedro thought it best to get out of Nogales immediately. With the animals and men well fed they left and Pedro with them. I went to Hotel Escobosa and turned in for a couple of hours after getting something to eat.

The Mexican cowboy, who could so easily have gotten me into serious trouble by shooting at the U. S. Patrol, came and begged me to let him explain why he did what he did. He had been caught smuggling twice before by the *gringos,* but the third time would be fatal. He continued, "I could see that we would be captured if you did not abandon the pack animals so I fired a few shots, the *gringos* dismounted, and we got over the Border." The man was almost stunned when I gave him a five peso bill and told him to forget the incident, for he did, after all, save the situation.

At four o'clock in the afternoon I thought it would be interesting to call on the U. S. Cavalry across the Border, and was well received by the officers after presenting myself. Smuggling, especially gun-running, became the subject of conversation and they told me a large pack-train had penetrated their patrol cordon during the night. On hearing this it was difficult not to smile, as we had gotten ten pack-trains over the Border.

The officer in charge of the patrol described the impertinence and audacity of the Mexican gun-runners, then added, "I wish there was no embargo on arms into Mexico as the revolutionaries need guns and ammunition." At this point I asked, "If you feel that way why don't you go easy and be more merciful in your pursuit?" to which the lieutenant leaned over and whispered, "We could have shot many of them last night and captured the whole outfit, but I gave orders to shoot high."

Returning to the hotel I was pondering over this remark. Was the officer making excuses for his failure or could he actually have stopped us? With this thought in mind, I was convinced that I had been riding my good luck a little too hard. At the hotel I found my horse well groomed, the saddle cleaned, and a man lying alongside my equipment guarding it as with his life. It was the cowboy of the night before. His name was Lopez, and he became my man Friday from that time on.

The following statement was published in an American newspaper that evening, December 2, 1913:

"It is reported to the Department of Justice Officers in El Paso, Texas, that the entire ammunition supply of this city has been exhausted. It is believed to have been smuggled across the Border to Villa's forces."

Thus ended my association with Pancho Villa, loved by the poor, hated by the *cientificos,* and feared by the federal army. He was hard, relentless and cruel at times, but he would give his shirt to help a friend.

Should anyone wish to sit in judgment on Gen. Villa he should, I think, consider the circumstances of his early life. His rugged upbringing moulded, naturally, his character to what it was. I have, therefore, added the following few notes on his tempestuous life.

The Story of Pancho Villa

Villa was born in northern Durango about 1882. His name was Doroteo Arango, but he changed it while in his teens to Francisco Villa to mislead the mounted police *rurales,* who were on his trail constantly. His father, a peon, died when Villa was about eight or nine years old. He left him a few acres of almost useless land, three sisters, two brothers, and his mother to take care of. The lad worked hard, but was forced to go to the hacienda store for food, and he sank deeper and deeper into debt.

A few years passed, but one day he left the hacienda and joined a mule train. Gradually he became an *arriero* (burro-driver, muleteer), and made more money than was possible at home, but he was hunted by the police as an absconder.

Within a few years he knew every pass in the Sierra Madre, every secret path, cave, and other hiding place in the deep gorges and ravines (*barrancas*). His friends were mostly Tarahumara Indians, and he spoke their language like one of them. Villa (Doroteo Arango), being fond of horses, became a famous bronco-buster in the State of Chihuahua. All this time he had saved his earnings and sent money regularly to his mother—sometimes he called on her himself.

The *rurales,* having heard of these visits, watched for him and one day captured him and he was sent back to the hacienda where, tied to the whipping-post, he was lashed within an inch of his life. He ran away again but was captured, and again the whipping-post. His age was now about fifteen, but he was a big and husky young man.

He escaped for the third time, and tired of the constant persecutions, he joined a famous outlaw. It was then that the Young Doroteo Arango changed his name to Francisco Villa, his comrades called him Pancho, and Pancho Villa it became.

Pancho made several other risky visits home

from time to time to see his family. On one of these sojourns, he found that his sister had been seduced by the land-owner (*hacendado*) for whom she worked, and the very man who had him flogged twice. Villa, now about seventeen years old, went after the man with murder in his heart, roped him, and then dragged the man along the road behind his horse until every bone was broken.

His bandit chieftain was eventually killed. but just before he died, he summoned the gang and told them that Pancho was their chief. Villa's followers were mostly escaped convicts, professional bandits, discontented cow-punchers and muleteers who, like himself, had fled from hacienda slavery and debt.

Villa's inner nature was slow and deep, but almost incapable of prudence for the tide of impulse, which at first gave him success, later overpowered him and brought unnecessary defeats. He was often swayed in the wrong direction by his impetuousness, and his lower impulses often brought him into trouble and several illicit unions. However, the peons and Indians looked up to him as a kind of Robin Hood, as he often helped them when in need. His exploits against the federal government became legends told around the camp-fires, inside the adobe huts, and treasured in the hearts of the simple ranchers, cowboys and muleteers, for like some of them, he was hunted like an animal.

This was the nature of the young man given to Mexico before the first thunder of the revolution had reached the ears of the outside world; his fame had spread to almost every corner of the land.

When Francisco Madero came out against Diaz

and preached "land and liberty," Villa joined Madero with all his men and was made a captain in Madero's little army.

One day in April 1910, a downcast and highly nervous revolutionary force under Colonel Orozco moved northward in the direction of the City of Juarez. In the lead were Francisco Madero, his brothers Gustavo and Raul, and others. The so-called Foreign Legion of about 100 men under Garibaldi acted as their escort. Behind them came the main column under Jose de la Luz Blanco. Far in the rear was Captain Villa with his guerrillas, fighting a difficult rear-guard action against a superior federal cavalry force from Casas Grandes.

No one seems to know what actually happened at Casas Grandes. The story goes that Madero, seeing his political hopes for the presidency slipping away from him, gambled all or nothing on an attack without ascertaining the strength and disposition of the enemy.

While the rebels moved forward, the federals held their fire but when close enough, they opened up with concealed batteries and raked the Madero troops unmercifully. The Foreign Legion moved back from the fight immediately. When the federals appeared with fixed bayonets, Orozco's men turned and retreated in haste. The federals sent a few squadrons after Madero and many peons fell under thelr sabers.

Pancho Villa was far away during the fight, but he turned up during the early stages of the pursuit. He engaged the enemy calvary and held them back long enough to save Madero from capture and the complete destruction of his force. The Casas Grandes affair seems to have been an unfortunate one because the rebels were inferior in numbers, short of ammunition and had no artillery.

Madero's men reached Juarez and took up position outside of the city. A strong and well equipped federal force, entrenched behind walls and protected inside of houses, was holding the town. Several of Madero's advisers wanted him to attack, but Madero, remembering his defeat at Casas Grandes, held back. Then, strangely enough, he proposed a two weeks' suspension of hostilities to the federal commander who, bottled up in Juarez, adroitly accepted. The truce was to remain in effect from April 22 to May 6, but what Madero evidently wanted was time for making a deal with the federal government. He issued a frenzied order to all revolutionary leaders within his reach, "Stop fighting! Wait for orders!"

During these secret negotiations, Villa had moved southward with a few men to tear up and dynamite the railroad tracks so as to prevent any federal reinforcement coming from Chihuahua.

The Utopian Madero thought he could march on Mexico City and take over the country without a fight. He had less than 2,000 badly armed men, short of ammunition and without supplies. The march of about a thousand miles was through hostile country, and he would have to face a regular army of about 40,000 men. Behind him he proposed leaving a well-equipped enemy force, twice as large as his own, to threaten his rear.

When Villa heard of the proposed withdrawal, he moved away from Madero and prepared to act on his own. He had a secret weapon, a bomb, made up of a number of homemade hand-grenades. These were given to picked men, and the order for the attack on Juarez was passed to his own men, secretly.

Villa's grenadiers moved forward and the federals, surprised and lost in amazement, were forced to retreat inside the city. Madero was also dumbfounded and, afraid that his negotiations with Diaz might fail completely, sent a messenger to Villa with strict orders, "Cease firing." But Villa could not be found; he was already inside the enemy redoubts loaded with grenades. Madero was too late. Tired of waiting, and inflamed beyond control, the Indians had moved forward and had begun to shoot.

Orozco, afraid of being outdone by Villa, sent his men into the fray, as did de la Luz Blanco, Garibaldi and others. The important Border City of Juarez with a garrison of some 3,500 well supplied federal soldiers was captured by the initiative of Pancho Villa on May 10, 1911. The total strength of the rebel force was about 1,800 men without artillery, short of ammunition, but with some homemade hand-grenades. Colonel Orozco, being the senior, was promoted to brigadier general and Captain Villa to a colonel, not for disobeying orders exactly, but for making a success of the insubordinant maneuver.

President Diaz resigned and left Mexico soon after the fall of Juarez. Madero moved into the capital with his staff, among them Villa. Villa got restless in the capital, however, resigned his commission and returned to Chihuahua. As there was peace in the land, he went into the cattle business, desiring to sell meat at a cheap rate to the peons.

After Madero's assassination, Villa was forced to give up his cattle venture or get killed, and returned therefore to his old hiding places in the sierra to raise troops to revenge Madero's murder. When rumors spread that Villa needed men, his name was enough to raise a force of several thousand, well mounted on stolen horses and armed after a fashion.

A few months after raising his little army Villa had cleared the northern parts of Chihuahua of federal forces except for the City of Juarez, which had been recaptured and strongly held by Huerta's troops. He wanted to take Chihuahua City; but realizing that other points must be cleared first, he marched with about 5,000 men on Jimenez, a railroad center in the northern part of the state on the road to Torreon. Villa made wonderful, though very risky, frontal attacks with his cavalry, but took the city and drove the enemy northward. The government troops tried to make a stand at Camargo and at La Cruz, but everywhere it was the same: Villa's cavalry charged against stonewalls like demons and drove Huerta's men into Chihuahua City, where there was a large federal garrison.

Villa, short of ammunition, stood in the outskirts of the city, which even he in a reckless mood knew he could not attack without inviting disaster. To remedy this, he picked a small cavalry brigade and made forced marches northward to obtain ammunition. When almost at the United States Border, Villa heard of a federal force concentrating behind him. Cursing his luck, he turned without getting the ammunition and moved rapidly southward with some 800 men. The federals, encamped with about 1,800 well armed men, seemed to be devoid of any knowledge of Villa's presence. His men and horses were weary and tired from severe marches, but Villa saw his chance and charged. The element of surprise made an almost certain defeat into an overwhelming victory. The amazed enemy broke in confusion which became a rout, leaving nearly half of the men in the field, dead, dying, or prisoners.

All federal officers captured were shot. It was reported they were placed one behind the other, two and four deep, then shot to save ammunition. That evening eleven long trains crammed with supplies for the federals were captured. Among the supplies were some field-guns with a few rounds of shrapnel in the limbers. The number of rifles and ammunition captured was great.

After weeks of continuous fighting, Villa decided on September 29, 1913, to capture the strategically important City of Torreon. It was garrisoned by over 5,000 well armed and entrenched regular government troops under General Jose Refugio Velasco. The towns located on the road to Torreon were also garrisoned and entrenched, especially La Loma, with 2,000 of Huerta's regulars.

It took two days of desperate frontal attacks to drive out the federals and eventually the town of Lerdo, on the very doorstep of Torreon, was captured. Villa's objective was now in sight and he attacked without hesitation. By evening of October 1, the City of Torreon, the railroad center of northern Mexico, was in Villa's hands. He shot some fifty odd officers and captured a great amount of supplies, including several trains, locomotives, over 500 rifles, 2 field-guns with 300 shells, but the small arms ammunition was scarce in proportion.

Bad news seeped in from various rebel fronts: General Obregon was seriously stalled in Sonora by the federals recapturing the City of Guaymas; General Lucio Blanco was likewise held up after he captured Matamoros, and other reverses. Villa apparently noticed the dawdling spirit of the rebels, for he made the capture of Chihuahua City a must. He moved on the place which was strongly fortified with a complex network of trenches, formidable redoubts, concealed batteries and machine-gun nests, manned by some 7,000 federals — most of them regulars.

When Villa reached the city, he had about 8,000 half-wild Apache Indians and cowboys, all suffering from that chronic disease among revolutionaries, "short of ammunition." As he wanted to gain time to obtain supplies, Villa offered the federal commander the opportunity to surrender. The note was sent. General Mercado, however, being sure of his men, and thinking Villa a mere upstart, wanted to teach him a lesson, did not reply. Besides, the note was tantamount to an ultimatum, therefore, unacceptable. Villa was restless, and as there was no reply to his offer, he gambled on his men being able to overcome the city's defences without ammunition—and attacked.

As luck would have it the federal army had for some years gradually fallen into a smug complacency, liked all the comforts they could get, and considered "night fighting" unorthodox and barbaric. Pancho Villa was barbaric and quite familiar with night-riding as a bandit, so he attacked the city by night—his only chance. The element of surprise was great, but fear of the man himself was greater, for the federals left their perfectly arranged front line positions and withdrew to the inner defences, where Villa met stiff resistance.

Villa suddenly realized he had made a mistake. He withdrew his men in a countermove using a stratagem as old as the hills. He moved rapidly southward, his men scattering all over the place as if in panic. Seeing the rebels retreating in disorder, Mercado sent his cavalry in pursuit. He did not inflict any damage, thanks to the mobility of the rebel units. Eventually the federals gave up the chase, returned to the city and reported that Villa's forces were in a disorganized rout, scattered for miles over the south, completely disintegrated.

When the federals gave up the pursuit, Villa turned and moved his men northward by a forced march. At the time General Mercado was telegraphing President Huerta of the great victory over Pancho Villa—which started jubilation throughout the land among the *cientificos*.

Adolfo Fierro, now Villa's right hand man, had for days been tapping the federal wires between Chihuahua and Juarez and picked up the information that a supply train was waiting in Chihuahua to be sent north to the Juarez garrison as soon as the road was clear of Villa's guerrillas.

When Villa was far enough north, he moved about 800 picked men east and captured the sleepy railroad station of Terrazas about 35 miles north of Chihuahua. Here Villa calmly telegraphed to that city, "The road is clear." and Mercado, confident that Villa was in retreat to the south, despatched the supply train for the Juarez garrison.

When the train reached Terrazas station, it was captured and some empty cattle cars found at the depot hooked on to it. Villa then wired to General Castro, the federal commander in Juarez, "The enemy is retreating to the south pursued by our cavalry; am sending you reinforcement of 800 men with all supplies needed," and signed it "Mercado."

By this time his men had thrown out everything from the train except the ammunition and other useful material. He embarked his troops and went off at full speed to Juarez, pulled into that city about midnight and found the garrison fast asleep in their billets, without a guard anywhere.

Villa with his 800 men got quietly out from their Trojan Horse and attacked the barracks packed with about 4,000 federal troops. By early morning November 16, 1913, the city was once more in his hands, but about 2,000 federals managed to escape. It was shortly after this astounding feat that I joined Pancho Villa in Juarez.

II

With Carranza and Obregon—Under arrest—The battle
of the Yaqui drums—Ambushed by Yaquis —
Navajoa and the Mayo Indians

With nothing further to do in Nogales after calling on the U.S. Cavalry, I opened a checking account with the First National Bank of Nogales from a letter of credit, boarded the train with my newly acquired Lopez and arrived in Hermosillo at noon December 3, 1913.

Hermosillo was a charming old town with a population of about 15,000, and located, one might say, in the middle of a cactus desert at an elevation of about 700 feet above the sea, and about 180 miles due south of Nogales. My hotel, the Arcadia, was an imposing looking building.

After cleaning up a bit, I wandered into the bar at five o'clock and found several people around, among them two American newspapermen who became my life-long friends: Timothy Turner of the Associated Press and George Weeks of the New

York Herald. Turner was a good-looking fellow in his late twenties, tall, clean-shaven, well dressed and could be taken for an Englishman. Weeks was also tall, handsome, wore a pointed beard, and was about 63 years old.

From these fine fellows, I learned that General Obregon's Headquarters were close to the hotel, and that Carranza was in town, which was good news as I had come a long way to see them. But they also gave a check on my enthusiasm when they informed me that no foreigners were accepted as volunteers, although they had Major Kloss, a German machine-gun expert, who later became a brigadier. There were also two American brothers named Smith who flew an awful looking biplane for the rebels.

Turner and Weeks both offered to intercede on my behalf with Obregon when they heard of my desire to join the rebel forces, and we made an appointment for next morning to see the General. At Headquarters we were received by Lieutenant Colonel Francisco Serrano, Obregon's chief-of-staff. He was courteous enough, but gave the impression that Americans were not particulary wanted, and I soon found him a *gringo* hater.

General Obregon came eventually, and he acted somewhat unnecessarily rude. He was short in stature, thick-set, and a man of about 33 years. He had a round cannon-ball type of head on which the hair was brushed down tight, the black mustache was short but turned up slightly at the sides. The rather small eyes were clear and piercingly penetrating. Taking it all in all, he was not a bad looking man. He came from near Huatabampo where he had a ranch not far from the Mayo River in southern Sonora.

When Francisco Madero started his insurrection against the reelection of President Diaz, Obregon, with the financial aid of Jose Maria Maytorena, a well-to-do landowner in Sonora, recruited some Mayo and Yaqui Indians into a unit which at that time was called a regiment. When Carranza came to Sonora on the invitation of Maytorena, now governor of the state, Obregon, with the governor's aid, became almost at once Carranza's right-hand man. The formation of the "Army of the Northwest" was begun.

Obregon's mannerism improved after awhile and he became quite decent but it was obvious he was trying to hide something. It took me several weeks to find out what, and then it was simple and understandable. He was afraid to expose to Americans his limited knowledge of military matters. But unlike many other generals, such as Pancho Villa, he was very keen to learn, and he did.

The general did not commit himself when I offered my services in the cavalry but said he would speak to the First Chief. We returned to the hotel. A few days later an invitation came for me to call on General Venustiano Carranza, the First Chief of the Revolutionary Army and the Constitutionalist Party of Mexico. When I got there Tim Turner and George Weeks had arrived for their usual daily news conference with Carranza.

I was introduced to Gustavo Espinosa Mireles, Carranza's secretary, a very likable fellow, who later became governor of Coahuila. In Carranza's entourage were three bright young officers: Gustavo Salines, Alberto Salines, and Julio Madero, all well dressed in plain but well fitting uniforms. (SEE PLATE VIII.)

75

The two Salines brothers were interested in flying and rose to be generals. Madero became Ambassador to Sweden and other countries.

When I was presented to Carranza his patriarchal figure gave me a distinct feeling of friendliness. He was over six feet tall, well built and must have been about 55 years old. He wore well fitting planter-like clothes, and his dignified and paternal bearing was reassuring in every respect. His dark spectacles rested on his somewhat large nose, and his long white beard gave him the sage-like appearance and wisdom of a Solomon.

Foreigners and Mexicans alike had warned me that Carranza's lofty and imposing bearing concealed arrogance, that he was proud, patronizing, stubborn, unemotional as well as incommunicative. But they all admitted that when he expressed his views they were usually much to the point.

I had been warned, but when I left after chatting for an hour I could not feel anything but friendly toward him. He was stubborn and would not let me join the cavalry, I had to enter the artillery because he had only two artillery officers. Not a word was said in regard to the wires between him and Villa, but he gave me orders to report to Major Merigo with the rank of First Captain as instructor of artillery and battery commander. (SEE PLATE XIV.)

George Weeks thought this appointment was something remarkable as all foreigners had been turned down except Kloss and the two American fliers. Neither Carranza nor Obregon accepted any more foreigners in the army during the revolution. My commission was signed by General Alvaro Obregon, as com-

mander of the northwest, December 9, 1913. (SEE
PLATE XV.)

Carranza was born in 1859 at Cuatro Cienegras,
in the State of Coahuila, where he had been a successful rancher before becoming a senator during Diaz'
presidency. When Madero launched his first objections
to the reelection of President Diaz, Carranza, seeing
his opportunity, moved over to Madero's side and
became one of his chief advisors. Among the intellectuals supporting Madero throughout his revolution and his tenure of office, the most outstanding man
was undoubtedly Carranza. Obregon had, at that
time, not yet reached the top.

Carranza was a member of the Madero Council
when the City of Juarez was captured by Villa and
Orozco in May 1911, and like Madero he did not
participate in the fighting. He acted as Minister of
War and when Madero became president, he appointed
Carranza governor of the State of Coahuila.

When President Madero was imprisoned by General Huerta and murdered February 22, 1913, Carranza,
as governor of Coahuila, came out against Huerta and
made a public declaration, "The government created
by General Huerta is unconstitutional." He then
packed his kit and began the war against Huerta with
two companions, little money, no credit and no weapons.
At this time Huerta had quite a large army, money in
the treasury, and all the credit needed from foreign
sources.

The revolution was making some headway, but not
too much because of the lack of a unified command.
When Carranza gave out his "Plan of Guadalupe"
in March 1913, as the Revolutionary Platform, it up-
held Madero's "Plan of San Luis Potosi" issued in

1910, and he became the leading spirit in the revolutionary effort. The rebel leaders present at the presentation of the "Plan" appointed Carranza head of the Revolutionary Party and recognized him as First Chief.

Jose Maria Maytorena, governor of Sonora and a strong Maderista, gave Carranza asylum in Nogales, a secure retreat on the northwestern border. In Nogales, Carranza gathered around himself a staff, the nucleus of the New Party, which for years thereafter dominated the destiny of Mexico.

Many men, good, bad and indifferent assembled around Carranza. His chief-of-staff was Colonel Jacinto Treviño, a very fine young man. Among the best were Alvaro Obregon and Plutarco Calles both in their early military careers. There were others, such as Luis Gusman, Alberto Pani, Lucio Blanco, Adolfo de la Huerta, Miguel Alesio Robles, Jose Vasconcelos and Manuel Chao. Among the junior officers was Lieut. Colonel Miguel Acosta, a very young man for his grade but an outstanding soldier, who became a prominent general later.

When Carranza moved his headquarters from Nogales to Hermosillo he had several generals on his staff, among them Felipe Angeles, a tall, slender, olive complected, handsome fellow who considered himself an Indian. Angeles was an unusual rebel because he was born and brought up as a *cientifico,* was the typification of a Spanish hidalgo, and most meticulous about his dress.

Angeles was educated abroad and went through the artillery schools in France and Germany. Unfortunately, and strangely, Carranza did not take advantage of his fine training. Both Carranza and Obregon were good men, but apparently, deliberately ignored all the ideas proposed by Angeles. Thus a military genius was wasted where needed so badly.

There were rumors that Carranza was in the process of making a deal with Huerta. In answer to an inquiry as to whether or not he was negotiating peace with the federal government as reported in certain American quarters, Carranza sent the following reply on December 8:

> "Answering your message of today, I have declared many times that I will not enter into any negotiations with General Huerta.
>
> V. Carranza."

General Obregon issued a proclamation the same day offering amnesty to all federal soldiers forced into the Huerta army, but did not include the officers.

The day after my call on Carranza I reported for duty at the old barracks and met Major Juan Merigo, the commander of Obregon's artillery. He was short, about 5'3", not fat, but had a well-fed look, a pouch that his well fitting khaki uniform was trying unsuccessfully to hide. He was not a bad looking man but vain, and reeked to high heaven with perfume. A cigar, lighted or not, was constantly in his mouth, and with this he strutted most successfully, swinging his English type riding crop.

He had been in the federal army, had a good classroom knowledge of artillery, but his field experience was meager, if at all. He became a general a year or so later, but ended up with a very unsavory reputation. Merigo took me around the barracks that seemed to have been built for defense against Indian attacks or revolutionaries. I was surprised at the scarcity of officers and non-coms, as there were only two second lieutenants and three non-coms in the whole outfit. The men, about 150, were mostly Yaqui Indians with no knowledge of artillery beyond opening the breech and pushing in a shell. The ten field pieces were of the 75 mm Montregon type and looked very efficient, though a few of them had broken firing-pins. With one thing and another, I soon realized that Merigo had something up his sleeve. He didn't want the guns fixed or any artillery officers, especially a foreign one and, therefore, resented my presence.

I had orders from Carranza to train artillery officrs, non-coms and men as quickly as possible, but under the circumstances, I decided to bide my time and say nothing for awhile at least. But it was not so easy to train men in gunnery when the material was that of half wild Yaqui Indians, many of whom could only speak Yaqui. These fellows were, however, most eager to learn. But I had to be a corporal, sergeant, and battery commander, all at the same time, showing them by hand and signs what to do. It was interesting but exasperating.

There was no time to put them through a proper course, or anything like it, and it was necessary to start at the end rather than at the beginning. A little drill and discipline I insisted on, to the chagrin of the two officers, but the men seemed to love it. I was astounded how easily these Indians, recently from the wild bush country, could learn quite intricate matters as long as they were allowed to handle the shells and try for themselves a few times.

When I returned to the hotel that evening, my new friends, the American newsmen, were waiting and, when told about Merigo, they did not seem surprised. Turner had known Merigo when with Madero and thought it was nothing but jealousy.

Soon after my appointment in the artillery I met Lieut. Colonel Miguel Acosta. He was tall, handsome, very bright and well informed young man of about twenty-five summers. As happens with kindred spirits, we met often and I found that he was second-in-command of the cavalry division now being formed. As a keen student on military matters he always introduced questions on cavalry formations and I confided in him, naturally, my desire to transfer from the artillery. He invited me to lunch to meet General Blanco, his chief.

General Lucio Blanco, was one of the more outstanding men who signed Carranza's "Plan of Guadalupe." He was about thirty-five years old, of medium height, dark complected with a black mustache, debonair, was good looking and well dressed but without any insignia of rank. He was buoyant of spirit and created the impression of strong vitality, and who makes friends easily.

Both Blanco and Acosta came from the State of Coahuila, the home State of Carranza. Blanco had some success when commanding troops in that state among other places and captured Matamoros from the federals. He had shown great and natural skill as a guerrilla leader, but had no military training of any sort. Then suddenly bad luck, or lack of experience, dogged him for some time and at Cerro Prieto the federals, under General Juan Navaro, cut his force to pieces. He followed Carranza to Sonora and Acosta came, apparently, with him.

It soon became obvious that Blanco needed someone to organize his cavalry into proper units, and while sitting there I was wondering why I had been sent to the artillery when I had asked for the cavalry. General Blanco must have been desperate for he asked me to draw up regulations governing the formation of a cavalry regiment, a kind of guide for each officer and N.C.O. This I promised to do if he could supply me with a man capable of putting my words into proper Spanish military terms.

When I returned to the artillery, Major Merigo was informed of the meeting with Blanco, and it annoyed him extremely. From that time on he began to place all kinds of obstacles in my way. He had me followed, and went so far as to have me arrested for seeing Blanco, but had sense enough to rescind the order before it was too late. At another time, he stopped me during field exercises with the battery and called out angrily in front of the men, "We do not gallop a battery into action in modern warfare, Captain Gray. That is a thing of the past." I thought there was something wrong with the man as two-thirds of the army had no guns, but carried scalping-knives, machetes, bows, arrows, spears and slings. Modern warfare indeed! I did, however, keep my own counsel and returned to the barracks with the battery.

One day I decided to move from the hotel to the barracks as it was inconvenient to get to the guns for early morning parade. I did not need to be there as I had distinct orders from Merigo not to attend these parades, except now and again, but I did so every morning except one. Besides, I had made up my mind to quit or tell General Obregon what was going on, for we were doing only a fraction of what we could do. Then it happened.

Merigo turned up for roll-call at six o'clock the morning I remained in my quarters, but I was looking down at the parade from my window. A messenger soon came with orders from Merigo for me to report at once to the commandant. When I reached the guns there was not a single word from Merigo, nor did he return my salute, but four men grabbed me from behind and tried to tie me down. As I did not feel inclined to permit this, two of the men got hurt, one with a broken collar-bone from a jiu-jitsu trick, learned long ago, in the art of self-defense. By this time Merigo had a substantial number of armed men around him, and I was marched between them to the Guard Room and there placed under close arrest in a small cell with an armed sentry at my door. I said nothing for it was necessary to remain calm as he could easily dispose of me inside the fortress-like barracks and no one would ever know. Apparently Merigo thought better of it as he trumped up four charges against me: 1. Constantly absent from early morning parade; 2. Disobedience of orders; 3. Striking and disabling a non-com; 4. Striking and hurting a gunner.

At noon a man brought me a piece of beefsteak and bread wrapped in a very dirty newspaper. The steak was full of maggots and it stank. When I showed the meat to the officer in charge he agreed it wasn't fit for a coyote but he couldn't do anything as it had been sent by the commandant, Major Merigo.

At about five o'clock in the afternoon, I began to realize this might drag on for weeks and pursuaded the officer to let me telephone to the hotel for some food. This was only a subterfuge to get hold of Tim Turner, and he, the good fellow, was at the barracks within an hour with some fried chicken, vegetables, and a bottle of wine.

There was an amusing incident in connection with Turner's visit. When he entered my cell-like room with the officer of the guard, I showed him the rotten meat and then threw the package through the door, hoping it would go through the window beyond. However, the newspaper opened up in flight and made a peculiar sound. The sentry, being half asleep, jumped to attention and presented arms to the rotten beefsteak.

Tim burst out laughing and we all joined him, but the Yaqui sentry couldn't see any cause for merriment. A few minutes later while trying to open the champagne Tim had brought, the cork went off with a tremendous pop and the officer, thinking I was shooting my way out of confinement, called out the guard, and we had another laugh in which the officer did not join, but the sentry did.

Major Merigo came to the barracks the following morning at my request. I had something to convey to him. He became most chagrined and troubled when I informed him that an American newpaperman, a friend of Carranza and Obregon, had been to see me and that by this time they knew all about the false charges, close confinement and the rotten meat. Then I demanded an immediate hearing or court-martial.

This was not pleasing to Merigo's ears for he realized I had forestalled him and he turned with fury upon the officer of the guard. As I had him in a distracted state and on the defensive, I told Merigo of my intention to ask for a transfer to the cavalry. No doubt this coward saw in my transfer a chance to get himself out of a bad fix for he changed in a second from a formidable enemy to an *amigo* and *compañero*. He withdrew all the charges and we walked out from the guardroom, with his arm linked in mine, as if we were old pals.

After parting with Merigo I made for General Blanco's headquarters and found him and Colonel Acosta discussing the reorganization of the cavalry. They were trying to make something out of our previous talks. Blanco chaffingly reprimanded me for not turning up as promised a few days before, and was aghast when told of my arrest. As this seemed to be the appropriate moment, I informed him of my firm intention to quit the artillery and leave Mexico if I couldn't get a transfer to the cavalry. Blanco was quite frank and said he needed my services, but would have to see Obregon first.

Here then we started laying down the minimum basic necessities for the reorganization of the Rebel Cavalry, including troop, squardon, regiment, brigade and division. Blanco and Acosta made notes constantly and within an hour they had enough information on paper to last them for several days. There was never an objection raised from Blanco, except when informed that N.C.O.'s and officer's schools should be started immediately. When Blanco wanted to know who was going to teach in the schools, my answer was, "Get me a transfer and we'll manage."

As I was leaving cavalry headquarters the governor of Sonora, Jose Maria Maytorena, arrived for a conference with Blanco and I had the pleasure of meeting him for the first time. He was short and stumpy in appearance, very well dressed, but like most politicians, perhaps a little too well-fed. He was known as a patriot who owned vast tracts of land, but thought of Mexico first and himself second, a rare and unique quality indeed among politicians at that or any other time.

He had taken up Francisco Madero's slogan, "Land and Liberty" for the peons and Indians and was striving hard to make Madero's "Plan of San Luis Potosi" work. He was trying to create small farms and do away with the hacienda debt-slavery for the benefit of the people, but he found strong opposition from some of the new politicos who had sprung up on the rebel side. He was also attempting the gigantic task of raising the standard of living among the poor, and hoped to develop the mining industry on a fair-share basis for the State and the owners. In all of these worthwhile efforts he had met no response except opposition from the large landowners.

Merigo, knowing of my efforts for a transfer and glad, no doubt, to get rid of me, agreed to my conducting the cavalry school every afternoon. To my surprise, he told me to start classes for both officers and N.C.O.'s in the artillery. These technical instructions were held every morning but the field exercises with the guns were before breakfast. The non-com class was getting along so fast that I could cut the program in half. It was remarkable how quickly these Yaquis learned when given a chance. Generals Obregon and Blanco started their lessons on strategy and tactics December 18, but it was kept as a strict confidential matter at Obregon's request, which was understandable due to his position as Corps Commander. But he was keen as mustard on learning.

About this time we received news which had caused some excitement in diplomatic circles, but received by us with jubilation. It was the telegram from the Queen of Holland to President Huerta in which she suggested that he resign for the good of Mexico and peace. It seems that Mr. Richard Conover, a reporter for the New York Herald, had in some way come upon this confidentially kept secret in the Mexican Foreign Office and published it in the Herald. Conover was arrested or forced to appear before Mr. Moheno, the Minister of Foreign Affairs, and was told he would be expelled from Mexico if he did not reveal the name of the informer, but he refused.

Gen. Huerta and Moheno then decided the American be treated as a spy, as he had obtained secret documents of the government. The political picture in the capital changed. Rumors were that Moheno would probably have to resign to clear Huerta and that Luis Menendez, a traitor to the peon-Indian cause, would take his place. It was also reported that Moheno and Carlos Pereyra had plotted against Huerta to have him removed from the presidency. People who knew Huerta thought he would dismiss Pereyra but that Moheno might be treated with the Law of flight (*Ley de fuga*) which is equivalent to "shot while trying to escape."

A few hours after hearing of Moheno's trouble with Huerta our headquarters received a message that quite a number of men stationed at the Mexico City garrison had rebelled. A number of destitute civilians, who trembled at the thought of provoking Huerta's vengeance, hesitated, but hunger overcame their fears and they joined the soldiers. This anti-

87

Huerta movement was apparently badly arranged for it was put down after a few hours of spasmodic fighting. There was a summary hearing but most of the soldiers and civilians captured were shot. To make sure that all those connected with the affair were punished, the military commander of the capital jailed a vast number of civilians who may or may not have been relatives of those who actually took part. Many of these were shot when they could not prove their innocence.

It came to our notice in Hermosillo, on December 16, that President Huerta had forced his lame-duck Congress in Mexico City to annul all federal laws that might prevent his own reelection. The same day we heard that the American Consul in Monterrey had reported the city under attack by the rebels under General Pablo Gonzalez, and that the federal soldiers were afraid of the outcome. They had reason to be afraid, as news had leaked out that our troops in Salinas and Victoria, not far from Monterrey, stood in readiness to march to his assistance if necessary.

We also heard that General Zapata was worrying the government, as Huerta had shaken up his command in Morelos by removing General Jimenez Castro and had appointed General Luis Canton in his place with orders to pursue the Zapatistas to the limit. From another source we heard that Zapata was recruiting men in the mountains of Huautla, and had attacked the federals several times at Huitzilac with demoralizing raids.

We were expecting with great eagerness about 1,000 Winchester carbines and 200,000 rounds of ammunition to come over the Border at any time and optimistically had made preparation for their distribution among the gun-hungry men. The bad news came on December 18, when the American press gave an acount of how the U.S. Border Patrol had captured a number of Mexicans trying to smuggle a large shipment of guns over into Mexico.

We lost not only the guns but also a large sum of scarce American dollars. There was an embargo on munitions of war, but there were also many degenerate picaroons in America with the sporting instinct of a bunch of skunks, who had nothing against selling us guns at fantastically high prices, exorbitant even when looking at it as blackmail. These men were paid in advance in American currency and sometimes for fake protection against interference by Border Patrols. No sooner than paid this blood-money, they informed the U.S. Authorities where and when to find the prohibited goods.

There were many bewildering as well as exasperating problems to deal with when forming a rebel army particularly when it is short of money, guns and ammunition. The gun shortage was indeed an acute one for the morale of the thousands of volunteers turned back for the lack of weapons. We did take the Yaquis and Mayos when they brought bows and arrows, and formed them into units under their own chiefs.

After the unsuccessful gun-running expedition, I reiterated to Blanco the necessity of the immediate formation of guerrilla bands to get ammunition and guns from enemy outposts, scouts, and small patrols. We also needed more information of the enemy and suggested sending trusted men to different ranches and villages to make friends with the people. At the same time they were to interest some of them in an espionage system, which should not be so difficult as most of the small working farmers were in sympathy with the revolution, and to inform the people that runners carrying information of the enemy were to be rewarded according to the value of the intelligence received.

On or about December 18, quite a number of Yaquis came from their homeland in the bush country somewhere around Cocorit to join our forces. They carried bows and arrows, knives, and some machetes. Several of them had white dots painted on their faces.

Tim Turner was informed one morning in Hermosillo that Chief Coyote Iguano, of the Seri tribe, had come from Tiburon (Shark) Island to pay his respects to General Carranza. As I wanted to know more about these people, I took Lopez as an interpreter and visited the quarters in which they were housed. I found them surprisingly tall in stature, well built and in perfect condition. They wore a light kind of upper garment which served as a shirt made of light cotton material. The slacks, of the same material, were rolled up over the knees. Four of them had head-bands to keep the straight, long, black hair in order. The rest kept their hair untidily hanging down almost to the shoulders, except for one who had hair a foot long down his back.

Two carried seven foot long spears, apparently used for fishing. The rest had round bows about four feet long or a little over, but one was almost five feet long. The arrows used were about three feet long with very fine tips, evidently used for fishing and bird hunting. One man carried what looked like a shield which was three feet long but only eight inches wide at the top and it was rounded at the bottom.

I never did know if this was a shield or, perhaps, a banner of some kind, as the man was shy and walked away when questioned.

Not long before the 1913 revolution, these Indians did a lot of damage to the settlers. They stole a lot of property and killed many Mexicans. The Seri had waylaid the Whites for years on the road from Hermosillo to Guaymas, and seemed to enjoy taking prisoners to secret caves and there torturing them to slow death, much like the Apaches and, if it comes to that, the Inquisition of the Christian Church.

The writer doubts very much if the Seri he has seen are Christians. Baptized, yes, but very few were Christians, at least not in 1913. The murderous Apaches that I met in Pancho Villa's outfit only a month or so before, and some of the Yaquis that I met later, were also called Christians. This makes one wonder what kind of yardstick is used when measuring Christianity.

The Battle of the Yaqui Drums

General Lucio Blanco and Colonel Acosta came to see me at noon, January 5, 1914, and informed me that my transfer to the cavalry had gone through that day. (SEE PLATE XVI.) The stumbling block had been Colonel Serrano, who did not wish to give Lucio Blanco any assistance. In fact, Acosta thought he wanted Blanco out of the way. General Obregon came to class that day and demanded more information on blockhouses, barbed wire entanglement, and the light emergency trenches used in the Boer War.

The Cavalry Division, still more or less in a

skeleton form, entrained at 9 a.m., January 8, for Culiacan, the capital of the State of Sinaloa. After waiting seven hours for Carranza, the train moved from Hermosillo at about four in the afternoon, with him and his staff safely aboard. The cowpunchers, making up our main force, were grumbling openly at the delay. The train stopped at Ortiz, a place about 30 miles north of Guaymas, where the troops under General Alvarado were inspected by Carranza. Alvarado had about 2,000 Yaqui Indians armed with bows, arrows, machetes and here and there a 30-30 Winchester.

The train moved on and we reached Santa Rosa about ten in the evening which was late for Carranza, for he disliked traveling at night by train. The cavalry was disembarked at once and bivouacked about 17 miles north of Guaymas. The troops around Santa Rosa were all Yaquis under General Cabral. Major Kloss and his machine-guns came along with the Carranza entourage, and so did Tim Turner and George Weeks.

We broke this camp about 2 p.m., January 9, and started off on the road to Cruz Piedra, a place located about ten miles east of Guaymas. A number of small wagons and carts made up our transport. The column arrived there late in the afternoon and found it occupied by some 1,500 Mayo Indians armed with bows, arrows, knives, and some guns, under the command of General F. Mendez. There were also many bands of Indians hanging around waiting to be accepted into our ranks.

On the small rise close to our camp at Cruz Piedra, we could see parts of the American and Japanese gunboats in the outer harbor of Guaymas.

The inner harbor was not visible but we knew the city was well protected with guns, mines, trenches, and two gunboats in the harbor. It was reported that the Japanese minister to Mexico was on a visit to Guaymas, which was not a good sign for us, as it was reported that an American Admiral, in cahoots with the Japanese, was cooking up an unsavory dish for the rebels.

While I was standing there looking toward the sea, Tim Turner and a Mexican friend came to have a look with the others. Suddenly, someone called out, "Look! There they come," and we could see a column of men emerge from Guaymas along the road in our direction.

No sooner were the federals spotted than drums from the Yaqui encampment started their weird tattoo signals. The Yaqui drum is a shallow tamborine-like instrument covered with goat or sheepskin on both sides. It is to all intents and purposes the "spirit of the tribe" or group to which it belongs. These groups vary, but are often two to three hundred strong. These war drums give out sounds not possible on the ordinary drum, and when need be, give out a great volume reaching far into the bush. The Yaqui headman, or chief, gives orders to his followers by different tattoos and they will move forward, retreat, move to any flank and in many other movements according to the drum beat.

While we were standing there, another column came out and it was obvious this was a show of strength and not a patrol action. The first column had grown in length and was of considerable numbers, probably three thousand strong.

Lopez had joined me for instructions and I sent him

back to Colonel Acosta to see if the cavalry would be needed. The Yaquis had by this time moved out toward the enemy, in full view from our position, and they advanced in their own tribal manner with no particular formation. At first they seemed to wander about as if lost. Then I noticed each man was taking care not to be seen from the front. They went from bush to bush, as by habit, even at this apparent great distance from the enemy. Some of them danced with a jump and stamping of feet while advancing. Their heads were bent down and their bodies stooped as if intensely interested in some trail. In the beginning, one could hear distinctly some of them chanting, a war song perhaps, and others laughed and looked exceedingly happy. Those with rifles carried them in the hand which was extended almost to the ground, due to their stooping position.

During this preliminary advance of some seven or eight groups, each with a drum, the tattoo was about the same. Then a single drum gave a signal, and each group drum changed its beat and with it the Yaqui manners. Their indifferent and don't care attitude became one of extreme carefulness. They moved like ghosts and disappeared out of our sight into the bush in front of us.

The federal commander had by this time deployed a force of about two companies in front of his advance guard which looked like the remainder of a battalion. All Indian drums were now silent, with only now and again a beat which was answered from some other point farther away each time. But the federals came on. Then came a series of beats from a place some distance in front of us, which were answered by short tattoos from places far away and on both flanks of the enemy. Then silence for quite a while.

At this time Acosta turned up to inform me that the cavalry was not to be used as this was a Yaqui affair, but that a regiment was in readiness in case of need.

Then came another drum beat, apparently from the chief in command, and all the drums started, then stopped. This time it was obvious that the Yaquis had reached both flanks of the federals who halted as if in fear and not by an order. One could see the officers through the glasses running up and down trying to urge the men forward, but they remained standing and refused to move. There was complete silence for a short while, and then several drums began to talk behind the federals. These drums seemed to give out weird and unholy sounds that must have sent cold shivers of fear into the enemy ranks, for the federals broke formation and began to run toward Guaymas, in disorder.

An officer made a gallant attempt to save his machine-gun, but failed as the Yaquis disposed of him and captured the battery complete with pack animals intact. Up to this point the only sound noticeable had been the drums. Not a shot had been fired. But now the Yaquis closed in on both flanks and played havoc with the federals. Some threw away their rifles to escape these dreaded Indians.

Ambushed by Yaquis

The cavalry left Cruz Piedra at noon, January 10. Before leaving, Colonel Acosta informed me that he had been warned of the possibilities of running into small parties of Yaquis running wild before we reached Fundicion, and he asked that I try to avoid a clash with them if possible. On the way south, the advance-guard, with which I was riding, found a good hand-car in an old railroad shed and it was difficult to resist the temptation to borrow it for I enjoy traveling on these hand-powered contraptions. Thus, it came about that four troopers, Lopez and I, started off in the hope of getting a shot at some game and seeing the nature of the country ahead.

We found game and some shooting too, but of a different kind than expected. About fifteen miles north of Fundicion, the hand-car ran smack into a stray body of Yaquis, armed with bows and arrows, who did not seem to like the looks of us for they attacked at once with a shower of arrows.

This was quite serious as the Indians had cut us off in the rear and were closing in to occupy the dense brush on both sides. When trying to rush the hand-car forward we found a number of braves throwing some large logs across the track and we had no choice but to jump off and take up position in the shallow ditch alongside the hand-car.

It was an uneven match from the start as our bandoleers were more than half empty before the scrap began, and the ammunition, although carefully nursed, was dwindling fast. Two men were wounded, one so badly that he could not move. The other continued to use his gun valiantly although bleeding profusely from a deep wound in the right thigh from which he pulled an arrow. While trying to stem the bleeding, I noticed our water bottles were almost empty, and just then a third man got hit in the neck which seemed to cause an internal hemorrhage for he choked to death a few minutes later.

When looking around for a way out of this mess, Lopez, who had been giving a good account of himself, offered to go out and negotiate with the Yaquis. But then an old warrior, who was next to me, asked to be heard, and Lopez translated: "These are young and untried braves against us who have scented blood for the first time. They will probably hang us up in trees and leave us there to starve and feed the vultures. It is better to fight on."

Feeling in sympathy with the old Indian, I decided to hang on. We hadn't fired a shot for fifteen minutes and then we noticed a sudden change, the arrows ceased coming. They apparently thought we were out of ammunition. We could see them, now and again, gliding almost carelessly, but swiftly, from bush to bush, nearer and nearer. Lopez and the old man had strict orders not to shoot until it was absolutely imperative to do so.

Suddenly, Lopez fired and hit one of the two Indians not ten yards away. Then we heard someone shouting an order upon which they all stopped and moved away from us hurriedly. A moment later, Acosta turned up deploying his men at a gallop, and the Indians vanished like ghosts into the bush. Their disappearance reminded me much of how the Zulu impi vanished in the N'Kansla forest, during the Zulu Rebellion of 1906, and I felt the same relief now, as then, to see them go.

Acosta had found our horses and was told of the hand-car. He sped after us with a squadron, as a report had come in that the Yaquis had found some *tequila* and were drinking heavily, which always puts them in a quarrelsome mood. The wounded were examined, but there was no sign of hard liquor on any of them. We lost two killed and two wounded, and found four dead and four badly wounded Yaquis in the bushes close by. I was rather amused later, when told that these Yaquis did not really mean any harm as they were only out for some fun while waiting to join our forces.

Before leaving the place, I picked up a few arrows and two bows as mementoes. One of the arrows had a hardwood point, another a very interesting black stone-point that might have been obsidian, but the rest had regular hunting tips.

While I was collecting these trophies, a very fine looking Indian spoke to me in Spanish, which was not much better than my own. He wanted to join our forces, especially the cavalry. When asked if he had taken part in the attack, he said, "Yes, I helped to put the logs on the tracks." His magnificent bearing and honest answer pleased me and I asked his name. He pointed to the sky where an eagle was soaring in the heavens, so I presumed his name was Eagle, and said, "Aguila," but he shook his head and said, "Tekwe." Later I found he meant to convey that his name was not Tekwe (Yaqui for eagle). However, the name remained his all through the war, and he seemed to like it.

By this time the rest of the column had arrived and so we continued our journey and marched into Fundicion at 9 P.M., January 10. This was a small station for ore shipments, and a community center for the employees of an American Mining company.

The cavalry boarded a series of trains and left Fundicion at 8 A.M., January 11, for Navajoa where we arrived at ten o'clock that evening. With us were Carranza, General Angeles, who was acting minister of war, generals Blanco, Alvarado, and Buelna. General Candido Aguilar was to arrive from Tampico two days later. Late as it was, our reception by the people was most enthusiastic with triumphal arches, flowers and bouquets for the First Chief, which pleased the old man. The women in the place seemed somewhat relaxed, friendly, and good looking, and our men made the most of it.

Carranza, with a large following, left Navajoa the afternoon of January 12 for Huatabampo, a town not far from the estuary of the Mayo River. Most of the general staff went with him, including General Blanco.

After they had all gone, I got a chance to check on the different units and found that reorganizing the cavalry was not going to be so easy as many of the officers were closely related to different generals or were their close friends. That afternoon the second of the officers' classes started and, to my surprise, all of them turned up. To save time and make it easier on the men, and also because I could not find anyone to teach me the proper military terms in Spanish, some of the more unessential details were dispensed with, to the great relief of all.

The town of Navajoa, located on the Mayo River almost in the center of the Mayo Indian territory, was an interesting place. Among other things, it had an old hotel with a shower in an outhouse which also served as a back-house. The Mayo boy fills the tank by getting up a ladder with a bucket, and you stand there while he pours in the water and grins at you from ear to ear, as apparently not too many people used the contraption. The place was swarming with Mayos, all carrying bows and arrows, waiting and hoping to join our forces against the government. During my trip through the town, I met two funerals which had resulted from smallpox cases, and I was told that there were many sick from this disease.

A number of Mayos from the outlying districts marched past in review before Carranza. They all wore breechclouts, leather sandals, carried bows and arrows, and a few machetes. A little later they performed a dance (the *Matachine*) for him. This dance is performed by all Indians in this region whether they profess the Catholic faith or not. It is a religious function and can hardly be called a dance of welcome to an individual, but it pleased the First Chief.

The dancers were dressed in rather grotesque costumes, each carrying a rattle and moved around dancing under certain leaders (*monarcos*). The leaders brought the dancers before Carranza and they bowed and shook their rattles toward him, symbolizing perhaps that they had accepted him as their chief. The music used in this homage came from a violin with one string, rattles, and a gourd held in a bucket of water without submerging the neck, while the man thumped on it with his hands, giving out weird sounds.

After the dance, a large body of local Mayos came out and demonstrated the usefulness and superiority of the bow and arrows over the rifle in bush fighting. In the middle of this most interesting maneuver carried out in the bush, someone felt that no one could see the Indians, and Carranza seemed to think the same, for he ordered the Indians to move out into the open.

The demonstration of the three hundred or more half wild Mayos became a fiasco. The Indians were disappointed and almost mortified at having to shoot their arrows, like children, at nothing. As a result, some of the *politicos* present thought it a waste of time to bother with these Indians as the bow was an obsolete weapon and could not stand up against the rifle. These skeptics almost convinced Carranza, and had it not been for Obregon, the bow and arrows might have been discarded, which would have been foolish, as we had no guns to give them.

In fact, without the bow and arrows of the Yaquis and Mayos, the revolution of 1913-1914 might never have been carried to a successful conclusion. All through the difficult days in the bush country of Sonora, Sinaloa, and Tepic, the bow was supreme. The federals with modern rifles and machine-guns were often forced to evacuate their positions. These remarkable Indians with their bows and arrows and long knives collected thousands of rifles from the federals. The bow brought us some of the first guns so badly needed for the fighting to come. Among those present at the bow and arrow demonstration were Carranza, Obregon, Blanco, Acosta, Tim Turner, George Weeks, Julio Madero and the Yaqui chiefs, Luis Espinosa and Ignacio Mori.

The Mayos speak a dialect of the Cahita (Bowman) language, not unlike the Yaqui dialect of the same language with a slight difference. The Cahita proper is an extinct or a forgotten language, but the Yaqui and Mayo dialects remain.

A guest member of the Carranza party had foolishly made some disparaging remarks about the Mayos to a particular sub-chief at the reception for Carranza, and there was a scene, but it was hushed up. Thinking no more of the incident, Acosta and I took six men and rode along the river to explore the country, scout, and see how the Mayos lived. About six miles from camp a shower of arrows greeted us from two sides. It was obvious that the Indians were shooting from quite a distance for the trajectory of the arrows was high and came down almost straight up and down, but we couldn't see a man. Acosta, cool but inexperienced seemed uncertain, so I suggested we run for it and this we did at the gallop. We arrived in camp with one trooper and two horses wounded, but not seriously. The following day it was reported that some of the Mayos were bragging about putting "a large body of cavalry to flight" at sundown the day before, in retaliation for the insults heaped upon their chief.

PLATE III

Gen. Alvaro Obregon.
Sonora, 1913

III

*Culiacan—Embargo on guns lifted — Gun and horse
thieves—Smallpox—The cavalry school—Two
American sailors—Rebel paper money—Heavy
fighting in Tepic—Federals hang all captured
rebels—Carranza to Chihauhau—Rebels short of
cash*

About a day or two after our experience with
the Mayo Indians in Navajoa the cavalry entrained
and we arrived in Culiacan at 11 A.M., January 21.
We camped a few hundred yards west of the railroad station. Smallpox was rampant in the city and
district which had threatened the troops for days
along the line of march. Personally, I got a room
at Hotel Rosales for a bath and a change of clothing.

Carranza's train came into Culiacan at noon the
following day. His welcome was not as hilarious,
perhaps, as had been expected, but there was a band
playing and a number of townspeople milling around.
Some of these had, no doubt, been forced to come
out by the military, but others came out of curiosity and to see the rebels.

As the city had only recently been taken over

by us, the so-called "best people" had fled fearing persecution. The 1st Cavalry Regiment lined the streets in honor of the First Chief. There was an occasional "Viva Carranza" to be heard and then a rather fat looking politician dressed in white clothes started to make a speech. He didn't get very far as some of the unsympathetic rebel soldiers began to laugh at his ludicrous appearance and Carranza, sensing it was the wrong man, moved on with his staff and guests. It may have been necessary, but it seemed to me that large sums had been spent unnecessarily on expensive decorations in Carranza's honor, which could have been put to better use, as we needed the guns, ammunition and clothing.

The officers' and N.C.O. lectures and general field training were resumed January 25, after three days of dinners, endless political speeches, luncheons, and elaborate balls every night. The troops were constantly reviewed by some general or visiting politician which interfered seriously with the training program.

The officers' class was practically at a standstill because of these *fiestas* which put them back from where they started. The N.C.O.'s schools, especially the lower grades, were kept open and it was a pleasure to see how keen these Indians and peons were to learn.

Carranza received many telegrams from Europe and the United States asking, some demanding, him to give up the revolution and make peace with the federal government. The suggestion was ridiculous, for the man to go was the murderer General Huerta. Should Carranza try to do what was demanded of him, he would have betrayed the peons and Indians and reneged on all his sacred promises. Besides, he would have been tried for treason by Huerta and hung, with the rest of us, in the nearest tree.

On January 31, we had two more smallpox cases among the troops, and Blanco ordered me to move to his quarters in town. It was a fine house belonging to some well-to-do man who had fled before our arrival.

A telegram from Governor Maytorena in Sonora, on February 1, informed us that 500 federal soldiers had mutinied in Guaymas and were fighting the others in the city. Fifty men and officers of the mutineers managed to break through to our side and reported the incident. The same telegram told of another mutiny among the federals at Cerro Prieto, where they had been fighting one another all day. The federals turned their artillery, which could be heard from the rebel position, on the mutineers inside the town.

There was an interesting character named Juan Carrazco who rode into Culiacan now and again. He was the leader of a mounted guerrilla band, refused rank, and dressed like any small rancher in his Sunday best. His men, sometimes referred to as the Carrazquistas, were a tough bunch of cowboys but most efficient in trapping federal outposts and small patrols. They shot the captured officers, but the soldiers were relieved of their guns, equipment, clothing, and then allowed to go, sometimes even without a stitch on.

This man had been of great service to Carranza in the capture of Culiacan, was in great favor, and could do almost as he liked. There was a report going around that Carrazco wanted to sport his own artillery and had gone out to capture some. He cunningly tricked the federals to send a field-gun with escort into the bush-country where it was captured. The Carrazquistas shot, carelessly enough, all the gunners and there was not a man among them who knew how to handle a field piece. The gun was brought to Carranza, and Carrazco gave up the idea of having his own Artillery Troop.

Culiacan was full of desperate thieves and we lost a lot of stuff. Two remounts were stolen one night, and three carbines the next. The soldier on guard seems to have been implicated as he had left his post and could not be found. That night two more carbines disappeared and the missing guard was caught during the evening of February 2, while trying to smuggle the carbines out of the town. He stole the guns, he said, for some friends located in the foothills of the sierra, long way east of the city.

Acosta, Tekwe, and I went into the lower parts of Culiacan to look for some guns still missing. We were well armed with revolvers and knives, but in a narrow back street we were surrounded and jumped on by a great number of men. It was obvious that we didn't have a chance, so we rushed at those in front of us with guns blazing and broke through. Our escape was almost a miracle for they fired several shots and threw knives at us at close range. None of us was hit, but the attackers lost at least two men who fell in the melee. It may, however, have been four as Tekwe, protecting our rear, fired several shots and had thrown his knife. When Tekwe threw his knife he could hardly miss a target the size of a silver dollar at ten paces.

On February 2 the First Cavalry Division consisted of two Brigades. The 1st Brigade had only one complete regiment; the 2nd Regiment was incomplete and lacked officers and N.C.O.'s with any knowledge on military matters. The 2nd Brigade was coming along slowly but lacked officers, N.C.O's and, worst of all, guns. The 3d Brigade was also in the making, but now only in skeleton form, with a few officers, mostly friends or relatives of generals and politicians. We had no transport but each man in the 1st Brigade carried three day rations, 100 to 200 rounds of ammunition, carbine and saber or machete.

We had been informed that the Division would leave Culiacan and begin its march on Mexico City within two weeks, and I was instructed to have officers and N.C.O.'s ready for the three brigades by that time, an impossible task. The idea was to raise and train another division as we went along fighting toward the capital. The training program was rushed, and it went on from before dawn to nightfall. We expected to capture guns and ammunition from the federals. To get to the right kind of men, we were to move from hacienda to hacienda, town to town, into Guadalajara, some 480 miles distant, and pick all cowboys we could find.

During the morning of February 3, the soldier who stole the horses and carbines was sentenced by a court to a seemingly severe punishment. He received twenty-five lashes immediately after the trial, in the afternoon another twenty-five lashes, and was shot an hour later in front of the whole garrison as an example to all other horse thieves. I felt they could have dispensed with the flogging, but Blanco had no say in the matter.

February 3, 1914, was an important day for us as Carranza received a telegram from Washington informing him that President Wilson had lifted the embargo on arms and ammunition into Mexico, "So that those in a revolt against Huerta could secure them."

That day we buried thirty-three men and women in Culiacan from smallpox, and there were three victims of vendettas or plain jealousy over women. We organized a special vigilante police to deal with these matters and they had strict orders to stop this unnecessary killing. The leader of the vigilantes was killed the first night out, with a knife in his back.

During the ten days following our arrival in Culiacan the rebel forces had grown tremendously; yet, we had turned away thousands of volunteers due to shortage of guns and officers of any value as such. The raising of the embargo helped us immensely, but we had to find American dollars somehow. We worked hard indeed to get them, sometimes a little roughly, perhaps, when we commandeered all the cattle we could find. Thousands were rounded up daily, shipped, and sold over the Border in the United States for cash. These buyers knew our predicament and were poor sports. We did not average more than $5 per head when they were fat cattle worth over $40 on the hoof.

The schools were doing fairly well, considering all the difficulties. The officers were backward, although some of them were good and could pass as instructors in the rudimentary principles of training men, which was important at the moment. Some officers were still objecting to the curtailment of their freedom during the day and simply hated any kind of discipline forced upon them. These malcontents were slowly being weeded out from the cavalry and given to the infantry. The rather amusing part of these transfers was that they went over to the infantry with promotion, because they had been half-way through the cavalry school, but flunked.

The rebel forces directly under Carranza on the Pacific coast were reported to be 25,000, but in reality we had only 15,000 and half of them not armed with guns. We were to raise another 15,000, and when they were in shape, another 15,000. These units were to be completed and ready for the field within three months. This gave us more time than the two weeks previously allowed.

Pancho Villa was said to have about 25,000 men, but he probably had about 12,000. The federal forces under Huerta were estimated to be about 40,000 on all fronts. He probably had about 30,000, but all well equipped. It was therefore difficult to understand why he was not more successful, in some places at least, for he had the railroad communication intact and we had little or no ammunition.

Smallpox showed its ugly face worse than ever all over the Pacific Coast, and 60 per cent of the stricken died. We buried from twenty-five to thirty persons daily, many of them soldiers. The City of Culiacan was fortunate indeed to have a German engineer and his charming wife to volunteer to take charge of the smallpox situation. They vaccinated as many as possible but there wasn't enough serum to go around for the army, let alone the civilians. One day he said to Turner and me, "You two should be vaccinated; come along, I have a few points put aside for an emergency and this is it," and he vaccinated Turner, Weeks and me. He was a fine fellow and I am sorry never to have known his name.

Due to the free and easy mode of living by the new officers, it was difficult to keep strict discipline among the troops as they, like the officers, came from everywhere in the country. Some of them knew the officers from childhood or had worked with them on a ranch. Some had private vendettas to attend to. Almost every night we lost two or more men, some went down with a knife, others by a gun. The military police and the vigilantes seemed powerless to stop it.

Rumors came to us on February 4 that the federals embarked 1,800 men at the coastal town of Altata, west of Culiacan. Later, it was reported that the federal gunboat went close to the shore but did not take any aboard.

Two American sailors, absconders from the U.S.S. Pittsburgh anchored in Mazatlan harbor, came one day and offered their services. They told how they swam three miles from the warship around the federal fortifications and eventually met some of our outposts and were brought to Culiacan. Although their story of swimming three miles through shark infested waters was a little fishy, I thought they might be used in the artillery as they were gunners in the U.S. Navy, and we were shorthanded. Carranza, however, did not wish to have anything to do with them and sent both sailors to the American Border under heavy guard. Blanco told me that many Americans had tried to join us, but as they were suspected of being "foreign agents," they had been turned down.

Bilimbiques or Rebel paper money

The question of raising money for the Rebel Army was a difficult one. The soldiers must be paid or they might return to the hills or their farms, and the civilians needed some kind of medium of exchange for the goods purchased by the army. Most of the money printed in Diaz' time had disappeared; taken away, hidden, buried in the ground. No one seemed to know where most of it had gone.

When the Constitutionalist Army needed anything, it was commandeered in the name of the Rebels and a receipt given stating what was purchased, price, when and by whom. These I.O.U. notes were to be honored by the government after the revolution had been won. This system worked well for a time, but it failed because these people could not continue in business when the promissory notes were not exchangeable for cash within a reasonable time. The soldiers also grumbled for something more tangible than a piece of paper difficult to negotiate in a store, bar, or eating-place (*cantina*).

Carranza thought it a good idea for the Revolutionary Party to solve its financial problems by printing its own money, rather than confiscating funds, cattle, property, and giving I.O.U.'s as they went along. Different kinds of plates were made. The paper was the best obtainable in Mexico, but it was the worst kind for bank notes. The printing presses began to work and Carranza had an endless flow of money of very poor quality, but it served its purpose for the soldiers were content, and it made life easier for everybody concerned.

We paid the soldiers one and one-half pesos per

111

day in paper money, given to him daily after the morning parade or drill, which was more money than the peon had seen for work on the hacienda. Bookkeeping was simple. Every regimental commander was given the money for his regiment, and he handed each company or squadron commander their amount, and they in turn passed it on to their subordinate platoon commanders.

There was only one signature for the whole regiment which was that of the colonel, and even that was dispensed with at times. He told how many men he had and was paid the money without question. It was a bad method as it brought on padded payrolls. It became noticeable that some of the senior officers were living far beyond their income, but no one seemed to care.

This method of overcoming one's financial difficulties appeared an excellent idea among the prominent as well as the lesser *cabecillas* (SEE INDEX), and they started their own printing-presses going in the art of making money.

There were dozens of presses working overtime in various parts of the country, each having its own particular type of plates, or no plates at all, but all the money was equally worthless outside of Mexico. When one of the generals ran out of paper, bad as it was before, he did not improve the looks of the bills when he resorted to rolls of toilet-paper. This had to be discontinued, however, because there was soon a shortage of that rare commodity also.

The merchants who refused to accept this paper money, jokingly called *bilimbiques,* were considered enemies of the State and were dealt with severely —sometimes their property was confiscated.

Among the more prolific producers of paper money were, of course, the commanding generals of large forces such as Carranza, Villa and Zapata. Orozco also printed large amounts while in control of Chihuahua during his insurrection against President Madero. But all of this money was not worth anything in the United States. When dealing with Americans, it was necessary to pay in silver or gold bullion, cattle, or U.S. dollars. One could, however, purchase in Mexico with these *bilimbiques,* gold, silver, mines, farms, haciendas, houses, cattle, and horses from scared people, and then sell to Americans and receive their dollars. This was done by crooked politicians who pocketed the money instead of handing it over to the Revolutionary Party for guns and ammunition.

When Carranza issued a decree that Mexico would not accept its own paper money for the payment of custom fees, Mr. Bryan, Secretary of State under President Wilson, fumed and protested vigorously to Carranza for not recognizing his own money. This, Mr. Bryan said, was a common law among civilized nations. Carranza's reply to Bryan must have hurt a little for it stopped immediately all further objections. In his quiet way, Carranza told the State Department in Washington that he had taken the idea from the United States, which had a similar proviso engraved on special issues of American dollar bills.

Tim Turner of the Associated Press thought he knew the origin of the word *bilimbiques.* There had been, he told me, an American by the name of William Weeks who employed Mexican labor in Sonora. He paid his men with chits or little tickets redeemable in goods or cash in the company store. When referring to these signed vouchers, the peon attempting to say William Weeks pronounced it *"bilimbiques."*

Carranza, or someone in his government on the Pacific Coast, made an attempt at silver currency and produced about 25,000 silver pesos in sand molds. The production was promptly stopped when analyses proved that each peso contained a great deal of gold, enough to make each coin worth about from two to four pesos. These homemade pesos vanished overnight after the discovery was made, but I managed to obtain one specimen which is kept as a rare memento from those days in Mexico. It was reported that Zapata made silver and gold coins, but I never saw one.

Who did it no one knows, but some rotter brought a great number of new American cigar store coupons and gave them out as American money to the peons and Indians for goods received. The peons accepted the coupons from the Americans in good faith on the face value of the numbers on the coupon. We tried to trace the culprit, but they were gone and the Peon-Indians suffered the loss of everything they owned by this dastardly act.

Fighting in Tepic

On February 5, General Blanco ordered me to leave all training programs and proceed south the following morning to join General Rafael Buelna, who commanded our troops in the northern parts of the Territory of Tepic. My duties were to try to calm down the impetuosity of this man, for he was inclined to be reckless as well as careless in the extreme, although successful. My job was also to try to persuade him to accept a few fundamental principles on military matters, such as strategy, tactics, administration, and to do what I could for this very young but brave soldier.

After giving orders to the new N.C.O. instructors who had just passed their exams, I took Tekwe and Lopez with me and boarded a small supply train at dawn, February 6, to join Buelna for two weeks. Our journey south was strenuous and troublesome, yet uneventful. We had to get off the train at Modesto, saddle up and proceed to Rosario by road because the important seaport of Mazatlán (Place of the Deer) was held by the federals. At Rosario we found a dilapidated old train which we took over and proceeded southward through Acaponeta and found Buelna about eighteen miles north of where the railroad crosses the San Pedro River, in the center of the Territory of Tepic, now the State of Nayarit.

Buelna looked quite young, about twenty-five, was clean shaven and seemingly very intelligent, but not strong physically. He seemed quite pleased to see me and had nothing against receiving lectures, but insisted on private tuition, which was understandable. He amused me one day when, in the middle of a lesson on tactics, something took his fancy. He jumped up and called a bugler and ordered "Boot and Saddle," as he wanted to try it out on the troops without letting the officers know what it was about. The maneuver became a fiasco as the officers were bewildered and the men seemed bored because Buelna didn't know enough to finish the exercise.

Most of his cavalry had been trained in our first

school in Hermosillo and along the road to Culiacan and were in fair shape. He also had a field-gun with a half trained artillery detachment. Buelna, a newly appointed brigadier, took orders from head-quarters in Culiacan. He began his operations against the federals in southern Sinaloa and drove them to within twenty miles of Tepic City. His officers bragged that the federals were on the run, that the revolution was practically over, and that General Buelna was now the leading military, as well as political, figure on the rebel side and would soon be the Minister of War, and president in time.

The attention and flattery of his officers affected the young man and he became a little too contemptuous of the enemy, which led to carelessness and indifference. Attacks were made without due preparation or consideration for his men, their provisions or ammunition supply. While advancing one day, I asked what information he had of the federals and found that he had none, nor did he have any intelligence service whatsoever, except what was brought in voluntarily by the local natives.

As his advance-guard and main body marched almost as in one unit, I suggested the advance-guard be moved farther ahead of the column and that it should be preceded by a screen of scouts deployed far out on a broad front, with flank-guards to be extended out away from the column. In this necessary precaution, Buelna thought I was over cautious and that it would be a waste of time. Then he added, "The federals are beaten and are in full retreat. We do not need all these tiresome maneuvers."

Buelna must have received more than his share of good luck because we moved on and he was successful without scouts, flank-guards, or reserves. One day he laughed at me and said, "You are the pupil now, learning how to fight in the Mexican way." I was learning, I thought, how foolish a young commander can be, for each successful performance made him more and more egotistical, as well as contemptuous of the enemy.

And thus we advanced as conquerors and occupied all the territory as far south as Santiago River. This in spite, or perhaps, because, of the fact that the men were green revolutionary Peon-Indians from the farms, desert regions, and haciendas, fighting against well equipped regular troops, superior in numbers, and led by officers with Chapultepec Military College training. We advanced, but catastrophe was inevitably staring Buelna in the face. His slack discipline had already undermined the morale of the men and he was a doomed man. Nothing could be done to help him for he was self-opinionated and stubborn—but brave. His officers, most of them good men in the field, were made up of former storekeepers, schoolteachers, and some cowboys with little or no military training like himself.

The relatively easy advance had undoubtedly affected their egos. The junior officers flattered their seniors, and to become popular with the men, they had permitted fully armed units to roam the country on their own without any fixed purpose, and they did as they pleased. The original idea was to scout and gather information, but during this time many unpleasant incidents took place such as rape, highway robbery, and even murders, but all this was generally suppressed by the commanding officers for political and other reasons.

When these men were called upon to return to their regiments, most of them did, but many being exuberant over the sudden power of armed freedom came reluctantly. Some returned ungracefully but they were harmless. Others were arrogant and inclined to lay down the law to their superiors. Thus the efficiency and discipline of the troops deteriorated quickly and the men reverted to type and often got out of hand. As an example: some of the men refused to go out on outpost duty, or scout any distance from the column because they thought it unnecessary. The result was that we often had no outposts, no scouts, and we were going like sheep to the slaughter. But no one seemed to know it, and Buelna laughed at my advice.

We advanced and had a decent scrap at Tuxpan (Tuchlan: Place of Rabbits), on the south side of the San Pedro River, west of the railroad. The federals captured 15 of our men and executed them immediately by hanging. When our men saw the whole line of their comrades hanging there, like scarecrows, their emotions exploded in a lust for revenge. "We will hang every federal," said one man, "No" cried another as if in pain, "that's my brother hanging there, we will castrate and then blind every one of the *cabrones* (cuckolds)!" The fight lasted about eight hours, when the enemy thought it best to evacuate their position.

We moved on to Yago, which was near the junction where the railroad crosses the Santiago River and it was captured after two days of hard fighting. The thirty federals captured by us were hanged and some mutilated, in retaliation for the hanging of our men at Tuxpan. Nothing could stop it as they demanded

118

not an eye for an eye, but two heads for one eye. Our casualties in these two fights came to thirty-three killed and about sixty wounded. Enemy losses must have been quite heavy because they left forty-two dead and wounded in the field.

We were moving ahead with success everywhere, but there was something radically, yet intangibly, wrong. Guerrilla warfare, so beneficial to us in the past, was getting out of hand, and the officers forgot or neglected all they had learned. These sturdy and willing peons and Indians were sent along the roads in close formation, without scouts or advance-guard. It was obvious that something had to happen sooner or later, because Buelna's head was full of the popular cry of his men, "The federals are beaten and on the run, Viva Buelna!"

The intangible worried me. The federals retreated in perfect order, well protected by scouts and patrols. I felt as if we were being drawn into something difficult to get out of, and here we were moving along in close formation without scouts.

On February 12, Tekwe called me about an hour before dawn and reported that all the vedettes, that I had personally placed at midnight, had dribbled back to camp during the night and that he had seen quite a number of mounted men south and east of us. I had requested Buelna to send out at least two strong patrols the night before, but the suggestion was ridiculed by him as unnecessary.

Knowing it was useless to inform Buelna, I aroused a regimental commander with whom I had become very friendly, and requested two squadrons to be saddled up for immediate duty, and to call all his men to arms. Then I went to Buelna and informed him. He became almost offensive and told me outright to keep my fears to myself. When I left him, my mind was made up to leave him to his fate and return to Culiacan and Blanco. Before reaching my horse I noticed the two squadrons filing into formation and ready to mount, and the inevitable happened.

The federals struck suddenly from the south with everything they had. It was still a little dark but they were inside our camp before the men could form into their respective units. As I could not leave the work of gathering our surprised and bewildered men, Tekwe was sent to the officer in charge of the two squadrons with orders to gallop out, circle around the enemy, and charge his flank without delay.

The next time I saw Tekwe he was leading a squadron at full gallop and charging the enemy flank, striking them behind their second wave of extended infantry not one hundred yards from where I stood. The charge had an astonishing effect, for the federals began to withdraw. Had they advanced another fifty yards, instead of retreating, we would have been at their mercy. It was, however, a fine sight to see this half-wild pagan Yaqui Indian leading the cavalry against an enemy vastly superior in numbers. Later I found that the squadron commander had been badly wounded while mounting his horse just before the charge, and it was typical of Tekwe to do what he did. This fine act of Tekwe was a pleasant contrast to the ridiculous sight of Buelna and some of his staff rushing about, in complete confusion, in their long underwear.

This surprise attack should have taught Buelna something about the value and the necessity of patrols and outposts. His pride must have been hurt, for he said not a word about it, and didn't even thank Tekwe for what he did. While getting the men together and having them fed, news came to us by friendly natives that large federal troop formations were crossing the Santiago River to the south of us, and that another federal force was doing the same over the San Pedro River north of us.

This was bad news indeed as we had no wagon transport, only the railroad train, for our supplies. After receiving the news brought in by Tekwe, I urged Buelna to retreat northward immediately with the train before the bridge at San Pedro River was blown up. He agreed, but valuable hours were lost by indecision and the useless discussions by the staff, some of whom were against the move. The infantry, our only field-gun and the supplies were eventually moved by the train toward Ruiz, a place located about where the San Pedro River runs under the bridge some twelve miles north of Yago.

Two squadrons went as advance-guard to the train in order to inspect railroad culverts, to see if they were mined or already blown up and, of course, to prevent a surprise attack on the train. These squadrons had strict orders to keep a mile behind the scouts, and the engineer of the train had instructions to stay about a mile behind the advance-guard. Three squadrons were detailed as a rear-guard, but as we were moving off, Buelna changed his mind and gave orders for them to remain behind to guard the Yago bridge, to which I strongly objected.

Buelna, who had gotten over the shock received during the early morning attack, was sure that the enemy's success was only a flash in the pan. He brushed my suggestion aside saying he would deal out a

121

severe blow to the enemy soon, and needed the bridge on his march on Guadalajara. I admired his guts but pointed out that the three squadrons left our rear somewhat vulnerable by remaining at the bridge.

Taking Tekwe and Lopez with me, I went with the advance-guard and managed with some difficulty to keep it at a proper distance from the scouts. This, however, made our pace too slow as the scouts were barely crawling along. As time was of great importance, I sent Tekwe forward to have a look and he came back with the information that the scouts had decided that a mile ahead of the advance-guard was too far and refused to scout more than two hundred yards in front of it.

This was disturbing, but as it was too late to halt and change the scouts, we continued. We had lost a lot of time, but we came eventually to a hill, around which the railroad track wound its way on three sides before going on to Ruiz. Our scouts, otherwise so excellent, but now seemingly out of hand, failed to go around both sides of the hill. They passed on its west side only and, of course, saw no one.

Soon after passing the hill we approached the San Pedro River and found the railroad bridge blown up. We had been hopelessly outmaneuvered as our rail communication with our own forces far in the north was cut, yet there wasn't any enemy in sight. Then we heard severe rifle fire behind us, and at the same time the unseen federals opened up at us from across the river with two field-guns and riflle fire from a large number of men.

We were too close for comfort with no artillery and only about 200 carbines. I moved the squadrons hastily out of sight and tried to stop the train from coming farther. I heard afterwards that the train had moved on toward the river, but after rounding the first two sides of the hill, the enemy, hidden on its top, opened a most effective fire on our infantry who, like sitting ducks and as close as sardines, were on top of the box cars not 250 yards from the federals on the hill. The engine driver stopped the train, then went on again, hesitated, and then began to back his train, exposing our men to a heavy fire at close range. As he was backing a culvert was dynamited behind him and our contact with the south was also cut.

In the middle of this mess the artillery officer made a gallant attempt to save his gun by unloading it from the flat-car. The infantry colonel in command of the train seemed to have allowed his men to help the gunners, instead of deploying them in an attack on the hill.

Long before the gun was off-loaded, the enemy had made a shambles of the place, panic took hold and our men started to run. It was a massacre. The federal general knew his job well for he had accomplished the difficult task of dividing the enemy into several parts and successfully mopping up each in turn.

When we turned and moved away from the river under artillery and rifle fire, continuous firing could be heard in front of us. As we approached the northern end of the hill we met a shower of bullets and were forced back under cover to dismount for action. We were about ready to advance on foot when we noticed our infantry running for their lives in disorder. Our contemplated assault on the hill was now out of the question, as we were too few and too late.

Then happened the almost unbelievable. Our infantry was scattered in flight in all directions and throwing their guns away. The train with the gun was standing abandoned on the track. My two squadrons were hemmed between the river and the hill and couldn't move without being exposed from two or more sides. Yet, with all these advantages, the federal commander moved away from the hill and left us to our fate. But as I couldn't tell from my position if it was a ruse, Lopez was sent to investigate and try to find General Buelna. He returned soon and said the enemy was moving away, but he thought they had General Buelna a prisoner as he had surrendered, or so one of our men had told him.

There was nothing else to do but try and find the three squadrons left at the Yago bridge, and thus strengthened, something might be done. While looking for and helping some of the stragglers, we ran into General Buelna with some 50 men. I was never quite clear as to where he had been when the train ran into the trap, except that he had been somewhere in the rear, for he was never timid in a fight.

When he saw the two squadrons intact, his young soul brightened up as he had been told that the advance-guard had crossed the river before the bridge was blown up, and that we all had been captured or wiped out. He had sent a mounted man for the squadron at Yago bridge with orders to join him at the village of Caramota that night. As Caramota was too close to the enemy, another galloper was sent with orders to cross the San Pedro where they could and assemble at Rosa Morada, which was located east of the railroad, several miles north of Ruiz.

The night of February 12 and the morning of the 13 were unpleasant and strenuous. Tekwe and

Lopez assisted me all night gathering stray bodies of infantry and directing them to cross the San Pedro River and assemble at Rosa Morada.

About three o'clock in the morning we came upon an abandoned ranch and as we all needed rest, we halted for an hour. It was a cold night and the two boys soon had a fire going in the middle of a room. Then they surprised me by producing four nice looking birds called *Chachalaca* (a kind of grouse) and a masked quail. These had been knocked down with sticks and stones during the day and were most tasty birds after roasting on small wooden spits.

While Tekwe was on horse-guard duty and lookout during the night he brought in some Cora Indians who were most friendly and said they came from somewhere near Acatán. All but one carried bows and arrows, a kind of sling, and a long knife. Their dress was primitive and all wore sandals. Several of them had joined the revolutionaries against the government, they said.

We arrived in Rosa Morada at daybreak and found the major and his three squardrons sound asleep without an outpost, patrol, or even a horse-guard. When the remnant of our infantry began to form, it was found that many had thrown away their rifles in their hurry to escape. As far as I could figure, we had lost all the territory from the Santiago River in Tepic to Rosario in Sinaloa, a distance of about 100 miles. Our casualties were heavy; 350 killed, 280 wounded, 300 odd missing. Also, about 1,000 rifles and carbines, 1 field-gun, 1 complete train, and all of our supplies. I include the train because the bridge was gone and we had to abandon it.

This disaster was a severe blow, but it could have been worse had the federal cavalry followed up their success. Why the federals left their perfect position on the hill has always been a puzzle to me, but they might have been short of water or overestimated our strength. This reverse may, however, have proved a godsend in disguise as it made at least some of the officers realize the necessity of discipline and having at least an elementary knowledge of how to handle troops above that of a guerrilla band. Buelna, realizing his mistake, and with his pride and swagger somewhat subdued, didn't need any urging to move his remaining men north, for we started out at once in a series of forced marches toward Rosario.

His infantry, with its strutting and bragging officers of yesterday, had been badly mauled and with their morale shattered they looked like a bedraggled caravan of second rate Gypsies. But in spite of all the reverses, the men shuffled fast along the road with an amazing cheerfulness and energy. These men had been through a strenuous day and night without food or rest, and the prospects of something to eat in the near future were slim.

Personally, I expected a pursuit by the federal cavalry at dawn, but was agreeably surprised for there wasn't an enemy in sight, and the opportunity of the federal commander to annihilate Buelna's column was lost for the second time.

As I considered my mission terminated, by our reverses and flight, I said *adios* to Buelna, whom I liked very much, and with my two men and three others leading spare horses, left at a fast pace, after the last man of the retreating column had left Rosa

Morada. We were lucky to find a box-car train in working order at Acaponeta, entrained the horses and made for Rosario. The three men and their horses were sent back to Acaponeta in the train with orders to rush the information of its existence to General Buelna as he needed it badly.

At Rosario we had to take to the open road once more because of the federals in Mazatlan. The distance from Rosario to Modesto is about sixty miles over a dirt road. The first part, as far as Villa Union, was not very bad, but the rest was over winding paths, sometimes a road, and sometimes none.

When we approached Villa Union our party ran smack into a troop of federal cavalry. They had, apparently, not heard of their success in Tepic as they turned and scurried off in a hurry toward Mazatlan, to our great relief. At Modesto we were informed that a rebel train with troops and supplies was standing at a siding not far away. As the train was en route to Culiacan, we got the tired horses into some box cars, and off we traveled in luxury, sitting among the animals, but having food for them and us. At one place the Pacific Ocean was in full view for miles and I couldn't resist stopping the train to have a swim. To make sure of not being left behind, I invited the engineer to come along, which he did. We arrived at Culiacan at noon, February 15.

Here we received news that Pancho Villa had cleared northern Chihuahua of the federals who had retreated to, and were entrenched in, Torreon, their last stronghold in northern Mexico. There were also rumors that Villa was tired of Carranza's proclamations and orders, which meant there was trouble between them.

Carranza, apparently anxious to see what Villa was up to, left Culiacan February 15 with his staff for the north. General Obregon went part of the way with him, and so did the American news correspondents Turner and Weeks.

Pedro, my Tarahumara scout when I was with Pancho Villa, returned February 20, which pleased me. He met Lopez and recognized him from our gun-running days, and then Tekwe came in. The three seemed to harmonize although one was a full-blooded Yaqui, one a full-blooded Tarahumara, and the third a Spanish-Indian mestizo. They were all good men.

February 22 was a day of remembrance as it was the first anniversary of the murder of President Madero and Vice President Suárez. The bonds which united the Mexican revolutionary elements after Madero's assassination were undoubtedly spiritual. It was a fascinating awakening of a people morally crumbling apart, but reunited by this crime, and without the thought of self. Men of caliber, education, position and wealth, came forward risking everything by bringing together the illiterate peons and Indians who had been slave-ridden for centuries by the iniquitous hacienda system of peonage. But the backbone of the revolution was the illiterate patriots who collected a few peons or Indians and, unfit though they were to lead, came to the standards of the real rebel leaders and offered their services.

The leaders needed men and, like a drowning man grasping for a straw, accepted anyone. The cowboy, peon, Indian or bandit, many unable to read, became colonels and generals overnight. But these patriots were not the men who did the damage to the revolutionary fiscal policy, pilfered the treasury, and lowered the morale of the rank and file by their actions. This was done by a new breed of patriots which came into existence, a kind of white-collar, money grubbing, selfish opportunist made up mostly of shyster lawyers and second rate politicians. Many of these must have served their apprenticeship in a queer kind of business, for they were experts at padding pay-rolls and diverting herds of stolen cattle to their own farms and haciendas which were also stolen.

The strange part of these parvenus was that they actually looked upon themselves as outstanding "patriots," but tens of thousands of cattle were confiscated from ranches and driven to the American Border for sale; rich gold and silver mines worked day and night and the miners paid with rebel paper money, so that the silver and gold could go into the war chest. Yet, there wasn't money enough to purchase sufficient cheap Winchester carbines and ammunition for the army. Something was radically wrong. Where the bulk of this money went was a question which bothered many of the really patriotic Mexicans who were busy doing the fighting. There were many exceptions, of course, for Carranza and Obregon had many fine men under them.

These men had a certain amount of influence with Carranza who, with some of the intellectual generals, came to an understanding how, and in what direction, the revolution should travel. The exaggerated hopes of the Madero revolution had practically died by the wayside, not in the eyes of the poor peons, but in the minds of some of these non-fighting educated men, and even, maybe, in Carranza's.

The leaders in the Carranza group, especially Carranza himslf, did not want any reactionaries such as General Huerta with Napoleonic ideas, nor did they wish to see a repetition of the French Revolution with Villa, Zapata, and the like, as Mexican Robespierres. They had good reason to fear the proletariat and the mob taking over, for the tatterdemalions had already taken charge of some parts of Mexico. Carranza, apparently, also wished to preserve at least some of the culture brought in by Porfirio Diaz, and wanted to bring into existence a more substantial middle class on which the government could lean for support against the extremist, either way.

Like so many others, including Madero, Carranza considered himself the savior of Mexico. There was no doubt that he was an intensely patriotic Mexican and did what he thought best for his country. However, like so many others in similar circumstances, he became easily annoyed at any opposition. Toward the end he wantd to crush any and all who did not fall in with his views. He was recognized in the north and the northwest as the First Chief, but there were many colonels and generals in the field of outlying districts who had never met him. Some of these *cabecillas* accepted the inevitable. Others took orders in a lackadaisical way, and others would not accept any of his orders, which annoyed him greatly.

The officer and non-com classes were started immediately on my return from Tepic, and there was constant drill and lectures for every unit from early morning to late at night.

The rebels were desperately in need of ammunition and we were scraping the bottom of the barrel to obtain the money needed, but there was not enough. On the morning of February 21, General Lucio Blanco approached me to lend the rebel government the sum of 10,000 (ten thousand) American dollars for the purchase of ammunition. As I did not have that amount in a dollar account, I gave him a check for $1,200 dated February 22, 1914, on the First National Bank of Nogales, and one for $2,000. It was agreed between him and me that the money was to be returned to me plus five per cent compounded interest when the revolution was over, or on demand should I leave Mexico before the end of the conflict.

With this amount and the money awaiting him in Hermosillo from cattle sales or gold shipment, Blanco left Culiacán by motor handcar for Cruz Piedra that same day. From Cruz Piedra he went on by horse to Maytorena station where a train was to take him to Hermosillo and Nogales, because the federals still held Guaymas.

IV

An ill-fated patrol—Hunted like a coyote—We capture
two Indian scouts—In Tarahumara Indian coun-
try — A short-cut with a climb — Down with
malaria—A short-cut with a chasm—Among the
Tarahumara—An Indian cure—A foot-race—The
return

Before leaving for the north on February 22,
General Blanco informed me that an Indian scout had
reported the existence of mounted enemy troops in
the foothills of the sierra in the northeastern parts of
Sinaloa, and ordered a large patrol to be sent to investigate. He also requested that the order as well as
the patrol be treated with utmost secrecy and that the
officer in charge be the only one told of the real
object of the expedition. Blanco seemed worried as
the federal victories in Tepic and their successful sorties on our positions elsewhere had forced us to give
ground, due principally to the lack of ammunition.
He thought the federals were now trying to make a
move against our flank and rear. Blanco, like so
many others, had to learn the hard way. I had repeatedly asked for extended patrols toward and into

the foothills of the sierra ever since our arrival in Culiacan, but had met with little or no support.

When Blanco had departed, I reported to Colonel Acosta, the acting Division commander, and conveyed Blanco's order for a patrol to the north. When I suggested taking the patrol myself, Acosta did not relish the idea, pointing out there was much to do in camp, but gave in on the condition that I take at least two squadrons, about 250 men. When I stressed the difficult terrain, and how that number would slow us down and be difficult to feed and water, he agreed on twenty-five men. We collected a mixture of Yaqui, Mayo and Pima Indians from Sonora, all of them good trackers, four special Mayo scouts and, of course, Pedro, Tekwe and Lopez. It was also decided to take a small freight train and go as far as San Blas as the first leg of our patrol.

To avoid the possibility of federal agents finding out our destination, we told the men the train was a rear-guard to General Blanco and we started at five o'clock in the afternoon the same day. Our transport consisted of one pack-horse carrying spare ammunition, another carrying cornmeal, medical supplies, and some coffee, and fifteen spare riding horses. The boxcars were filled with fodder and we let the horses eat all they could on the way as we had no means of carrying fodder after leaving San Blas.

As the track had been cleared we made good time reaching San Blas by midnight. The engineer got orders to park his train somewhere in San Blas and await our return or to move upon receiving orders from the cavalry. By three o'clock in the afternoon, February 23, we were ambling fast along the road

Indian recruits, mostly Yaquis. Sonora, 1913.

to El Fuerte, a town north of San Blas on the Fuerte River. We acted so quickly and silently that it is doubtful if anyone in San Blas knew of our coming and going except the railroad personnel.

We deliberately avoided the village of Tehueco because one of the men thought it was too friendly with the federals. At Badaja de Monte, a queer little village, we managed to get some fodder for the horses after which we proceeded to El Fuerte, about seven miles farther on, and got there about noon. No one seemed to know anything about federal troops in this area, so Pedro and Tekwe were sent to investigate but brought back nothing new.

Two Mayo scouts were sent in advance to Choix, a town northeast of El Fuerte and close to the Choix River, which is a tributary of the Fuerte River. The other two scouts were sent to Yecorato, about thirty miles by road, east of El Fuerte. The rest of the men had a good meal and rested until eight o'clock in the evening, when we moved toward Choix.

Before leaving, two of the Mayo scouts reported they had unexpectedly during the day run into some of their own tribe living along the river Fuerte, but none of them knew of any federal troops in this region. On the road, the men received instructions as to what to do in case our little force was surprised and dispersed by the enemy, for we were entering a difficult terrain and could easily be taken unawares as we were traveling fast. They had orders to scatter as fast as they could in all directions, like a guerrilla band, when I made a circular movement over my head with a hand, which was the old signal for "retire." They should then work their way back to the train at San Blas and, if no message arrived from me in six days, return to Culiacan with the train.

We reached Choix early in the morning of February 24, after advancing rather recklessly along the road all night. We had done about fifty-five miles in twenty-four hours, changing horses now and again, but without seeing or hearing of a federal soldier. Pedro and Tekwe did not seem to like the local enthusiasm for our cause and advised caution. There was something in the wind which these scouts did not care for. As every man in the party was a hand-picked veteran from Sonora, there was no question as to the reliability or loyalty of any one. A few scouts went out on fresh mounts and the rest turned in for some sleep next to their horses and guns in a corral.

The Mayo scouts sent to Yecorato turned up at noon with the information that at Baimena, a village south of Choix, they picked up a rumor that some mounted men had moved northward the day before. If this was true, they could hardly have gone anywhere except through this town of Choix, which confirmed Pedro's suspicion of the local people.

Leaving Lopez in Choix with three men and the spare horses, except the two we brought with us, the troop started out on the difficult paths to try and ferret out or at least locate the mysterious mounted men and ascertain who they were and how many. Pedro became quite excited when learning of the plan of operation and mentioned he had come down this way from the *barranca* country only two weeks before from his home near Urique, adding, "I have hunted this sierra since I was a boy and scouted almost every gorge when with Pancho Villa."

After crossing the river and riding northward from

Choix, the ground rose and we came to Tasajera, but no one here had seen or heard of any federals. Not feeling very content with the large gorges of the Choix River behind me, I decided to have a look down there myself. A guide was obtained and, leading our horses, he took us over a stony path down to the river a few miles to the southeast. A bitterly cold wind was blowing but we saw a great number of bluebirds all around us. When I asked Pedro about these lively little fellows, he said they were plentiful in certain parts of his homeland and that villages were named after them.

When we reached the river, two horses were lame, so I sent them back down the river to Choix to exchange them for fresh mounts. We found the north bank of the river so difficult that we crossed over, which was not an easy operation, through large boulders and deep water-holes.

Once on the south side, we found many tracks of shod horses and men which we followed upstream. A mile farther on we came upon several campfires, not more than two days old, and the scouts thought there had been about thirty horses in the party. We searched up the canyon but found no more spoors, so this party must have gone down the river. We returned to Choix by following the river downward and reached the town, after a strenuous trip, during the afternoon of February 25.

Lopez, being a good scout, was on a sharp lookout but had not seen or heard of any mounted men. The mysterious troop, whose campfires and tracks we had seen, had either by-passed Choix and gone farther down the river toward Matalo or Vaca, villages located northwest of Choix on the River Fuerte, over a difficult and stony path, or they had gone north to Campo, or some other place on Mesa Colorada.

It was arranged that two Yaquis and Pedro were to move toward Mesa Colorada to scout as far as the Fuerte River. The Yaquis had removed all trace of military equipment but carried carbines and remained mounted. Pedro went on foot dressed in his Tarahumara trousers of light material, sandals, a shirt and a colorful blanket. He was armed with his ever present sling, knife and a six foot long hardwood stick, pointed very sharp at one end. It looked like a spear but could also have been a planting-stick.

Pedro, wishing to work alone, went off at a jog-trot at 3 a.m., February 26, and the two Yaquis followed an hour later. Soon after them came our little band of horsemen walking and trotting right through the desolate but interesting country which surrounded us. At Tasajera no one knew any more than they did yesterday morning and so we continued to El Nacimiento farther north. Nothing indicated that human beings lived here and every step forward was a hazard, a perfect place for an ambush. The stone-bound ground, with rocks lying here and there and everywhere as if from a violent eruption, made scouting toward the flanks difficult and slow, and without any advantage to man or nourishment for the horses.

We rode to Mesa Colorada where one of the Yaqui scouts awaited us behind some large rocks. He indicated that about fifty mounted federals had been close to Campo the night before but had moved westward down the river. He also said that the local people were afraid to speak about troop movements. We went down to the river where there was a crossing which led to Mesa de Santa Rita farther to the north. There wasn't a trace of the enemy, but to be sure I turned the troop eastward and went up the River Fuerte instead of down.

As we were moving along, I was wondering what had happened to Pedro and shortly thereafter he turned up with the news of two bodies of federals which he had seen, one down the river, 150 strong, and another up the river with about 250 men.

As there was no time to lose, I wrote a note to Acosta and sent it with a Yaqui scout to San Blas where he was to take our train to Culiacan. In my report I proposed that he send a regiment of cavalry by train to San Blas and work from there. I also suggested that all railroad bridges and culverts remaining intact should be guarded as the enemy could play havoc with our supply line from Hermosillo to Culiacan. The scout, leading a spare horse, went off within fifteen minutes as fast as the ground permitted.

The sun was already casting its beams obliquely for it had traveled almost two-thirds of its course toward the west. When I looked up into the sky, the light white clouds were showing rosy tinted edges and beyond, in the center of infinite space, so intensely blue, was a great eagle soaring without moving its wings. Ahead of us, toward the east, could be seen a number of vultures circling round and round also without moving a wing but ready to come down to pick out the choice tidbits, the entrails, eyes or other delicacies from whatever was dying on the ground below. Pedro thought the *Wiru kompari* (Godfather vultures), which he called them, must be on the other side of the federals where some animal had been slaughtered or a prisoner shot.

The messenger had no sooner gone when I ordered the men quickly back to the mesa, but at this moment the scouts began to arrive from all directions to report that the enemy, by an extraordinary coincidence, was advancing on us from three sides and, by what they said, outnumbered us about 15 to 1. It was now doubtful if the Yaqui galloper could have gotten through to San Blas, and so drastic measures had to be taken for we could not fight in our present position. Calling the men close to me, I got Pedro to explain that the only chance for some of us to escape was to disperse in all directions as previously arranged and make for San Blas. There were loyal murmurs against separating and my heart felt warm toward these fine fellows but I had no alternative. The agreed signal to scatter was given and they were gone.

Three of us remained as Pedro and Tekwe refused to leave me. Pedro proposed that we cross the river at once and make for some caves he knew farther up in the sierra. There are no roads or paths, he explained, so the federals cannot follow us in any great numbers as the terrain is bad and horses can't get through.

It was an excellent plan and we rushed for the river and abandoned the horses, but I insisted the saddles and bits be removed from the animals before letting them go, which worried Pedro as we lost valuable time. Each of the two men took a carbine, ammunition, water bottle, haversack slung over his shoulder and a serape. Besides my carbine, I had a revolver with ammunition and an old hunting knife, a British army haversack containing bandages, quinine, aspirin, matches in a watertight box, two large bars of chocolate as an emergency ration, a pocket compass and an army pannikin. All of this weighed far too much for the struggle ahead.

Pedro had also stuck to his long stick which came in handy when I slipped into a deep water-hole between high rocks. The stick probably saved me for the boys could not have pulled me out without this spear-like instrument. While we were struggling over driftwood and great boulders, a shot was heard, then another, after which a lively rifle-fire began to pepper us. As we got on the other side, a machine-gun had been mounted and opened up recklessly. They didn't come very close to us and I could not help thinking, with a sigh of relief, that they were inexperienced machine-gunners as the range was not over 400 yards.

As we disappeared in a donga-like ravine, I looked back and could see plainly a troop of about thirty men trying to ford the river with horses. We could have shot quite a number of them as they were only about 200 yards below us, but deep thinking Pedro read my thoughts and said something about wasting time and ammunition, and then added, *"Jefe,* (Chief,) the Mexican Cavalry are no good on foot, especially in the mountains. We have a long and difficult trip in front of us. Let us move onward." It was good advice and we moved on.

Hunted like a coyote

We climbed up and down a seemingly endless series of gullies. The ravines and small *barrancas* were full of rattlesnakes. We left them severely alone. There were also a lot of birds around but we had no time to study them for every second was needed for

141

escape. It was getting dark when we reached a protecting heavy underbrush where Pedro called a halt. He examined the ground carefully and led us over a creek, then up a ravine, taking care that we walked on stones all the way. Here, high up, we found the two caves Pedro had mentioned, but they were so close to one another and joined that it was practically one cave.

Pedro told Tekwe to gather some firewood and then he entered the large cave carrying a handful of dry material looking like spunk, also dry twigs, all of which he had picked up on the side of the ravine leading to the grotto. In a few minutes a fire was burning and then Tekwe came with an armful of dry wood which he dropped on the fire. He went out again and soon returned with two large dry logs.

Interested in how Pedro started the fire, I asked if he had matches and he produced a flint-lighter which he called *birina*. It consisted of a broken file some three inches long and a piece of flint the size of a small hen's egg. To demonstrate he took a piece of punk and lighted it with the second strike of the steel. The two of us agreed, when with Villa in November, that Pedro would always name things in Tarahumara as his knowledge of plants, animals, birds, and the tribal legends of his people was astounding. He was a master as a teacher; had the gift of making me understand, and was most patient when I could not always follow what he had said.

One of the caves could easily give shelter for about thirty persons and the other about ten. When I expressed regret at not having brought all the men, Pedro said, "Don't regret, thirty men from the plains would have retarded our progess and not half of them

142

could have escaped over the river with federals so close and in such supeior numbers."

The caves had obviously been used before as there were many old campfires about. Pedro said he had taken shelter here several times; the last time about four years back when guiding a surveying and prospecting party. Both the men examined the old markings on the floor and agreed no one had been there for several months.

When I sat down, Pedro warned me with a grin to look out for the *machiri* (scorpions). When I looked around with a burning stick, not less than a dozen of the nasty little fellows could be seen quite close and several almost under my rump. The boys didn't seem to mind them, but took care to brush the ground with a small bush before sitting down. I followed their example and kept an eye open for those that might approach. I did notice that a scorpion does not like the fire but creeps up from behind you.

We divided the little food we had plus some berries (*amuri*) collected along the way by Pedro. They were not bad tasting. Then I produced the two bars of chocolate and divided them but suggested we keep this for an emergency as we did not dare to fire a shot at any game.

After this parsimonious meal, Tekwe went to the creek to replenish the water in the bottles and returned with the news that he had heard two rifle shots not far off. Taking all our equipment we emerged from the cave to listen. It was pitch dark and a cold, damp wind came from the northeast which made one wish for the cave and comforting fire, scorpions or no scorpions, since some of my clothes were still wet.

Pedro did not like the look of things and wanted to move on at once toward the Urique River. He knew of an old Indian path a few miles farther on and thought it better to stumble along in the dark than fall into the federal hands. This made sense but I noticed Tekwe had become quite stiff in the legs after sitting down, for we had climbed like monkeys about 3,000 feet over boulders and through ravines. However, we moved on and found a thick underbrush farther up and not far from the cave, where I suggested we spend the night, as my back and legs were aching. There was also some shelter from the cold night wind and one could see down the ravine as far as the mouth of the cave.

We capture two enemy scouts

Each of us was to take turns on the look-out and we would move out at three o'clock the following morning. Tekwe seemed relieved and Pedro acquiesced on condition he take the first watch, but he didn't fool me, for it was obvious that he knew I was overtired. Before turning in, my two companions interpreted the shots to be a signal and expressed surprise at the federals coming so far and so fast. "And," Pedro added, "they must have Indians from the sierra as trackers because no federal cavalryman from the plains could follow us."

He woke us at midnight and said that two men had entered the cave but they were not soldiers, and that he had scouted the area and there wasn't another soul within half a mile. We realized the necessity of knowing more of these men, for should they be

144

Indian trackers in the service of the federals, "They must be eliminated," said Tekwe seriously with a movement to his long knife.

It was dangerous to fire a shot, but we couldn't leave these men to follow our trail with federals to back them, and so we had to get them out of the cave by a ruse. Tekwe was sent toward the creek and fired two shots as the enemy had done a few hours earlier. Pedro and I took up position behind some rocks close to the opening and were ready to act. The two men came out running, and it took less time than telling about it to make them understand that struggle was useless.

When Tekwe returned, the men were disarmed and their hands bound. We led the captives to our camping place and questioned them while Tekwe stood guard in case the shots had attracted others. Our prisoners were of the Odami tribe from near Tahonitas, a place far south in the State of Chihuahua. Pedro explained that the name given was the name these Indians call themselves; other people call them Tepehuanes, but the Tarahumara refer to them as "the insect that walks like a stick" (*Saero*). The Tarahumara *saero* is a specter insect of Phasmidae Family, also called "walking-stick" in the United States.

The men were dressed much like Pedro except that their trousers did not pinch in at the ankles. Each carried a light colored blanket with a broad stripe at both ends and they wore sandals. Both men carried a 30-30 Winchester, ten rounds of ammunition and a long knife.

These Tepehuanes did not at first concede they were in federal employ, but eventually admitted they

145

had been so for over a month. Pedro, with a flare for the dramatic, asked with a great deal of contempt, "How can you be in the federal service fighting hundreds of your tribe and thousands of other Indians struggling and fighting for land and freedom?" The reply surprised me not a little as one of them pointed to me and said, "We were offered fifty head of cattle each if we could bring about the capture of this Americano who is training the Indians in the White man's method of warfare to kill other Indians." When asked how many federals managed to follow us up the sierra, the leaders of the two said, "Nine," and they were all recruited from the Durango mountain regions and had camped by a small stream about twenty minutes from the cave.

Pedro, not quite satisfied, asked them why they had left the federals and come to the cave. To this they answered simply, "We found some *tequila* in Choix and as we did not wish them to know, we came here and drank it. Otherwise you could not have captured us." When asked if there were any more trackers with the federals they said, "One," but added, "They think we are out scouting and will not move before we come back."

It was now a question of what to do with these fellows. They were a fine type of men, proud as could be and did not ask for any mercy. When I suggested taking them with us both my companions thought this was not practical. When I proposed to give them 100 steers each in exchange for our safety, Pedro said, "They will not believe you and think it is a trick." Valuable time was passing and then Tekwe came up with an idea which I accepted. He proposed that we remove all their clothing, including their

146

sandals, and that he remain behind with them for an hour or more before cutting them loose. Then he would follow us.

We left after Tekwe had received instructions as to the direction. The going was tough but we had been out in the dark for so long that we could see objects quite clearly several feet away. We halted several times when Pedro placed a stone or carved a trail-mark with his knife for Tekwe. Pedro never seemed to let up. He climbed vertical rocks like a monkey, turned around and lowered his stick for me to grab and pulled me up. We were now in the forest zone and the trees gave some shelter from the cold wind.

I missed my pocket anneroid which had been stolen several weeks before, but I guessed we were about on a 7,000 foot level. During the early morning hours Pedro had bagged several small birds with stones and sticks. He knocked them down on the ground as if by a gun and never seemed to miss, even at twenty paces. At one place he killed a rat (*okiri*) with a stick from about ten paces. It was a mountain-rat, or pack-rat, the best tasting food in the sierra, Pedro said. I could have shot a dozen wild turkeys (*chiwi*) during the first two hours after daybreak while on a small mesa but I didn't dare to jeopardize the safety of Tekwe for there still was no sign of him.

In Tarahumara Country

At about eight o'clock we stopped and I thought Pedro had lost his way when he began to build a cairn of stones about two feet high. When I asked

147

what time he expected Tekwe to catch up with us and what he thought the Tepehuanes would do, the answer shocked me a little. Pedro thought these men could easily walk to their camp without sandals and that Tekwe would be a fool to let them go, and added, "These men are working for the federals. They are after our scalps and will stop at nothing to catch you dead or alive. Why worry about what Tekwe may do to them?" This was the first time I had an inkling of what had happened to these men. I wasn't happy about it, but these faithful companions had acted in the manner they thought best for our safety.

When the cairn was finished, Pedro gave me a beckoning gesture and moved carefully, avoiding treading on soft soil for about a hundred yards, to a steep, overhanging cliff from which place there was a wonderful view all around. Then I noticed the cairn was in the open and could be seen from quite a distance from many points. Here my companion put down everything he was carrying and made a mark on the ground not far from a protruding shadow made by a small tree, and said, "We must leave here when the shadow reaches this mark, whether Tekwe comes or not, for he should have caught up with us long ago."

I was in the pink of condition, and had gotten over the stiffness of the night before, but was glad indeed to put down my guns and other paraphernalia as they seemed to weigh a ton. By this time Pedro had begun to clean the birds and the rat, but when drawing the rat, he said, "The Rat becomes a Bat eventually or after death," then added most solemnly, "When the Rat becomes a Bat, no man can touch it without proper medicine, for like the Dead, the

148

Bat moves about at night only, and is therefore bad medicine."

When the game was drawn he gathered some dry wood and prepared a fire in the back of the cave-like overhanging cliff, and filled the water bottles from a near-by spring which was oozing forth from the crevice of a rock. When he returned, he seemed much concerned about Tekwe, and then a crow gave a screeching call in the distance. Pedro brightened up, went out in the open and answered the mating call, lighted the fire and began to roast the birds on long thin twigs as spits. He gave me the rat to do, and when it was almost done, he touched my arm and pointed toward the beacon he had built, and there was Tekwe approaching the monument. Once there he turned in our direction and walked straight south to our hiding place, so arranged by the never-failing Pedro.

It was obvious that Tekwe had traveled far and fast, so we said nothing before the meal was more or less over, and I will praise the taste of a pack-rat. Later I found it is considered a great delicacy among the Indians who generally roast them without being drawn or skinned.

Tekwe related to us in a few simple words what had taken place; "After you had gone, I took care of the two federal spies in the manner I know they would have taken care of me. Then I scouted around the federal's camp and found them ready to march, but they seemed to be waiting for something, perhaps the Tepehuanes. There were nine of them under a young officer of high rank. He must have been a colonel. Apparently the two shots worried them, so I proceeded once more to the west of their camp and fired several shots, then ran back to our camp and here."

Pedro was beginning to keep an anxious eye on his sundial for the shadow was close to his mark, and then Tekwe said he was ready to go. It was now close to noon. Before starting, Pedro informed us that after another day or so of climbing up and down mountain sides we would begin to descend for several hours, cross a river, then ascend for several hours to a mesa, close to which was a village belonging to his tribe where he was known.

Somewhat cheered by this information, we started off, but we had a stiff and difficult climb and came into patches of snow on the north side of cliffs and among the trees. We went through a defile or pass (*napuchi*) and there I was sorely tempted to shoot an apparently irritated large brown bear in front of us, seemingly unafraid but growling.

When I unslung the carbine, Pedro rushed up and gave me an interesting lecture on his ancestors. He said, "There are two kinds of Bears (*ohi*); one is a real Bear and the other a dead Tarahumara or a sorcerer who has made himself into a Bear. It is therefore no use trying to kill a Bear for meat, for it may be a Man-Bear. All Bears of a light brown color are our grandfathers, or at least one of our ancestors. We do not kill an ancestor for food or any other reason." We did not, of course, have a bear-steak that day, or any other day, on the expedition.

When we came to a place where water was seeping from the rocks, I halted for a conference to make a stand instead of running. Pedro, backed by Tekwe, was afraid of being outflanked by a superior

150

force in the high sierra, which might make escape impossible. We continued after a brief rest.

That night we took shelter under a cliff and had fragrant pine needles, collected by the boys, for beds. We had been through a steep valley and up again to our camp, which gave us a little shelter against the cold wind and a good view, but there was no sign of the federals. The following morning I awoke at dawn and found my two companions already gone to have a look around.

Sitting there I noticed the stars, so bright during the night, were gradually getting paler. One could see the mountain peaks towering above the mist like so many spires of castles in the land of dreams. But I knew the sinister shadows hid deep and treacherous fissures and precipitous formations on the side of the forest-clad mountain. As darkness retreated in favor of daylight, these foreboding black spots disappeared gradually and brought into view a wonderful panorama. In an open place I could see a few deer close to some woods. Above us, as far as the eye could see, there rose rugged naked cliffs, and here and there a lone tree which seemed to struggle to survive against heavy odds. There was a deep silence. But high up on the barren rock, jutting dangerously over the seemingly bottomless chasm below, stood two men. I shrank back under cover of the rocks for they were not my two companions. A second or two later came a welcome thick mass of mist which concealed our camp from view of our persistent pursuers.

When I ran back under cover, every possible arrangement was made for a quick departure and

I divided our meager meal into three parts. Suddenly there was a shot which echoed startlingly several times in the adjoining hills. Fearing the worst, I picked up the gun and took cover outside and soon thereafter my friends came running in their jog-trotting manner. They had come upon the fresh tracks of two men, doubled back away from the camp and fired a shot in the hope of leading them off the trail.

A *perilous climb*

We left hurriedly and the mist covered us as would a wet blanket. Tekwe took us deliberately over some soft damp soil toward the west and being last he tried to obliterate our tracks with a small bush. We came on some rocky ground but found more soft soil beyond, over which he made us run, and, as before, he tried to cover up the spoors, though with less care. This was quite a stretch but it brought us to some solid rock formation free from vegetation. Tekwe now signalled to Pedro who took over the lead and led us in a semicircle toward the northeast, taking care, very good care, this time not to leave any tracks.

When we stopped for a rest and a bit to eat before noon, I asked Tekwe why he was so careless when covering up our tracks that morning. Tekwe spat on the ground, which was a habit when he was not quite sure how to answer, and said that the federals were mere city-bred soldiers so he did not dare to cover the trail too well for fear, "They might not see the covering up," and then spat again. This time with an unmistakable contempt for the federals.

Pedro had taken charge of the direction and he

knew a short-cut. He was merciless and would not allow a stop except for a drink at an occasional nice-looking spring, and they were few and far apart. Eventually we came to the foot of a formidable rock formation that seemed to tower perpendicular and fear-inspiring, indeed, above us for at least five hundred feet. On the one side was a deep crack in the earth, a crevice several hundred feet straight down from where we stood.

I thought we were trapped. While surveying the possibility of escape by climbing this straight-up-and-down face or trying to descend into that dark looking hell-hole below, equally vertical, Pedro told us, "We must climb this face for there is no other way out. It is steep, but we must get up there without delay, for should the federals have more trackers, they might catch up with us before dark. If they do, we will be forced to ascend during the twilight and we will be shot down from this rocky face like mountain-rats."

During the few minutes rest while adjusting the carbines before starting, I asked Pedro, "What about coming down again if forced to do so by the terrain above?" He answered, "This place is too steep to try and come down while carrying 'long-guns', without risking a fall into the canyon. I have been up there before, we must make it. Let's go!"

It was late in the afternoon when we began, but heavy red clouds could be seen in the west reflecting the fire-like tracks of the sun. It was warm climbing but the air seemed to be cooling off with the coming of evening. About halfway up this formidable cliff, our advance became more and more difficult. When we halted for breath, Pedro cautioned me not to look down, for come what may, we could not go down in the dark. When Pedro said it was a steep climb, he should have added "difficult," but that is the way with these Indians. We climbed up and up and my hands were bleeding from desperately grasping the sharp rocks. Not far from the summit we were forced to halt on a narrow ledge to get our second breath, for we were high up in the mountains.

When we were about to move on, Pedro pointed below and there in the deep shadows of dusk a number of men could be seen, like little dots, coming toward the base of the cliff. Unslinging the carbine, I sent a few shots at them. They ran for shelter and opened up at us in return, but all shots went high, and we hastened to the top. By this time it was too dark to observe anything below, but we sent a shot now and again, until it was too dark for them to climb. Although we knew the enemy couldn't get up that cliff at night, we, tired as could be, moved on with Pedro leading and soon entered a forest. As we went along, the forest became thicker, and here and there the ground was so swampy that we sank down over our ankles in the bog. It was black in there, so we halted. I often wondered how Pedro could find his way in pitch dark and have come to the conclusion that he, like the Bushmen and other tribes in Africa or Malaya, did it by the highly developed instinct of the animal.

Down with malaria—A short cut with a chasm

The next day we climbed up and down constantly before coming to a pass. An hour later I knew I had a touch of ague, and soon thereafter my knees began to buckle under me and refused to carry the burden.

Pedro looked back several times and could see that something was amiss when Tekwe relieved me of my carbine and ammunition.

After awhile, I couldn't move any further. I ached all over and knew my intermittent African malaria, which had plagued me for six years, had me in its grip. Pedro came back, felt my skin and pulse, shook his head and looked worried for the first time since he joined me. I told him the shaking and pain would disappear by the afternoon of the following day if I could lie down and take quinine every two hours, alternating with aspirin. He looked up at the escarpment behind us and said, "We must go on because the federal officer is gambling for high stakes and will not give up the chase."

Tekwe said something while unslinging his carbine and began to retrace our steps, running westward. Pedro now reverted to his favorite role, being that of a peyote-shaman. He opened his medicine bag and produced a *peyote* (*hikuri*) plant and said, "this is *hikuri waname* (Cactus Family; genus *Lophophora*) the most powerful of all medicines, chew it well and swallow, it will soon make you feel strong, but hurry—the enemy cannot be far behind." Having seen and heard of *peyote* in northern Chihuahua, but never eaten the stuff, I did what he asked and found the mescal-button he had given me was unpleasant to my taste—almost sickening.

Then we heard two shots, one after the other, and Pedro led me hurriedly behind some large rocks, where I slumped down, as I was unable to stand. He unslung his gun and stood watch looking toward where Tekwe had disappeared. While sitting there helpless, I gradually realized the tired-to-death feeling was disappearing. I felt refreshed, but it was a peculiar, though wonderful, feeling, as if being in a happy state of exhilarated intoxication. This was almost immediately followed by drowsiness and complete exultation and contentment. I seemed to see or dream wonderful things, in which many beautiful women took part, then blackness.

How long I was under this influence is doubtful, but Pedro shook me back to consciousness and told me that Tekwe had returned after taking care of one of the enemy. Then both had been away for an hour to lead the others on the wrong trail. Pedro gave me another piece of *peyote*. They took everything from me and loaded it on themselves. I felt much better, and being refreshed, I was keen to go, although I knew it was the dope in the plant that did it.

Pedro, wishing to save time, now told me of another short-cut which could save us the arduous task of crossing a steep *barranca,* but it meant jumping over a wide crevice. When we reached the place, I found we had the choice of climbing down like monkeys for some four hundred or more feet and then up again on the other side, which looked like a perpendicular wall, with dubious results and loss of time, or jump over the abyss.

While contemplating the best thing to do, Pedro made a running leap and was over the yawning gape as easy as a mountain-goat. I tried to guess the width of the open space and thought it about ten feet.

Then I looked down into the chasm and it did not inspire me much as the effect of the *peyote* had worked off and I was suffering from fever and had a terrible headache.

Tekwe must have noticed something, for he called out to Pedro, who came flying back like a springbuck, and gave me some more *peyote*. While sitting there helpless, the boys jumped over several times carrying the guns, ammunition and water bottles. When the *peyote* had taken effect I made a running jump with rather shaky legs, but having nothing to carry, it was not so difficult. However, ever since that time, I see that hell-hole under me when I jump over a ditch.

Everything went well for about two hours after the leap. Then I began to have severe shivers, cold sweat, and another peculiar headache. Pedro seemed to know what was happening for he gave me another piece of *peyote* which I ate but found difficult to swallow. This time the stimulating effect lasted longer, almost three hours, but the boys would not allow me to get sleepy, and then the malaria took hold of me once more.

Looking around, sick as I was, or perhaps because of it, I could not help noticing the grandeur of the surroundings, how nature seemed to have squandered with a lavish hand the best it had in this wilderness, terrifying yet beautiful. We crossed a river close to a tremendous gorge with walls standing perpendicular on each side of the river, which was rushing happily but madly, it seemed to me, in a southerly direction.

I was led and half-carried to a small cave which Pedro said he had used many times in the past. It was off the beaten trails and the entrance was protected from view by trees and thick bushes. A dozen yards outside, I noticed what looked like a man-made pool of water, kept full by a trickling stream. As soon as I was inside the cave, I began to take quinine and aspirin to make me sweat. The two boys needed a rest as much as I, if not more so, for they had helped by carrying my guns and often half-carried me all that afternoon. While sitting inside of the cave we heard an angry growl, then a whistling kind of sound and a roar outside. Pedro, sitting on watch close to the entrance, did not move for a minute or two, then went outside. When he returned, we found it had been a puma having a drink, and it had either gotten our scent or was disturbed by some other animal.

The boys stayed with me all night but in the morning I awoke to find both their blankets over me and they were sitting there in the cold without any cover. As we were about to leave, I suggested two of the three carbines be placed in a cache somewhere, and these two friends risked their lives once more for my sake, for they hid all the carbines and ammunition so as to be able to carry me. Tekwe, being a fairly good revolver shot, took my Webley pistol and ammunition.

When we began to climb, dark shadows along the mountain side indicated deep cliffs and dangerous crevices which made the place appear in an exaggerated form, uninviting and spooky to my sick brain. The picture soon changed, however, for looking back on the mountain tops from across the river one could see the pale gleam of rose-colored clouds getting brighter. Then high up some steep cliffs were hit by a sunbeam. The sun came like a golden arrow across the sky which penetrated the gloom and darkness below and cheered me immensely.

I was helpless by myself for every bone ached. I shivered with chills and my teeth rattled; the fever refused to break into a sweat. The boys gave me a hand all the way and often carried me. Up and up we went and eventually came to a mesa where Pedro left me with Tekwe and went off running for help. I must have passed out, for when I came to, I was lying on some goatskins inside a small house. They had carried me several miles to a Tarahumara village. I thought of the day and made it out to be somewhere near March 2.

Pedro informed me that three members of the village had backtracked our trail as far as the river and one had come back with the information that they had not seen anyone. The other two had orders from the chief (*serigame,* headman, *gobernador*) of the village to go to the top of the western range to scout. They had taken bows and arrows and would say they were hunting if they met the federals.

My two wonderful companions had only one thought in mind, to get me well as soon as possible. Pedro, being a shaman, did not want me to take any more quinine. He said, "It has not done you any good and I have sent for a famous healer living in a village about ten miles distant. He will be here before nightfall." The man arrived and strangely enough his name was also Pedro. These two wanted me to go through a Tarahumara "cure," which I was against, as I had seen shaman cures in Malaya, Sumatra, China, as well as cures by African witch doctors and did not wish any part of it. In the end they got me to agree to a "sweat-bath," as I knew

159

it was necessary to sweat before the malaria would break away. The bath was arranged for the following morning.

About midnight my two friends Pedro and Tekwe came with four men and carried me down a steep incline and placed me in a very small lean-to structure on top of some undressed goatskins which stank terribly. Tekwe, now dressed like a Tarahumara, informed me that the sweat-bath had to be postponed as the federal officer who had followed us from Sinaloa had crossed the river with six men and was on his way to the mesa.

"We will not cover you up now," Pedro said, "but will come back and do so before the federals reach the village. This is a storehouse and the federals might take a look inside. Here is your water bottle, but do not answer the call of anyone." Before he left I wanted to know if there were any Villistas in the neighborhood and received a negative answer, but Pedro said, "You have given me an idea. I will drop a hint to the federals that there are Villistas not far off. It might make them leave sooner."

At dawn Pedro brought me a cold soup-like dish which he called *kobisi* (pinole) made from corn. It was quite stimulating for I had eaten little for two days. The stuff reminded me of Kaffir-beer in Pondoland and Zululand. When finished he covered me with ten or more undressed goatskins and left me with the warning, "Do not move until one of us tells you, as they might be federals." They stank, as only raw goatskins can stink, especially when one is sick and covered by them. I felt terrible from the fever no doubt also from the after effects of the *peyote,*

160

and I did not dare to relax for fear of falling asleep, which I needed so badly.

About ten o'clock in the morning I heard voices of two or more men. They passed within a few feet of the building, then returned and opened the wooden lock which held the door in place. One of them crept in but did not stay long; he rushed out with the words "it stinks," leaving the door open. Before long the place was swarming with rats and other friendly creatures, which made it difficult for me to remain still.

I must have moved a little when I felt something crawling on my legs, as a number of hides slid to the floor with a rustling sound which made several rats disburse through the open door. As my legs had been exposed and there was no need to try to hide, I sat up, badly in need of fresh air, just as a federal soldier appeared in the doorway. His gun was pointed at my chest not five feet away, but I was too sick to care what happened. The man seemed surprised at seeing me appear from under the skins, as he hesitated, which decidedly saved me from a somewhat ignoble death among rats. Tekwe rose up from behind some large rocks about fifteen feet behind the soldier and threw his heavy hunting-knife like a flash of lightning; the man sagged to the ground with a groan, without firing his gun.

Tekwe, working fast, relieved the man of his rifle and ammunition, and threw him over the edge of the near-by, almost perpendicular, precipice which protected the storeroom from all sides, except for the narrow path leading to the village. Then he hid the gun and ammunition and told me he had come down to keep guard over me, as the federals were snoop-

161

ing around everywhere and had also taken the village chief as a hostage. With this information he left with the words, *"Jefe,* there are only six of them left. If they don't free the chief and leave today, we must, in some way, dispose of them and quickly."

Pedro came after a while and brought some evil-looking green broth, which I later found was a concoction of herbs boiled with the meat of a female rattlesnake. This had a peculiar, almost sickening, odor of oozing vegetation, but it stimulated me considerably. When questioned, Pedro admitted having added, among other things, a good portion of home-made corn-liquor, a kind of strong moonshine.

He then unfolded their simple plan to get rid of the federals. If this did not work, all of them would have to pay the penalty for intruding on the privacy of his people and arresting the chief. Being without guns, his people couldn't do much during the day, but would try to frighten them with the nearness of a strong Villa patrol. If this ruse failed, he and Tekwe would have to eliminate them, one by one, and with this cheery news he left me.

While sitting there helpless without a gun, and as sick as any dog could be, I realized what had made me so uncomfortable under the hides. The skins had only recently been brought in and had not yet been cleaned of the large pieces of fat remaining in places. Every skin was covered with worms, maggots and other crawling insects, many of which had transferred their affection to my person.

Tekwe, with two local Indians, came soon thereafter with bad news. The federals had tried to arrest the fifteen year old son of the chief and when he tried to escape, they shot him. They would, no doubt, come down here soon to look for their comrade, and with these remarks they helped me from the store-house to behind the large stones and some bushes, where Tekwe had been before.

Shortly thereafter came two short barks of a dog, which was repeated once. Tekwe and his men took cover behind the stones quickly, each placing some arrows near-by for immediate use. He bent forward toward me and whispered: "This is going to be easy. Only two Huertistas are coming down to look for their lost comrade." Ten minutes went by and then two federals approached the store-house. They halted with their backs toward us, not five yards away, and dropped with arrows through their backs without uttering a sound.

Their guns, ammunition and other paraphernalia valuable to the Indians were removed, including shirts, pants and shoes, before they followed their comrade into that abysmal hell-hole of the *barranca*. When he returned from this gruesome but necessary work, Tekwe made a rather long speech, for him. *"Jefe,"* he said, "there are only four of them left, but they must be disposed of today before they notice that three of them have gone to their Happy Hunting Grounds. What orders have you for us?"

Feeling very sick, I could hardly speak coherently. My answer may have been wrong. I said, "Do as you and Pedro think best." With this they left for the village armed with the three guns taken from the federals. Less than two hours later Pedro, Tekwe, the chief, and a dozen men came carrying the four remaining federals. Tekwe, knowing my weakness for soldiers being in a line, was most meticulous in having the dead men in a perfect line, for my inspection. The chief was standing there looking down on the federals, and I wondered what he thought as his revenge built upon the tradition of centuries had been robbed by the quick action which circumstances had forced upon my two friends. A few moments later they were stripped of all clothing and their naked bodies thrown over the edge of the cliff.

The men had brought a kind of wicker chair (*kosiberaka*) without a back, and two long poles according to Pedro's orders. In this sedan I was carried back to the village as a cannibal chief might well be carried, I mused in a sick kind of reverie. I was restless, and a little unhappy over the method used by my faithful friends, who knew no other way to dispose of the federals. But when I thought of the unnecessary murder of the chief's son, the 100 head of cattle on my head, and their unmerciful pursuit of us, I let my regrets go by the wind. But, maybe, I was too sick to reason.

After the excitement of the small engagement had passed and the stink of my clothes had been more or less removed, I began to think of ourselves and what we should do. My malaria wouldn't break; it was aggravated by the *peyote,* the strenuous climbing while under the influence of this unusually powerful stimulant, no sleep and no quinine.

Late that afternoon, the chief and two other important members of the community came and thanked me for freeing him and his people from the Huertistas. I had personally done nothing, but when I looked away from these angry faces the sun sank over the mountains, and I knew that Huerta's control of the Indians of this part of the sierra was a thing of the past.

Pedro and Tekwe would not even discuss any of my problems except for getting me a sweat-bath at once. The preparations for the cure were so interesting to watch that I almost forgot my illness. When a sweat-bath is necessary to cure fever, evil, or other ailments, the smoke made from cedar branches is the best, said Pedro.

First they dug a hole in the ground, about two feet deep and three wide, and in this way they made a large fire on top of which a number of large, round stones were placed to be heated. When the stones were hot enough, the fire was removed and branches of cedar placed on top of the stones. On top of the branches was placed a thick layer of cedar needles. Two woolen blankets were placed over the hole and I was led under them to sit on the needles over the almost red-hot stones.

After about an hour both the shamans came and looked at me and they did not seem satisfied. They removed the blanket and rubbed me with some ointment on the shoulders, chest and back. Pedro told me with pride he made the ointment from a large rattlesnake (*sayawi*), and that it would make me sweat. The steam created by the hot stones reminded me of a Finnish steam bath (Finnish bastu).

The shamans covered me up once more and I sat there for another hour or so. It was exceedingly warm underneath the blankets, but the cedar needles and branches became pleasantly fragrant on the hot stones, which diverted my attention. Suddenly, however, I felt relief and realized I was sweating pro-

165

fusely, but my head was throbbing fiercely as if it were on fire. When I was removed from the hole, they placed me inside a small house on some goatskins and covered me with several blankets.

After about an hour the two shaman-doctors looked me over and had a consultation. Pedro came forward with a piece of bark about the size of a fifty cent piece but twice or more in thickness. He broke off the bark from a short stick about two inches thick and three long, probably the branch of some tree. He told me this would help the fever and requested that I chew the bark thoroughly and swallow it with plenty of water.

This was repeated three times with intervals of about half an hour, but the last time the bark was a larger piece, almost that of a silver dollar. After a while I got drowsy and realized it must have been an opiate of some kind. The pain eased, but I became a little alarmed when finding froth around my lips, a heavy brown saliva running down both sides of my mouth, which I could not check. Then a pleasant, relaxing kind of feeling came over me. I did not seem to care any more. Then oblivion, as unconsciousness took over.

When I came to my senses once more, I felt weak but the fever was gone and my head was clear and cool. Pedro came in and gave me some delicious soup, which he proudly said was made from the same kind of rat "that you liked so much the other day," and informed me that I had not moved for twenty-four hours. Before allowing me to get up, he brought some cedar branches, lighted them, and let the smoke pass over my legs, to counteract the possibility of witchcraft, he said. When I got up, I felt fine but was a little groggy on my pins.

As I wished to return to Culiacan without delay and to send a messenger to Colonel Acosta, I summoned my two companions, now discussing the revolution with the village elders while cleaning their guns retrieved from the cache down by the river. The boys strongly advised me to remain in the village for at least two more days as I needed the rest. They had also made inquiries about another road farther south which was easier to descend from the sierra through the *barrancas* into Sinaloa than the one by which we had come.

A *Tarahumara* Foot-race

While sitting there talking things over with the boys, the headman of the village came and invited me to witness a foot-race between his young men and those from another settlement the following day at noon. Having heard of the Tarahumara prowess as long distance runners, and seen what Pedro could do, I decided to stay because once upon a time I had tried to be a miler when stationed in Pondoland, just prior to the Boer War.

This was to be the foot-race the Tarahumara call *rarahipa* (with the foot throw; run with the ball). It is a combination of a foot-race and a game, played with a ball. It can be played by two men, but it is usually run in teams from separate localities, the one team against the other. The idea of the game is to kick a ball along the ground over a pre-arranged course, which in most cases has been used for gen-

167

erations. The course itself may be only a few miles long, up to ten or sometimes more, but the Indians run around it about ten or twenty times, depending on the arranged distance.

When I got to an advantageous point of the course on a borrowed burro, there were groups of people scattered all over the place and some seemed to be very busy. Each team had a shaman manager with one or two assistants, who took every conceivable precaution to protect his team against sorcery, and every effort was made to bewitch their opponents. This particular race had a course of about four miles, to be covered eight times by the runners, or equivalent to about thirty-two miles in all. A race of a hundred miles without stopping except for medicine, is quite common and races are known to be a hundred and fifty miles long.

One of the participants in this race carried a peculiar looking rattling-belt (*somaka*). It was about three inches wide, made of leather, and had a number of strings hanging down, each of which held a section of a reed and a cleaned out deer hoof. The deer hoofs and the reeds rattled against one another and were supposed to keep the runners awake so as not to fall into crevices or over a precipice while running. It is known that some men have gone to sleep while running and broken their backs by falling down some deep crevice. The rattle of the deer hoofs would also make the wearer of the belt as fleet as the deer. The belt is slung over the back and tied in front with a leather strap so that it and its trappings hang behind the body.

Pedro made it quite clear that when a team loses a race, it is not because of the superiority of the winning team as much as the more powerful medicine of their shaman, which made the losers weak in the legs as well as short-winded. One of the shamans was washing the legs of a runner not far from me and this, I was told, was a medicinal wash made from the boiled branches of a cedar bush. It is usual to do this for three days prior to a race, and now this man got it for the last time, to make his legs strong.

Each team had a ball (*komaka*) about three inches in diameter and usually made from the knotty part of a small tree or branch or from the root of an oak or soft pine, which was kicked off at the same time as the opponent's. Each team ran after its own ball and the first one there kicked it again. The ball could not be touched by the hand unless it went into a deep hole or crevice where it could not be kicked. Should this happen it was thrown out by hand or picked out with the cane carried by each runner. This cane or stick (*risora*) was about an inch thick, three feet long, and made of a bamboo-like reed which had a few pebbles enclosed to make it rattle while in motion. The ball of one team was painted white with markings in red and blue to distinguish it from the opponent's ball.

One of the teams, sometimes both, distinguishes itself by having its members' legs painted with white stripes, which was done by the visiting team in this race. Pedro informed me that the painting of the legs is called wind (*ikaka*) and that it used to be a "cure" by the shaman to make the runners as fast as the wind. Just before the race the young looking village shaman offered a sacrifice of corn-beer (*tes-*

güino) to the ball so that it would not get into too many crevices during the race, and to make the runners on his side strong.

Should a runner get tired during a race, due, of course, to witch-craft, he stops in front of his shaman and his legs are rubbed with a medicinal salve made from the ground roots of an unidentified plant (called *sinonowa*) mixed with suet. To make sure of his team winning, the shaman will also mix the leaves of another unidentified plant (*kochinawa*) with the leaves of the tobacco plant (*pewaraka*) and then smoke it toward the runners of the opposite side to make them sleepy and cut down their staying power.

Magic was also used against the runners. Certain herbs were thrown into the air and their evil intent carried by the wind to the other side. Other herbs were openly shaken in front of the opponents to make them weak from the fear of the magic. Pieces of a ball-cactus (*wichuriki;* genus *Mammillaria*), were used by one shaman to make his runners light of foot and increase their speed. This plant was greatly feared due to its supposed magical powers. I did not see any graves looted of bones, but Pedro informed me small pieces of human bones are sometimes buried in the ground along the course, as running over human bones makes a man tired and weary.

I was informed of many other powerful medicines sent out by the shaman against his opponents, but this was not enough, as he must also protect his own runners against the Wizards and Witches (*Sukuru-ame*). The most powerful of these protecting medicines was made from an unidentified small ball-cactus (*bakanawa* or *bakanori*). The root was chewed

170

and then rubbed on the legs of the runners to make them light of foot. There seems to be no evil medicine which cannot be countered by another. For instance, the dried blood of the bat (*sopechi*) and the dried meat of the turtle (*muri*) was mixed with some cultivated tobacco (*wipaka*). This mixture, which is considered a very powerful one, was smoked by the shaman toward the runners of his own team to protect them against the evil smoke sent out by their competitors.

To a Tarahumara, the most important and interesting place on the race course is where he can place a bet. Each team had a kind of director and they arranged the various articles bet, as each bet must be matched by something of equivalent value before the race. These men also paid out to the one who won immediately after the race. Those who win on a race are expected to give the winning team a certain part of their gain or its equivalent. The Tarahumaran is an inveterate gambler and might gamble everything he owns on a race or game of chance. Without a second thought he will bet his only goat, cow, sheep, bow and arrows, down to his one and only blanket, even his breechclout may be missing, all lost on a race or game.

Looking at the gathering of Indians around me, I felt that one of the outstanding features about them was their free, easy and independent style of walking, and then, perhaps, their hair and the way it was kept. Some had the hair hanging down loose over the shoulders. Some men had a head-band of white cloth, the women a similar band, but in red. Some had their hair plaited, others wore a hair ribbon made of fine material beautifully woven in dif-

171

ferent colors, mostly red, green and white, alternating. Their hair was straight, long and black, and shining as if dressed with some fatty matter to make it glossy.

All of the men wore sandals (*akaka*); some, but not many, had trousers (*sarawera*) of white, loose fitting material and tied around the ankles. The others, although it was cold, wore nothing but their breechclout (*sitabacha*) and blanket (*kemaka*) woven on a homemade loom in different colors. On top of the trousers or breechclout they wore a belt or girdle (*puraka*).

The women wore a skirt (*sipuchaka*) of a white material, very wide at the bottom and billowing like a balloon-jib in the wind. The women seemed very proud of these skirts, for they wore a number of them at the same time, not so much to keep them warm but to show off their wealth. Some also had a shirt (*napachaka*) of the same material as the skirt, but I understand these were of foreign origin and worn only by those well-to-do. Very few ornaments were noticed among the women. Only two wore necklaces (*korogaka*), one of them made of colored glass beads, the other of a kind of seed. Two women had pretty ear-beads, strung on short strings and fastened to the ears, with a small shell hanging below the beads as a kind of pendant.

Every man carried a kind of leather bag or pouch with a long narrow leather strap attached, which was put over the head and suspended from the shoulder like a haversack. One or two men had this strap tied around the waist. The head village shaman-doctor, although a pagan, wore a large crucifix hanging on a rosary. Pedro questioned him for me, and he considered it a talisman, a kind of amulet, a charm against evil, and a sign of being successful and wealthy. It looks pretty, he said, and can therefore be considered an ornament among the non-Christians. His rosary, which carried the large crucifix, was made from hard, bony, capsule-like seeds known as Job's-tears which grow in the warmer *barrancas.*

For some reason, blamed on witchcraft, the race did not start before five o'clock in the afternoon. One man from each team threw his ball as far forward as he could on a given signal and each team followed. The first man there kicked the ball of his team and so it went on over the thirty mile course. It was dark by eight o'clock, with heavy clouds overhead, but it wasn't too dark because of the many fires made along the course. A shaman next to me was working on the legs of a runner under the light of a torch made from resinous pitch-pine. Many torches could be seen carried everywhere and some had been stuck in the ground at several points.

I was beginning to feel the strain of standing around after my illness, not mentioning the "cure" I had been through, and should have been asleep on my goatskins long before this, but nothing could have dragged me from this fantastic scene. Pedro, noticing my distress, had somehow obtained a bottle-gourd full of maguey-beer (*chawiki*) which he offered me to drink. It was most refreshing and invigorating to a convalescent and must have contained a strong stimulant for I was all over my weakness in a few minutes.

Six runners made up each team at the beginning, but only three in each team remained running in the last circuit. They were all running smoothly and with ease in a style similar to our own long-distance runners. When they came within about half a mile of the finishing line, a lot of boys, girls and grown ups were running behind them carrying torches—it was a remarkable scene indeed. The visiting team won by about 200 yards, which wasn't much for that distance. They had run about thirty miles over rough terrain in crudely made sandals and carrying paraphernalia in about five and one-half hours.

Tekwe had gone for the burro and we were preparing to return to the village when I decided to give each runner a present. When leaving Culiacán I had taken enough paper money to pay thirty men for two weeks and some for my own upkeep and feeding the horses and men. All this money was intact and feeling generous with the notes the rebels had printed only a week or so before, I told Pedro, who carried the money in a bag over the shoulder, to give each runner of the winning team ten pesos, and five to each of the losers. Fifty pesos were given to help defray expenses of the food and drink at the *fiesta* by the race-course, which had been free but must have been paid for by someone or by the village. This action created much more excitement than I had expected, for the people had never seen or heard of anything like it before.

There was to be a pre-birth *fiesta* and, of course, all-night dancing in our village in honor of the visiting team. Due to my presents the inevitable happened, I was invited and it was no use saying no, so we returned to the village. I wanted to lie down on the goatskins for a rest but Pedro thought this might hurt the feelings of the villagers, so I took another good drink of maguey-beer and followed my companions to the dancing-place (*awirachi*).

It was an interesting *fiesta;* the dance (*rutuburi*) was led by the shaman-chanter (*saweame,*) who seemed to shake his wooden rattle (*ariki*) constantly. But by two o'clock in the morning I was too fagged out to continue. The weakness after the illness and the cure itself began to tell, and as I felt myself sinking into a coma, I asked the two boys to help me back. Pedro shook his head but assisted me to a near-by wall where I squatted down like an Indian against it. When I woke, it was broad daylight and once more I found their blankets over me snug and warm. It must have been very cold for them, but I felt better. All around me I noticed people eating, drinking and some dancing. They appeared happy though tired. When I asked Pedro to offer my apologies for falling asleep, he almost giggled and informed me that everything was all right for the villagers thought I had imbibed too much *tesgüino* which meant having had a good time.

We came back to the village, which was close by, about 9 a.m., and, feeling refreshed, I began to prepare for our return to Culiacán, although my legs were weak and my boots felt like lead. While arranging for two men to carry my things, a deputation from villages scattered far and wide came to see me. They represented about three hundred men who wished to come with us and join the Rebel Army.

Needless to say, I was delighted, and the matter was settled at once. They were divided into three groups of one hundred each, and three men recommended by the chief and Pedro were appointed temporary company commanders. They received orders to report in Culiacán in seven days time, and not before. They were also told not to move as a company, but split up into small parties of six or seven men so as not to be conspicuous. The leaders received fifty pesos each to help them along, which was all I had to give them.

The return

When this was settled, a special runner was sent with a note to Colonel Acosta in Culiacan, giving a short resume of what had taken place. We started out at noon on the southern route, via Ignacio and Morelos. The party consisted of Pedro, Tekwe, two porters, myself and a friend of Pedro, who came as a special guide. We climbed up and down through a pine forest, crossed a rapid river and a large gorge. These men seemed to be guided by a remarkable instinct, for they always reached a fair place to ford, or a crossing over some turbulent cascade. They miraculously found old paths apparently unused for ages which we followed, but suddenly the path would dead-end abruptly. Not all of these paths were welcome.

After we had descended some distance, we came suddenly to a lovely valley. Everything was green, quiet and peaceful. There was water in the creek and I had to halt my companions, as this was Shangri-La. The boys did not relish the idea when they came upon a smooth path leading downward along the creek. We followed it for about a mile when we came to the foot of a perpendicular formation, high and threatening, which seemed to defy us to pass, and there the path ceased to exist as mysteriously as it had begun up in the valley. My Indian trackers had to be forced to search the trail for tracks but couldn't find any. The path was, nevertheless, perfectly smooth as if in constant use.

The path practically ended by the high, palisade-like rocks, from which water ran freely from a crack with a pleasant sound. My Indians did most certainly not like the looks of the place as Pedro came and asked permission to move on quickly because evil and supernatural forces were at work around us. He thought it the home of the dead war heroes of his tribe, and it was courting bad luck to disturb them. This place was mentioned in the legends, he said, but he knew of no one that had been there. We moved on around the cliffs, but I noticed the boys did not halt anywhere near that path or the valley when they stopped to eat.

In one gorge we came upon a number of terraces, built one above the other. They reminded me of the agricultural terraces seen in the hills of Java and Japan, the only difference being that each of these Mexican ones had been built across almost dry gullies (*arroyos*). Each terrace-wall varied from five to eight feet in height in the center, and about fifteen in width. The stones were laid with great care and skill, without mortar and yet not one stone was out of place. These walls seemed to have been filled in behind with soil, sloping down to the top of the wall, but this could, of course, have been the work of erosion processes from above.

Pedro and his friend were scouting ahead of the party, but Tekwe made camp for the night at a prearranged spot, near a spring with clear water coming out of the rocks—as from a tap. A number of partridges had been knocked down with stones by one of the porters, and a pleasant meal was in store, but I told Tekwe to pluck and draw my bird before roasting, which he thought would spoil the taste of the bird. The man who did the hunting had brought his bow (*ataka*), and the arrows (*waka*) he kept in a quiver (*Koma*).

Pedro and his companion returned a little later with unpleasant news. They had run into some Indians from Tubares who told them that Pancho Villa's patrols were searching the sierra to capture a Carranzista patrol which had come up into the sierra from the low country. Pedro thought the federals who had chased us had been mistaken for Carranza men, but suggested that we change our course and return to Sinaloa by going southwestward, which meant very rough country, but relatively safe. He also knew that Villa and Carranza had serious trouble between them, and capture by the Villa patrol might be unpleasant, for they would probably shoot all Carranzistas on sight.

During supper Pedro told me of a lost Spanish mine at the bottom of a deep gorge half a day away, which he wanted me to see. And now for the first time he mentioned the legend of a Lost Spanish Community around a gold mine in the sierra. I had heard of this before, for it had been discussed several times in the Hotel in Culiacán, but I didn't know it was also an Indian Legend.

We started out early next morning on a forced march and crossed Rio Fuerte (one boy called it Rio Urique) west of San Francisco by nightfall, and I sincerely hoped never again to be forced to meet such formidable *barrancas* and rough country. After the first two hours we came upon a trail which was fairly good, but among other spots there was one in particular at which the trail was not three feet wide for about a hundred yards. On the one side was a perpendicular drop of well over a thousand feet, and on the other rose a wall several hundred feet in height, with pebbles and small stones rolling down from the top constantly, which was most unpleasant as one expected an avalanche any minute. This very old Indian trail was made possible by a fault in the rocks which had been improved on by man, and yet these winding, breathtaking trails are a pleasure to move on in comparison to the many cross-country jaunts on the Indian short-cuts.

After crossing the river and being on Mesa Colorada once more, we looked for signs of our disaster some two weeks before but there wasn't even a vulture in sight. Clean picked bones of six horses and, perhaps, of men were scattered about but no signs of clothing, guns or saddles. At El Nacimiento we came upon a Mexican with a small pack-train of horses which was commandeered and we rode bareback into Choix arriving by noon, with very sore seats.

The two Tarahumara porters and the guide refused to return to their homeland from Choix as they

179

wanted to see the great and famous City of Culiacán. To do this they joined the rebel army and were running happily alongside the horses.

We had a pleasant surprise in Choix as Lopez, anticipating difficulties, had moved the spare horses westward for safety and they were now grazing in the lowlands not far from the road to Agua Nueva. He told us that about 300 federals had come through, but, as they had only three prisoners, he remained in hiding in the hope that some of us might turn up. Lopez had not seen any other federals, but rumors had come in of heavy fighting near Yecorato, in the south, where the enemy had been badly beaten. I knew then that Acosta had received my message and sent a strong force. Lopez also thought the train had returned to San Blas with reinforcement, in the hope of picking up the remainder of our little force.

Hoping this was true, we started out with borrowed saddles and each man leading a spare mount. We changed horses several times and made that long journey by nightfall. The locomotive wasn't exactly cold, but it took us two hours to get up steam. We then sped crazily toward Culiacán and reached there, after a few delays, at ten o'clock the following morning, March 10.

Colonel Acosta's reception was full of enthusiasm. He gave a lunch party of welcome, at which the whole town seemed to have been invited. At luncheon he told the guests of my note from Mesa Colorada, and how the dispatch-rider successfully arrived by train though badly wounded. The fight at Yecorata was wonderful. He said, "We caught the

180

federals more or less in the open and attacked them from three sides.   Only about twenty escaped."

He also told how the federal gunboat "Tampico" had mutinied and had come over to our side on February 24 at Topolobampo, a small town with a good harbor, south of San Blas in Sinaloa.   Everything went fine, but when the gunboat steamed out a few days later to engage the other federal warship "Guerrero," our newly acquired pride and joy, the "Tampico," received a broadside.   Five shells hit her waterline and she was forced to run onto a sand bar to save herself from sinking.

Among Acosta's guests in the hotel that day were two Americans, Shepley and Leek, pleasant fellows and the kind of Americans we like to see in Mexico.

V

An ambitious sergeant—A patrol into the foothills of the Sierra—The cavalry school—We move south—A narrow escape—Talk of war with the United States

During dinner on the evening of my return from the land of the Tarahumara, Colonel Acosta told me of a sergeant sent to Rosario two weeks before to recruit men for the cavalry. Reports and rumors reached him that the sergeant recruited over 300 men, but had also elevated himself to the rank of general. He had mysteriously obtained a number of guns, and ignored all orders to return to Culiacán. Acosta was apologetic, for he knew I needed rest after days of arduous traveling, on top of which came the tiresome luncheon party at noon. He asked me, nevertheless, to proceed to Rosario and bring the recruits back as well as the obstruent sergeant before General Blanco returned from the north. "Pick what men you need," he said. "A train is awaiting you at the station with steam up."

Not knowing the local status of this ambiguous

but ambitious sergeant, or what kind of opposition might come our way, I picked ten good Yaquis, some spare horses and boarded the train about two hours later with Pedro, Tekwe and Lopez. We arrived at LaCruz at three o'clock the following morning. The railroad track was bad, in fact terrible in places, as several culverts and bridges had been blown up by the rebels to retard the federals, and we had no material to repair the damage.

To get over this difficulty we graded off the banks, and laid the rails into the dry creeks which were often quite deep and broad. When we came to one of these places, the train would stop, back some distance, get up steam and then move forward at full speed down these shaky inclines into the river bed, and then up on the other side by its own weight. This kind of traveling with men and horses inside of boxcars is disconcerting enough in the day-time, but simply nerve-wracking at night, so it was quite a relief to stop at La Cruz to replenish the firewood for the engine.

We continued at daybreak and reached Modesto at two o'clock in the afternoon. As the seaport of Mazatlan was held by the enemy, we unloaded the horses and started out for the town of Rosario some sixty miles to the southeast. We halted at Potrero to call on General Jesus Carranza, who was in bed with several wounds. The one in the right side gave him much trouble. He complained bitterly of the pain and was in great need of the medicaments we brought him.

I told Carranza about Pedro's skill as a herb-doctor, and as he knew how famous some of the Tarahumara doctors were, he asked for him. Pedro came, looked at the nasty looking festering wounds, and went to work with a speed and skill which might well put any M. D. to shame. He knew beforehand of the wounded general and Pedro, always a shaman-healer, had collected some herbs not found in his medicine bag. He ground one of these plants, mixed with water, and washed the wound carefully. Then he pulled his long wicked looking knife and calmly cut away some small pieces of apparently dead flesh, then washed the wound again.

He took some leaves from a plant of the Logania Family (genus *Buddleia*) out of his medicine-bag and warmed them in the hot ashes and placed them directly on the wound. Then he called me outside and mentioned that the leaves were three weeks old and might not be "as strong" as from a fresh plant, but he hoped they would cure him anyhow. As a final move, this extraordinary Indian produced the stem and leaves of a plant of the Vervain Family (genus *Vitex*) which he broke into small pieces and boiled with some water, strained it, and made Carranza drink a good size potion to reduce his fever. Less than half an hour thereafter the general was asleep for the first time in several days, and we continued our journey at once.

We made a stop at Nevadillo about five miles north of Mazatlán for a rest, but continued at midnight. We passed through Villa Union, east of Mazatlán, and arrived outside Rosario that evening. As men and horses were tired, and not wishing to alert the "general" and his men, we bivouacked some distance north of the town near the Rosario River. What struck me as peculiar was the fact that we had not seen a scout, outpost, or patrol belonging to us or the enemy since we left Potrero. The country seemed deserted. There wasn't even an outpost in the outskirts of Rosario, which was a small but important rebel post.

My indefatigible scouts Pedro and Tekwe did not like the looks of things either, and insisted on going into town at once to see if anyone was there, and who. They dirtied their hands and faces, stripped themselves of all military accoutrement and with dirty clothes, went into the town, looking like very tough *hombres* indeed. They returned an hour or so later with the information that the sergeant had taken over command of the district, made himself a general, and was at this moment giving a *fiesta* in his own honor. He had recruited about 400 men, but as some had only recently been let out of different jails to join his "command," there were many professional murderers, drunkards and outlaws among them and, as respectable Pedro expressed it, "Many of them are evil looking!"

Tekwe said there were also several Yaqui, Mayo and other Indian volunteers who were discontented, although permitted to roam the country side and do, as well as take, what they wanted. These recruits had plundered different houses and obtained an assortment of muzzle-loading guns and about forty Winchester carbines.

Both of the scouts advised caution and that we do nothing until the *tequila* and *mescal,* which was given out free and liberally, had taken effect. Tekwe thought we could count on the Yaquis to go with us if we let them know our intentions, but this I was against as it was too risky.

The two Indians returned to the feast after we

had agreed to move forward and halt at a certain place about two hundred yards from the town. If they did not return by midnight, we were to move in and see what had happened. Just before the appointed hour, a coyote called, and shortly thereafter an owl, which was the agreed signal, and the two men were among us again. They came like ghosts, unseen and unheard apparenly, even by the Yaquis in our party.

The *fiesta* was going strong and many women were present, they told us, and most of the men were already asleep. The "general" was drinking heavily but the *tequila* did not seem to affect this half-breed traitor, Pedro said, although he was showing signs of inhibition.

We moved into town. Pedro and Tekwe, once more fully armed, had their lariats in hand as I wanted to take the "general" alive if possible. By the time we reached the place of the feast it was close on one o'clock in the morning and not a guard or outpost was encountered. As we entered it was obvious that only about a dozen men could stand up unaided. Some fifty men and women had gone to sleep leaning against one another like pigs. Some had fallen to the floor. Others had left the place before our arrival.

The "general" was sitting half drunk in a large, plush, green armchair, as if on a throne, with a cheap but flashy looking woman on his lap, when we made our presence known. Tekwe had come in from another entrance, and was swinging his rope and let it go when the "general" began to fumble for his guns, which was not an easy thing to do efficiently with a woman so close. It was a good throw, the "general" and woman were pulled from the chair and looked funny struggling on the floor, but Tekwe had the man hog-tied like a steer in a few seconds. The half dressed woman was released, and she disappeared through a doorway as fast as her shaky legs permitted, to the amusement of all present.

There was no opposition to speak of from the drunken men, except for one who tried to make a sneak draw, but was stalled in mid-air by Lopez. We made no further arrests as it was difficult for so few to handle so many, but their guns were removed and placed in a room under guard. The men who could understand what was going on were told to disperse, but to turn up for inspection the following morning at ten.

The sergeant who had been such a braggadocio as a general became a miserable whimpering wretch after the arrest and begged for mercy constantly. Tekwe, who never liked this type of man, told him he would hang by the neck within an hour if he did not reveal where his loot was hidden. We eventually found the stolen property, and I estimated it was worth over 20,000 pesos, which wasn't so bad for a sergeant to collect for himself in two weeks. Among the various articles were a number of gold wedding rings, brooches and several articles of great artistic value stolen from haciendas. There were also two large silver candlesticks taken from a church. The cash money in his possession was surprisingly small, only 1800 pesos in rebel and federal bills. These I distributed among my men, giving them fifty pesos each. Pedro, Tekwe and Lopez received 100 each.

The rest was kept to defray the expenses of our return to Culiacán.

Apparently some or all of the jailbirds got scared during the night and left the city, for only 310 men turned up in the morning. The "general" had done rather well by his followers; he had appointed a lieutenant for every ten men, and a captain for every twenty. There were no majors or colonels, but a raft of non-commissioned officers, all of them sergeants. There were more officers and sergeants than men in the ranks.

Almost everyone in his party produced paper money in denominations of fifty and 100 pesos each, signed by this harum-scarum "general," amounting to 17,000 pesos. It was amusing as well as tragic to see these *bilimbiques,* as they were written on sections of toilet paper. As the men seemed quite concerned over this so-called money, I promised to intercede on their behalf with General Blanco.

As these men had not been organized into any kind of military formation, they were divided into three groups, each under its own leader but under the command of Tekwe, who was given the temporary rank of major, with two of our men as his second and third in command. Provisions were purchased and packed on spare horses. The Winchesters were distributed among the Yaquis, Mayos, and Tepehuanes, and the column started out on foot about three o'clock in the afternoon of March 13, destination Modesto, some sixty miles to the northwest. This is not a very long march for ordinary infantrymen but a terrible distance for some of these Mexican cowboys.

My little party, with the "general" securely bound, moved on after the rear-guard of the other column had left. When we passed the bedraggled looking outfit, catcalls and violent threats were vehemently hurled after him by a great number of his former followers.

When we were about six or eight miles along the road, we noticed a lot of deer in the hills near the village of Guajolote (Wild Turkey). In view of the fact that the scouts had not encountered any enemy patrols, we halted and went hunting. The place was simply teeming with deer and we had eight of them, skinned and ready within an hour, when Tekwe's column caught up with us. The unexpected ration of meat cheered everyone considerably, and on we continued in a more buoyant mood.

We arrived at Potrero early in the morning of March 15 and found General Carranza much improved and his fever gone. He asked to see Pedro, the Tarahumara doctor, and gave him fifty pesos. Carranza was now under the care of a Mexican doctor sent from Culiacán. He had strong reinforcement and orders to hold Potrero at all cost against any surprise sortie by the federals in Mazatlan, only about thirteen miles distant. When told of the sergeant coming along as a prisoner, Carranza felt that I was too soft with this renegade, and added, "You are making a hero out of him. Try him and hang him before you reach Culiacán."

We moved on to Modesto within the hour and found the train standing where we had left it a few days before. The crew was absent, but the engine was hot and more or less ready to pull out. From a track repairman, we found that the men had gone to the beach to look at the Pacific Ocean. Off I went with Pedro to bring them back.

When we returned after a swim about two hours later, it was reported that the "general" had tried to escape, but the Yaqui guard threw his knife after him and he died. Not knowing what to do with him, and not wishing to take the trouble to bury him, the body had been carried about a hundred yards from the station and left there for the coyotes to take care of. I found the body and there was no doubt that he had been killed by a knife in the back. His death coincided with Tekwe's remark to me in Rosario before we left: "Señor, this imposter may never reach Culiacán, for he will try to escape. Why don't you let the men deal with him in their own way and save you a lot of trouble?"

The train pulled out early in the afternoon and we arrived in Culiacán, March 16. When I informed Colonel Acosta of the "general's" inglorious death, he smiled and remarked: "It may be for the best for it saved us the trouble of a court-martial and a firing-squad." Acosta then informed me of the latest news from Carranza headquarters. It appears that General Villa, needing money for the campaign, took possession of the "El Desengaño" mine in the State of Durango sometime in January last. The United States, representing Spain, sent a note to Carranza demanding an explanation on the confiscation of the mine by one of his generals.

Carranza's answer to the United States on March 12 was more or less in the following strain; Spain could not expect any reparation or indemnity, since

Spain had recognized the Huerta regime. Spain was nevertheless invited to make a direct representation to him (Carranza), but had no business or right to make a claim through the United States.

General Blanco returned from the north on March 18, and appointed me commander of the 2nd Regiment of Cavalry in the 1st Brigade, but without promotion in rank. He reiterated for the third time that my promotion was a foregone conclusion and blamed G.H.Q. for holding it back for some unaccountable reason.

A Patrol into the foothills of the Sierra

On the 19th there was another change in the over-all plan as something had gone wrong. We heard that strong enemy patrols had been seen in the hills east of us. Blanco told me to take as many men as I thought necessary and proceed eastward into the foothills of the Sierra Madre, locate and destroy, or drive out, the strong enemy patrols which had been reported by some strange Indians. One of them, a very old man, said, "They were in such large numbers that it was impossible to count them for there were more soldiers than days in the year."

By all accounts it was obvious that the federals were getting active on our flanks and it worried Blanco. This advance south could hardly take place with an enemy of unknown strength on his left flank as well as on his right, for the federals still held the important harbors of Guaymas, Mazatlan and San Blas. Besides, the gunboat "Guerrero" was constantly patrolling up and down the Pacific Coast and shelling our communications whenever possible.

Again I brought my Three Musketeers, Pedro, Lopez and Tekwe, for they were unsurpassed as scouts and trackers and could always find something tasty for the pot such as a bird, squirrel or venison when food was scarce. Thus, with two squadrons, we started out by following the paths up the Culiacán River and did not find it difficult to reach the village of Imala, where no one had seen or heard of any federals for some time.

From here scouting across country was more difficult. One squadron was assigned for scouting work over a wide front which meant long and winding footpaths that could separate each troop considerably. Due to the terrain, my own party was forced southward slightly, but as I wanted to reach the village of Junta, we tried to move north again but failed to get there, as we had to look everywhere for hidden troops. As we turned to rejoin the others the tracks of two shod horses were plainly seen pointing in an easterly direction toward the sierra. Pedro maintained that these tracks were not more than a few hours old. Later we came across some soft ground with hoof prints about ten days old of a force in which there were 25 to 30 horses traveling south. Two of my companions followed the tracks for awhile then rejoined me.

On the evening of March 22, I sent orders to all scouts within reach to come to the small settlement of Higuera on the Culiacán River due east of Culiacán. About fifty men turned up, but they had no news of the enemy nor had they seen any tracks, so I presumed the enemy was hiding somewhere. The scouts had reported the rest of the squadron had gone up the valley toward Torno, so a man was sent after them with orders to join the column at the small settlement of Cofradia, located on a tributary of the Culiacán River, the following evening. In the meantime I took a small party and tried to follow the enemy tracks toward Platanar, near the Durango border, but found more time was needed. As the paths and Indian short-cuts were hard on the horses, I turned toward Cofradia after two horses had gone lame.

The creeks were dried out in most places and Pedro pointed out that the deer had started to move into the sierra for water. The stone-bound dry ground over the hills, as well as the deep and rough dried out arroyos and river beds, harrassed our animals as there was no grass to speak of, and very little water. Water was found here and there, but it ran into the ground and disappeared, appearing again farther down, to vanish once more and for good into the sand and stones. We tried digging below one of these spots, but had to abandon the experiment when, four feet down, the wall kept caving in. Pedro remarked that this condition of the creeks was a common occurrence even in the larger rivers during the dry season.

While resting the horses and waiting for some of the scouts, the legend of the Lost Spanish Mine was again brought up by Pedro, who seemed to be crammed full of Indian tales. He mentioned that we were about in the locality where the early Spaniards passed through on their way from Culiacán to reach the *barranca* of Bacis Quebrada, in the neighborhood of which the supposed rich mine was located. As an afterthought, Pedro said, "I don't know if there is any truth in these stories, but there must be something to these legends for they have been repeated for many generations among different Indian tribes, and White prospectors have been looking for the place for a very long time."

All the scouts, except two, turned up at Cofradia and none of them had seen any federals. That evening Tekwe was worried as the two missing Yaquis were not only close friends, but he knew them as excellent scouts and he claimed that one of them at least would have come to report. Fearing the worst, he asked permission to go and look for them. He was refused, but I promised we would all look for them in the morning.

We moved out before dawn the following day with a whole squadron scouting on a wide front. Not far from Higuera, Tekwe, guided by circling vultures, came upon the two men hanging in a tree. As we had passed the place only the day before, I presumed the enemy must have come there after our departure. Tekwe pointed out that one of the men was wounded badly in the thigh, and he reasoned that when the other came to the wounded man's rescue, he was captured and they were hung together.

After examining the ground like bloodhounds, all the Indians agreed there had been about twenty-five federals and that they had brought the two men in the afternoon of the day before and hung them. Tekwe requested permission to follow the federals with ten Yaquis, and he was allowed to do so after he had given his word to rejoin us before dark at Cedros, about six miles to the southeast. He went off and we followed, more on the alert than ever, scouting far and wide. Before we reached Cedros we heard a lively rifle-fire ahead and pushed forward with increased speed as I was afraid Tekwe needed help. But Tekwe had encircled the place, and coming from the south he drove a federal sergeant and eight men toward us. The Yaquis didn't need our help to finish them off. Hot for revenge they rushed in and killed all of them, but lost one of their own in so doing. They were still not satisfied, for they wanted to get the federals alive, and I was grateful they did not.

After the skirmish I noticed several horses were lame and many had bleeding fetlocks, so we halted in a suitable position to take care of the animals. At noon I took advantage of our enforced detention by taking ten men to drive in some deer that were roaming around everywhere, which also gave me a chance to look at the terrain and check on the outposts. Within two hours we had all the meat needed for the two squadrons and the men feasted that afternoon.

No fires were allowed during the night and it passed without incident, except for the infernal prolonged howls of coyotes and the barking and yapping from, it seemed, several packs of wild dogs. We started out at dawn for Sacata, in the southeast, to try and locate the enemy. The hills were dry with hardly any grass, but there was seemingly unafraid game everywhere. The deer stopped eating, looked at us from not a hundred yards away, then went on feeding. Everything indicated that this part had not been

196

visited by man for years, as did the few empty and abandoned ranches. The whole of this part of the country was deserted except for the game, and, wherever a stone was turned, scorpions.

We had traveled for about an hour when a messenger from General Blanco caught up with us with orders to return to Culiacán immediately. After recalling the scouts, we turned around and made a forced march to Culiacán and arrived there in the evening of the same day. During the evening Acosta told me that a colonel with 150 men of the federal army had deserted in Lower California and landed at Altata, a coast town west of Culiacán, to join our forces. This may seem small and unimportant to outsiders, but to us it was a great stimulant, for it indicated that the morale of the federals was beginning to crack.

The Cavalry School

The morning following our return to Culiacán, it was gratifying to see the schools and drill-grounds crowded with aspirants for commissions or promotion to higher grades. These schools, so much ridiculed by most of the generals, were not considered a "must" by most of them. The schools had succeeded far beyond my own expectation, for it was only Blanco, Obregon and Acosta who could see the necessity of them.

Most of the middle class, as well as the Peon-Indians, seemed to be starving for knowledge of almost any kind, a chance to get on. When given the opportunity, they fought hard to reach their objective.

On March 25, Blanco asked me to try and double my efforts in turning out officers, but apologized when he saw the training program. When the field exercises and the regimental economy tests took place the following day, three former captains were promoted to lieutenant colonels, six captains became majors, and the top twenty students from the ranks were given the grade of captain. Two of these could not read or write, but were promoted because they passed as numbers 1 and 2 in the field tests. Both of these fine leaders were colonels two months later.

The rest were made lieutenants, but three of them were reduced to the ranks a few days later because they could not carry the quantity of *tequila, mescal,* or moonshine gin they consumed. It was amusing, but typical of the revolution, that when I met one of these busted lieutenants sometime later in Jalisco, I found he had been promoted to brigadier general in the infantry because he had been through the cavalry school. We had a drink together to celebrate old times, but as before he kept on drinking and ended up very intoxicated. He was, however, a good soldier in the field when liquor was not obtainable.

The non-coms came out almost better than the other officers; in fact, several of them, being former sergeants, were given commissions. Needless to say Blanco was elated, for it completed the formation of the 1st and 2nd cavalry brigades with all officers having some technical training. Some of the officers, relieved by the new men, became attached to headquarters staff to attend the most intensive training probably ever attempted in a rebel army. Those who

PLATE VII

Gen. Miguel M. Acosta.
Photo about 1920.

PLATE VIII

*l. to r. Captains A. Salines, J. Madero, G. Salines on Carranza's Staff.
Hermosillo, 1913.*

passed on top were made instructors as we needed officers for the four more brigades to be formed.

General Blanco, although extremely polite at all times, surprised me during the morning of March 28 by turning up on the parade ground to bring me back for breakfast. While eating he asked if I would accept the appointment as his chief-of-staff. Again he mentioned my promotion and that it was held up at Obregon's headquarters by Colonel Serrano, for the papers had not yeach reached Obregon, but my promotion to major was confirmed.

Blanco seemed much put out by this and other delays and unloaded some of his trouble to me during breakfast. When finished he added a note of warning by saying, "Serrano hates all Americans which includes you, because he thinks you are an American agent sent to spy on us. Look out and never go out alone at night."

During one of the lessons, Obregon appeared intensely interested in trenches and barbed-wire entanglements and kept asking questions for more details. When the lesson was over I told him of the many stories going around about him, and asked if it was true that his name was originally O'Brien. He smiled and told of the rumor of his ancestor being Michael O'Brien who served with the last Spanish Viceroy in Mexico. When the Viceroy returned to Spain, after the War of Independence, O'Brien got permission to remain in Mexico and he became a subject under Emperor Agustin in 1821 or 1822, but moved to the Pacific Coast and settled there in what is now the State of Sonora. The word O'Brien gradually became

Obregon, but he did not seem quite sure whether this story was true or not.

Carranza purchased two airplanes in the United States, which were smuggled into Mexico and flown by two American brothers named Smith. During the fighting around Guaymas in the early part of 1914, one of them dropped some homemade bombs on the federal positions. One of these dropped about two hundred yards behind the advance trenches and killed a woman and two children carrying food to the trenches.

A tremendous howl went up in Mexico City from the already scared government. The German, British and American ministers did not investigate but complained bitterly that the Articles of Geneva Convention had been violated, and there were threats of intervention. A few months later in the same year the Germans and British, who had protested the loudest against the rebels using aircraft for dropping bombs into the trenches in Guaymas, were doing the same thing on defenseless cities and killing civilians by the thousands in Europe, in which the United States joined with even greater vigor a few years later.

We move south

On April 3 we received the wonderful news of the capture of Torreon by Pancho Villa the day before. The news was received with mixed emotions by the senior officers on this side of the sierra, especially by Obregon who appeared pleased but was actually put out by the constant successes of Villa, whom he seemed to hate from the bottom of his heart. With the fall of Torreon, I received orders to re-double my efforts to turn out new officers as we were going south as soon as possible to forestall Villa, apparently, from going into the Capital.

It was interesting to note the difference between Obregon's and Villa's method of fighting. We had trained the Carranza troops to try to use common sense strategy to overcome an enemy, to wear him down by constant feint night-attacks, night and day sniping, and cutting off his supplies. Pancho Villa was too temperamental and perhaps too primitive for strategy, for as a rule he would not wait and brought his cavalry into play constantly in frontal attacks, charging like a Don Quixote against fortifications and stonewalls in an incredible manner, but he won and kept on winning against every rule of common sense.

Through March, the recruits were drilled all day or whenever possible and the officers courses increased from two to five classes daily. Every one seemed to be running around with his nerves on edge. About noon April 18, a rumor was flying around Culiacán that Mexico and the United States were at loggerheads over something unpleasant, no one knew what, but it created quite a furor and nervous tension among the officers.

That evening Blanco received orders from Obregon to prepare to move south against some federals who had moved northward and threatened our lines. The 1st and 2nd Cavalry with Acosta and myself began to entrain long before dawn April 19, and pulled out of Culiacán at 8 a.m. We hoped to make Modesto by nightfall but got there at midnight. The horses were removed from the train immediately, and two dynamiting-gangs went out to mine a few of the bridges still standing between us and the enemy at Mazatlan as a security measure. Our scouts and patrols went everywhere, but did not see an enemy patrol although they went within four miles of their main position.

Many infantry units including Yaquis and Mayos arrived during the night. Brigadier Pablo Gonzales was left behind in Culiacán to raise money for the campaign, which meant putting the printing presses into full gear making paper money.

Early in the morning of April 21, Lieutenant Colonel Miguel Acosta was promoted to full colonel. He should have been made a brigadier general for he was so superior to any of the junior generals around that it was almost amusing. After Acosta's promotion had been promulgated, I told Blanco of the wonderful beach three miles away, and without hesitation he took the senior officers of the staff with him and cantered to the Pacific for a swim. We could see the enemy six or less miles away.

As the officers and men did not seem quite themselves due, I thought, to the nearness of the federals, I remained behind to see personally the scouts and patrols started. While doing this, I found it necessary to strengthen our outer defenses at a certain point and took one hundred men and placed them in two bastions that we dug, one on each side of the road leading from Potrero to Mazatlan.

A Narrow Escape

When returning to camp late that afternoon, it was necessary for me to ride through the infantry lines, but as the place seemed littered with boxes and other stuff, I dismounted to walk the remainder of the way. No sooner was I on foot when a number of infantry officers closed in on me in an obviously hostile attitude. When I stepped back to see what it was all about, a rope was dropped over my head from behind, and I was tied hand and foot with the lasso.

The hate displayed in their faces matched their foul insulting remarks that boded nothing pleasant. While I was wondering what it was all about, they carried me aside and threw me somewhat carelessly under a bush, and placed an armed guard over me, with an officer in charge. No one seemed to care or notice what happened to my horse which was frightened and trotted on to the cavalry lines, which gave me certain relief.

One of the guards was a talkative fellow and tried to tell me there was serious trouble between the United States and Mexico, and that war with America was imminent. When the officer in charge returned, he displayed intense dislike for my person. He refused to give me water and kicked me several times. When it was almost dark, I noticed Pedro and Tekwe mooching around and taking in all details.

Somehow I had expected one of them to notice my saddled horse and look for me, and here they were taking not the slightest notice of my presence nor coming anywhere near me, but they knew where I was. Suddenly they left, and I was sure Acosta or Blanco would come with a regiment if need be. Later, I found they did not dare to mention my name as the men might have killed me instantly.

About midnight, when I was stiff from the cold and cramped position, someone touched my arm. It was Pedro. The guard standing only four yards away had not heard this Indian tracker who squeezed my arm and disappeared as silently as the darkness itself.

About two o'clock in the morning there was a slight dull sound, and Pedro was at my side cutting me loose. A few seconds later Tekwe joined us and both men helped me, as I was very stiff. Soon we came to a place where twenty armed Yaquis stood, and they half carried me in a round about way to the cavalry lines.

The following morning it was reported how a soldier on duty had been found dead, mysteriously stabbed inside our lines, and dragged into some bushes. Not a word was mentioned of my capture and escape, but Acosta discovered that the officers had intended "to dispose of the *gringo* spy before daybreak." He also figured that the Mexican extremists were afraid to bring this matter into the open, as they were in the minority.

The scouts had not seen an enemy all morning, and so many of us spent part of the day at the beach while waiting for mule and horse transportation for the ammunition. Some of us hunted rabbits in the dunes or the many ducks in the lagoons. But as the game had to be shot with soft-nosed bullets, it didn't leave much meat on some of the birds or rabbits. It was all very pleasant, but I was still a *gringo* outsider to all except my own crowd.

We broke the Modesto camp early April 23, and passed through Potrero, Nevadillo and Conche, where the road branches off to Mazatlan only five miles away. Not an enemy patrol or scout could be seen. Someone made the remark that the federals were scared of our show of strength and had pulled in their outposts. We bivouacked that night at Palmilla about eight miles from the enemy.

We continued the following morning, but as a strong enemy patrol had been reported east of us, Acosta and I took a regiment and scoured the country far and wide without seeing a soul. We were east of Roble, but north of Villa Union, when a native runner came from Blanco with the message of warning that a federal cavalry brigade was advancing rapidly on our right flank, but he gave no orders.

Our position was unpleasant, as men and horses had been traveling far and fast, and we had neither food nor water. The 1st regiment had off-saddled and was resting behind a low hill stretching for a few hundred yards east and west. On the left was a deep arroyo difficult for horses. On the right were remains of some old buildings without roofs, some fallen walls of an ancient corral and some tangled underbrush, but no water anywhere.

It became a question whether to hold on or evacuate for a more favorable position, but this latter had its drawbacks, as it was almost too late to move without disclosing our strength. Acosta wanted to saddle up

at once and move to the rear, but a lesson in concealment and the element of surprise was brought home
to him in a few words. He saw the point, declared it
risky, but dispatched two dismounted squadrons to
the top of the rise. There, behind whatever cover they
could find, these men had orders to remain and under
no circumstances show themselves or open fire until
ordered to do so.

Acosta, Pedro and I took up position behind some
bushes on the left flank where we had a clear view
of the oncoming enemy. The federal cavalry, of about
a regiment in strength, came up the gentle slope in
close formation without scouts or advance-guard, and
I wished and itched for a good old Maxim-gun in
my hands. Apparently the federals thought us far
away, for they were talking aloud and laughing. When
about 150 yards from our position, Acosta could not
hold himself and gave the signal to fire, although I
begged him to let them come nearer. With the first
volley some thirty men dropped. The federals evidently
suspected an ambush for they wheeled and galloped
away in disorder leaving thirty dead and thirty-three
wounded on the ground. We had one man wounded
by an accident.

The other squadrons had saddled up during the
fight, but could not pursue as we didn't know the enemy
strength in the neighborhood. Besides, our horses were
not in good shape. The scrap took only twenty minutes,
but before it was over more than a dozen vultures were
circling high overhead waiting for a square meal. We
continued on our way and reached Villa Union during the evening.

On our arrival the following telegram forwarded in a letter was received by an Englishman in this town from the American Consul in Rosario, about thirty miles to the south:

Rosario. 21-4-1914. Mr. Showers. You are officially. notified that General Huerta has refused to salute the American Flag demanded by Admiral Mayo as an apology for the insults offered in the arrest of American sailors and that yesterday President Wilson laid the matter before congress so that proper steps might be taken to enforce the nation's rights. You are reminded that the President heretofore advised all Americans to leave Mexico until order was restored. If all who now heed this advice come to my office in Rosario, provided they have no better means, every possible effort will be made to provide an exit. Answer forthwith Notify Parks.

(Signed) James W. Keys
Special Agent of the United States.

Mr. Showers tried to telephone the American Consul but couldn't get through, so he and Mr. Parks left at noon April 25, for the waterworks, where Showers was in charge of pumping water to Mazatlan through an eighteen kilometer long pipe-line from the Presidio River to the civilians and federals in Mazatlan. Another telegram arrived for Showers, from the American Consul, ordering him to come to Rosario at once. It came after he had left, but we forwarded it to him by messenger.

The 1st Cavalry left Villa Union that afternoon for Escuinapa station, located some miles south of Rosario. Rumors reached us before leaving that the

Yaqui Indians were restless in their homeland in southern Sonora. The 2nd and 3rd Cavalry, following us from Villa Union with General Blanco, arrived at Escuinapa about 4:30 p.m., and were received with band music and a parade by the Generals Jagers and Buelna.

We were hurriedly making up a mobile column in Escuilapa for a push south on Acaponeta. At this moment, we had a force of 5,400 men; not strong, but those armed were fairly efficient as rebels go, and they were keen for action. The column was made up of three former more or less independent units. General Jager had 2,000 men, Buelna 1,000, and ourselves 1,900 but all were not armed.

Into this very mixed and little-disciplined body, we were trying to impress the importance of inter-communication, the necessity of outposts, patrols, scouting and intelligence work. This was not easy as many of the officers could not see the need for any of it. They all agreed on the scouts, as it suited the cowboys, and as such they were good when not tempted to get into a *cantina* in some village and get tanked up on *tequila*.

During the reception for Blanco, there was a noticeable resentment against orders, almost rebellious in nature, in the infantry ranks. Apparently the lukewarm attitude among some of the officers in their loyalty to the rebel cause, so brilliantly illustrated in the Tampico incident and the American occupation of Veracruz, had already reflected with detrimental effect on the discipline of our troops.

There had been smoldering displeasure for some time against certain orders, especially those regulating women following their men on the line of march and in battle, While the officers were squabbling over the question of joining Huerta against the United States, this bitter resentment among the peon-soldiers was manifesting itself in trifling but serious retaliations against such commands, These seemingly unimportant transgressions of orders were generally condoned by the junior officers, because they were either inexperienced or afraid, but sometimes it was also overlooked by regimental commanders and even by brigadiers.

We should take into consideration that in some instances many recruits were obtained in a somewhat unorthodox manner. When some of the revolutionary leaders entered a town, previously held by the enemy, they threw open the local jail and made the inmates join their ranks, but this method of obtaining replacements did not, of course, always bring good recruits. However, it sounds worse than it really was, as most of them had been imprisoned for some petty offense such as belonging to the wrong political party, being related to a rebel or, perhaps, defying the impossible demands of the Church. These political prisoners, usually poor men but perfectly decent citizens, were nevertheless thrown in jail and mixed with common thieves, murderers and bandits. All of them made excellent though sometimes ruthless guerrilla soldiers.

The rank and file of the revoutionary army was otherwise mostly made up by the younger generation of peons and Indians of different tribes. On the Pacific Coast we had thousands of Yaquis and Mayos, some Pimas, Tarahumara and Tepehuanes. Farther south in Tepic some Coras joined us. In the Chihuahua area there were many Apaches, some Tarahumara and Tepehuanes under Villa, and in the deep south Zapata had Guerreros, Tarascans, and a mixture of Tepehuanes, Tarahumara, Coras and Otomis.

All these people had a deep-rooted grudge and hatred for the *cientificos,* for they had been exploited, robbed, and their land and homes taken from them by the Whites.

The rebel soldiers also saw and felt the noticeable change in some of the leaders, many of whom at one time did actually entertain a sincere desire to help the peons. But, as the generals grew more and more powerful, this desire to help seemed to cool off. Their slogans became shop-worn and did not ring true.

Pancho Villa and Zapata lived on a very high plane, equal to that of any *hacendado,* but these two did keep on fighting for the land promised the people and were not looking for political or other lucrative positions. Obregon promised land and so did Carranza, but it became obvious that these two were playing for higher stakes than originally intended, and the chips used in their gamble were the lives of Peon-Indians, who had to wait.

As a rule the real peon-soldier had no particular interest or knowledge of the world beyond his horizon. He was usually completely indifferent to anything outside his family, cornfield, nearest village and *fiestas.* The Indian soldiers, who had lived away from the influences of the haciendas, were quite different as they had broader vision and interests, such as hunting and fishing, and some had agriculture and trade for their existence. They all made good soldiers for the kind of fighting on hand.

We heard of reports from the United States, how the federals and the Church in Mexico were accusing the revolutionaries of being bandits, an uneducated scum of anarchists, who intended to confiscate all the land, mines and property of the rich, should they succeed in the revolution. We were also supposed to be murderers who executed our prisoners wholesale without trial, to satisfy our thirst for blood and revenge upon the educated classes.

Some of these accusations may have been true up to a certain point among the Villistas and Zapatistas, but seldom among the Constitutionalists under Carranza and Obregon. It is true that we shot traitors, but we preferred to hang them in a tree as it was more effective, and there was no waste of ammunition. When we hung or shot a man in the ranks, it was not because he was a federal soldier. He had been a spy.

When the federals hung or shot one, ten or more of our men, which was done constantly, we sometimes returned the compliment by doing the same to a similar number of federals, sometimes, I am sorry to say, with interest. However, we also shot some of our own men for outraging women, but that did not make us blood-thirsty anarchists.

The transportation and commissariat of the rebel army were taxed to the limit, often caused by camp followers. It was almost impossible to move troops without them as most of the women had left their homes with the men to join the revolution. There was nowhere else for them to go, the men wouldn't come without them, and it was dangerous to let them go because they might fall into the hands of the federals while their men served with the rebels. They came along anyhow in the beginning, carrying their bundles of food, pots, pans, and clothing on top of their heads or on their backs with a carrying-strap. Sometimes they were allowed trains of boxcars. They climbed inside or on top, and underneath they slung hammock-like contraptions between the wheels. This was usually the favorite place for the young boys.

These women came by the thousands. They were of happy disposition and most thoughtful of their kind, but demure by nature. They foraged for corn and other food while on the march and frequently arrived in camp ahead of the troops and had tortillas and whatever there was to eat ready for their particular men. These remarkable women would constantly risk their lives to get food to the firing line, and take the guns in place of their men while they ate their meager fare.

It was difficult indeed to give orders for these women to stay behind after they had become part and parcel of the army. The 1st and 2nd Cavalry Brigades did not have much trouble, for the women were forbidden to come from the start, but a few did come along with the infantry behind us.

If a man was killed, the woman would often pick up his gun and continue in his place. As a rule, however, she would later attach herself to another man and work for him. There was nothing crude or vulgar in these unions and perfect decorum usually prevailed. Some women rose to be captains and some colonels, but the higher ranks were generally self-appointed by women leaders of bandit gangs who came and fought on the rebel side.

Talk of War with the U.S.A.

On April 30 while in Escuinapa we received the news that the United States had occupied Veracruz. The American version for the invasion differed somewhat from that of the Mexican, the details of which we need not enter here. The attack cleared, however, the reason for the somewhat peculiar behavior of some of my rebel friends which had puzzled me a great deal.

The United States, apparently looking for an excuse to remove Huerta, ordered the Atlantic Fleet into Mexican waters. In the meantime the Hamburg-American S/S Ypiranga was approaching Mexico loaded with munitions of war for General Huerta from Germany. When this leaked out in Washington, President Wilson was informed of it, and he gave his vital order, "Take Veracruz." The American Fleet went in and captured the town, on April 21, 1914, and over two hundred Mexicans, mostly young Cadets of the Naval Institute, were killed along with twenty-one Americans.

Although the occupation of Veracruz actually helped the rebels, Carranza objected strongly and wired Washington to the effect that the American invasion of Mexican territory violated all treaties and endangered the sovereignty of the country, and asked them to get out.

When the discord between the United States and Mexico had reached an impasse, almost a state of war, President Wilson, worried, no doubt, over his hasty action in invading Mexico, invited the representatives of Argentina, Brazil and Chile, as well as Carranza and Huerta, to meet and try to settle the difficulties in Mexico. The three South American nations accepted and so did Huerta. Carranza accepted, but with a proviso that only the international differences between the United States and Huerta be discussed. He specifically denied the right of the mediators to meddle in the internal affairs of Mexico and insisted that there could be no cessation of hostilities between the rebels and Huerta, not even a temporary truce. Carranza's representatives returned and the mediation effort was a failure.

In Mexico City, General Huerta, the prepetrator of all the trouble, sat pondering what to do. He was not in an enviable position for a general. Villa was victorious in the north, Carranza and Obregon were moving forward through Sonora, Sinaloa and Tepic in the northwest and west. Zapata was doing just as he pleased in Morelos and other southern states. Rebels were also moving in on Tampico in the east and now the United States troops had landed in Mexico and threatened the whole Atlantic Coast.

Instead of using his senses, Huerta tried to drown his failing strategy and disappointment in whiskey, but it didn't work, for his faculties became more and more benumbed by liquor, and chronic diseases were fast destroying his fine physique. While in drunken stupors Huerta had made many serious mistakes in the past, including murder. The worst was, of course, the assassination of President Madero and Vice President Suarez, but there was also Gustavo Madero and hundreds of others who stood in his way. At another time he ordered his troops into the Chamber of Deputies and forcibly disbanded them when the Chamber would not follow his dictation. The last act may be overlooked, however, until we know all the facts.

Now this capable soldier of a bygone day sat alone, but he was scheming hard to overcome his difficulties. His warped and liquor-soaked brain, his body now rotted with disease, was struggling and calculating with his old cleverness, and the cunning of an Indian, which he was, to save his tottering throne and win a complete victory over the rebels. And thus while in a drunken state he conceived a "brilliant" idea. He would force the United States to intervene in Mexico. He did not think that America would do anything drastic, but if it did, all the better, for it would solidify Mexico and the rebels would rally under his banner in war against the aggressor. While so employed, he apparently calculated he could easily deal with the more obstreperous rebel leaders and eliminate them one by one. It was easy. With this hopeful but distorted and treacherous plan in mind, he did not try to negotiate further, but deliberately ignored the demands of the United States. The Mexicans were jubilant over his patriotic stand.

Telegraphic dispatches from Carranza to Blanco used strong words condemning the United States for landing in Veracruz. He sent the same proclamation to all commanders in the Constitutionalist Army. He also demanded that Huerta, the man with whom he was fighting for the control of Mexico, do something, as the American occupation of Veracruz was an infamous transgression of Mexican sovereignty.

Many reports and rumors came fast and furious in tone from all corners of Mexico. Some asked advice. The most sobering one came from Pancho Villa, who disagreed with Carranza as to the seriousness of the Tampico incident or the occupation of Veracruz by the United States. He told the First Chief that he didn't give a whoop what Huerta did, and suggested that Carranza let Huerta stew in his own pot.

Everyone here talked of war with the United States, and someone seemed to be pouring oil on the fire among the officers, for they were actually imagining they could beat the Americans, drive them into the sea, and force them to return at least some of the territory lost in the war of 1846-48. Carranza and some others seriously talked of joining forces with Huerta. As far as I know Carranza never faulted in morals or deportment, but the voice of hatred for Americans rose to a terrific crescendo calling for a united Mexico to drive the *gringos* out of Veracruz. This may have influenced him.

Not all revolutionary leaders felt it necessary to join Huerta, although perhaps fifty per cent of them did. There were many men such as General Lucio Blanco and Colonel Maguel Acosta who were much against any affiliation with the man. I spoke to two Yaqui chiefs, and they were surprised and disturbed at the very suggestion and spoke loudly against the idea. The rank and file of the rebel army did not seem to care much what happened, but the Indian scouts did not wish to have truck with the federals at any time, except to fight the revolution to a successful conclusion.

Whatever the effect on the people of Mexico, the capture of Veracruz by the United States brought out an interesting moral side among the rebel leaders by the inecorum created. These *cabecillas,* although perhaps in different military camps or political affiliations, all fought for the same principal and uttered the same cry, "Land and liberty for the peons and Indians." Some expressed their views with greater spiritual daring, bitterness or passionate poignancy than others. Some talked a lot but did nothing, while a few hoped for advancement by the destruction of their military or political rivals by either fair or foul means.

On the other side of the political fence was General Huerta, a sworn enemy of the common people, yet he needed only to devise a simple scheme, a strategical trick, for the destruction of the rebel cause. Some of the rebel leaders could not see or sense the proverbial Sword of Damocles hanging dangerously over their heads. They forgot their promises to the Indians and were openly discussing the pros and cons of walking into the trap, while others were actually advocating joining this Devil incarnate, an enemy of the Indians and peons, although almost a full-blooded Indian himself. One might here quote the befitting words of Omar Khayyam, "O Thou, who didst with pitfall and with sin beset the road I was to wander in."

Very few persons in Mexico or in the United States know how perilously near Huerta brought America into war, for had his reputation been less jaded, the plot would have worked. A few years later, while in France with my regiment, I began to think that Huerta's move was master-minded by the German General Staff, to pre-occupy Washington and keep the United States out of the affairs in Europe. To Pancho Villa, Lucio Blanco and Alvaro Obregon should go the honor of doing more, than all others combined, to avert the terrible catastrophe that inevitably would occur by joining Huerta in a war with the United States.

After the occupation of Veracruz by the U. S. forces I became, for a while at least, a mere tolerated alien. I was not a *compañero*, not even a friend in the eyes of some. The opinion of the officers changed like a pendulum, right and left, depending on who spoke last and most convincingly. But the good will of Blanco, Acosta, the rank and file of the cavalry and Indian scouts, never faltered.

VI

Whatever the cause for our stay in Escuinapa from April 25 to May 1, it was good for the troops because it improved considerably their conception of what a military organization should be. However, some of the units still did not seem to care. As an example; on visiting the outposts one morning I found them badly placed. Some had left their posts to eat, leaving the front wide open with the enemy only a few miles distant. When I reached General Buelna's headquarters he was not there but most of his staff was suffering from a hangover from a *fiesta* the night before.

That afternoon the cavalry units were issued three days ration of flour and *penoche* (a brown sugar). We had no meat but hoped to pick up some along the line of march, for we were due to move at midnight. The enemy patrols exchanged a number of shots with our outposts in the southern sector that evening but nothing serious occurred.

The 2nd Cavalry entrained and left Escuinapa at one o'clock in the morning, May 2, and arrived at Copales at six, a distance of about twenty-six miles. Here we joined forces with an infantry regiment acting as an advance-outpost. Copales consisted of nothing but a burned bridge and a pump for delivering water to the locomotives, but the pump had been destroyed and the water which should have run in the river did not exist. It had dried up. A water-hole was found some distance up the river and the water had to be carried to the train by hand.

The country was dry and desert-like everywhere. The people who lived in these parts had left to take refuge in the mountain regions to the east to escape the war-zone and forced enlistments, and in order to get water. Some were fighting with us. Others had been forced into the federal army.

The enemy's main force was located inside the town of Acaponeta about twelve miles to the east-southeast. Their patrols contested vigorously all day the positions of our newly placed outposts only a mile from the camp. During the night scouts reported the federals moving about in force east of us. As the information was rather vague, some Indian scouts and special patrols were sent out at midnight. At dawn I took Pedro and Tekwe and went southeast for some reconnaissance and contacted a vigilant enemy about three miles from Copales. We withdrew and moved east and found them not so well protected there for they never saw us or they ignored our presence. It was, nevertheless, easy to make sketches of the terrain as well as their positions, after which we returned to our lines.

When we returned to our outposts, I was met by the sergeant in charge who seemed to have been waiting as he came forward and declared that I was under arrest and demanded that I dismount. His behaviour was insulting, insubordinate and threatening in the extreme. His men closed in all around me and I spurred my horse when one of the men grabbed its bridle. The horse, not used to the spur, reared and knocked the man down and I galloped off in the direction of headquarters for an explanation. Here I was met by the officer on duty, Major Bocanegra, who immediately challenged me with the remark, "Where have you been, *gringo?* Did you make a call on the enemy in Acaponeta?"

It took all my will power to restrain myself as I did wish to punch this bounder's nose badly, but I kept silent and rode to the cavalry lines with my two Indians. Tekwe was surprised that I didn't shoot the man but was even more surprised that the outpost did not shoot me in the back when I broke their attempted arrest. "They no doubt would have done so," he added, "but didn't because Pedro and I were ready for them, the cowards."

General Blanco and Acosta arrived with the rest of the 1st Brigade at six o'clock in the evening of the same day, May 2. I handed Blanco my report and sketches of the enemy position. He seemed pleased and surprised. I doubt if he ever had a military sketch in his hands before. Later in the evening he handed it to General Obregon who studied it carefully for a long time.

When I narrated to Blanco my experiences with the outpost and Bocanegra, it angered him considerably, and he said he would take the matter up with Obregon. Then he surprised me rather by saying, "It seems peculiar that all the men who have attacked your loyalty to the rebels are Obregon followers. You started to give him lessons on military matters when he was a brigadier but now he is the C-in-C. Do you think it is possible that he or someone under him wants you out of the way because of this?" He evidently regretted what he had said for he added, "I wish that remark had not been made for I know Obregon likes you—No! It is Serrano's doing."

The plan for the encirclement of Acaponeta was ready. The cavalry was to move eastward to Mariquita, about eight miles north of the enemy position. One squadron was to move south from there and make a forceful but feint attack on the city, then withdraw and join the regiment which in the meantime was to move eastward, then south, in an encircling move around the town, and take up position at Motaje on the railroad some ten miles south of Acaponeta to prevent the enemy from escaping or retreating by rail.

Three Bad Shots

When making the usual round of the outposts that evening, I was shot at by someone from behind in the section under Major Bocanegra which formed the second line. As the bullet whizzed by, much too close for comfort, Tekwe said something to Pedro and vanished as if into thin air. He returned shortly thereafter with an empty shell of a 30-30 Winchester. He held it up then threw it away with the remark, "You are lucky, señor, that we have such poor shots in the infantry!"

After completing the round of the outposts we returned to camp without any further trouble, but found the place under a nervous tension because a sergeant had been found knifed to death inside our lines of vedettes and patrols, but not robbed. Remembering Tekwe's absence and finding the shell after the shot, I sent for him and he came grinning from ear to ear. No questions were asked. I just looked at him and could find nothing but a fine specimen of a man who was loyal to his last breath. He knew what it was about for he said, "That man tried to arrest you but failed. He shot at you twice at very close range and missed, but he would not miss next time. He deserved what he got. It was either you or him."

The cavalry had practically been standing to arms all night but were alerted quietly at four o'clock in the morning of May 3 to advance and take up the positions allotted them. When daybreak came and no advance was made, I went to the advance-guard to see what was going on and the officer in charge referred me to a colonel from whom he had received orders not to move.

Thinking something had gone wrong, I proceeded to General Blanco's advance headquarters and found him in conversation with this particular colonel who, by the way, looked more like a shyster lawyer than a soldier. Blanco was obviously embarrassed when

I asked why the change in plans without informing his chief staff officer. He did not answer at once but the colonel said, "The plans have been changed as the C-in-C considers it advisable for the cavalry to advance from the west instead of from the south in case the enemy has discovered our intentions." With this remark he bowed to me with a supercilious smile which infuriated me, for it and his remark were loaded to the muzzle with insinuations and insults of the worst kind.

The tension was diverted by a shot and another bullet whistled close by but did no harm. The colonel departed in a hurry and escaped my answer which was perhaps for the best at the moment. It was clear, however, that someone was after my scalp.

I left my orderly, Francisco, behind with my dispatch box and baggage when the cavalry began to move at 9 a.m. We crossed the Acaponeta River at noon and continued to San Felipe and eventually halted around a railroad bridge at five o'clock in the afternoon. The bridge was marked No. 932A.

The next morning, May 4, when leaving camp with Pedro and Tekwe to try to locate the federal advance positions, Major Bocanegra, accompanied by a lieutenant, came and requested permission to go with us. It was obvious that he wanted to keep an eye on me, and I decided to let him have a run for his money and conveyed the idea to the two scouts who could not suppress a grunt of pleasure, but the dangerous glint which flashed from their eyes boded no good for these two men and I almost gave up the idea.

When we came out in the open the major asked, "Where are your so much talked of scouts? Where is your advance-guard?" He was shocked to his foul soul when informed we were the scouts, advance-guard, main body, as well as rear-guard all in one, out to try and locate the enemy's outer line of defense or at least their outpost. Bocanegra, swivel-chair type of staff officer that he was, did not relish the idea at all and wanted obviously to return but could hardly do so and we continued along an old road.

When we reached Colorada, located a few miles south of Acaponeta, we had not seen an enemy and I was just about to turn away from the town, when Bocanegra, evidently fearing a trap, lost his nerve, turned his horse around and called out, "I am not going any further without troops," and galloped away as fast as that poor animal could go. His adjutant remained with us which pleased me immensely. As we had been a little foolhardy up to now for the benefit of Bocanegra's nerves, I slowed down and advanced more carefully. We were now about a mile or so from Acaponeta and we had not encountered any outposts nor had we seen a single scout.

Suddenly two enemy vedettes broke away from behind a broken down house and galloped toward the city. When Pedro, with a broad grin on his handsome face, suggested that we chase after him, the young officer complained of terrific pains in his stomach. He was invited to dismount and wait for us behind a wall but he almost shouted the words, "No! You crazy *gringo!*" and with this remark he wheeled his horse and followed his superior in a cloud of dust. I was a little disappointed in this fine looking young man who apparently was cast in the same mould and was of the same quality of material as his chief, Major Bocanegra. My two Indian companions could all but conceal their contempt.

We rode on for a hundred yards or so when I decided to defy fate no longer and turned homeward toward the camp. This was a lucky hunch, for a troop of federal cavalry appeared and chased us down the road. A few shots were exchanged from horseback but no harm was done. When we arrived in camp I found Major Bocanegra had reported to General Blanco that I was either crazy, in league with the Devil, or in cahoots with the federals. Blanco had a good laugh when I got Pedro and Tekwe to tell how Bocanegra had galloped off, scared as a rabbit, with his adjutant following.

Blanco requested me not to act against Bocanegra at this time and sent me on a reconnaissance, as we had to locate the disposition and movements of the federals in the west and northwest. "Take the 2nd Regiment and go at once," he urged. The importance or urgency of this trip was, I think, to get me out of reach of these tough *gringo* haters.

Instead of a regiment I took Pedro, Tekwe and Lopez and left Motaje at noon. We rode northwestward toward the Acaponeta River and located a federal cavalry patrol of about fifty men dismounted and relaxing on the other side of the river, watering their horses as if there wasn't a rebel in the land. Lopez was sent with the animals into a thicket and we crept forward to have a look. As we were sitting there snug behind cover observing the federals, Pedro touched my shoulder and pointed to where my own saddled horse was mooching toward the river, straight across from the enemy, for a drink.

The situation was embarrassing to say the least but Tekwe, not liking the looks of things, offered me his horse and suggested we get out of there the best way we could as he could manage very well on foot.

Moved by his generosity, which inspired perhaps the impulse, I got up and walked after the horse and waved to the federals, caught the animal, mounted and rode away with another wave. I had gambled on my uniform, for it was not of rebel cut, and it worked, for there seemed to be no suspicion among the federals. But after riding about a hundred yards someone was calling me urgently to halt. I didn't consider it prudent to do so, or even to look back, but spurred the horse and galloped hell-for-leather toward the hill and bushes over very stony ground. They opened fire as I was entering the wooded area. I wasn't hurt but my double-brim Australian hat was knocked off when I entered the bush.

The enemy patrol seemed to have become uneasy over this incident for they gathered their horses quickly, mounted, and cantered toward the north. Tekwe retrieved the hat and it seemed good for use although it had a nasty hole through the double crown.

Pedro followed the patrol running on foot. We followed discreetly at a distance and saw the patrol join a regiment about three miles away. They all turned then and galloped toward Acaponeta. We returned to headquarters after dark, and the information we bought in made it possible to complete our flanking maneuver of the enemy at Acaponeta by midnight.

The feeling of distrust, almost hatred, for all foreigners, especially Americans, among a great number of Mexicans of the middle and educated class was getting worse. Toward me they were getting somewhat violent. Their emotions and personal jealousies seemed uncontrollable at the moment, which made work difficult, so I asked General Blanco to relieve me as his chief-of-staff. The request was turned down, but he said, "After the fall of Acaponeta we will take up this matter again."

When I left his quarters someone took a pot-shot at me from out in the darkness but missed. Tekwe, who never left my side, disappeared but returned shortly thereafter with the remark, "That man was mounted. He shot at you with a revolver and galloped away." Blanco, hearing the shot, came out hurriedly and seemed much perturbed at these murderous attacks.

Drums Before Acoponeta

The new order for the attack on Acaponeta was issued before midnight, May 4, and was much the same as the original one. General Jager was to move on Acaponeta from the northwest; General Buelna and Colonel G., (I cannot remember his name) from the north; General Blanco and Colonel Acosta with the 1st Cavalry, which was partially dismounted, from the south. On the left wing of the 1st Cavalry was Yaqui Chief Trojiño with some Yaqui and Mayo braves. Our total attacking force did not exceed 1,400 armed men in the front line, the rest of our 4,000 men had no guns.

The rebel forces moved forward before dawn and the seige of Acaponeta was on before any one realized it. Some of the federals tried to break through eastward but were outmaneuvered by Colonel Acosta with a reserve squadron.

The most important and interesting part of the siege took place when some Yaquis and Mayos were sent out to different points around the town with about twenty of their war-drums. When in position each drummer made two beats on his drum to show he was there. When all had been located, the drummer with the Chief gave a signal and then began their weird and terrifying tattoos from twenty drums. The soul of the tribe, hidden within the drum, was speaking to the warriors and giving them orders to advance and to destroy their enemy. The drums could be heard moving slowly toward the city, nearer and nearer. Suddenly the nerve of the defenders snapped. They had counted twenty drums, each representing approximately 250 to 300 Indians, or about 5,000 Yaquis. The commander sent out two officers under a flag of truce stating he would surrender, but not to the Yaquis.

The condition of the surrender was granted, but it had to take place immediately as the Yaquis might get out of control. The officers returned, but treacherous characters almost caused a disaster. Before the actual surrender a messenger came with a verbal message for General Blanco that General Jager's men had moved in and occupied the center of the town. Thinking the show was over, Blanco, the most gallant officer in the rebel army, rode with his staff ahead of the advance guard right into the middle of the city but there wasn't a sign of Jager or his men.

As we halted, about 500 fully armed federals marched out from some houses and a church and lined up smartly in front of the twenty of us. It did not look very healthy, but at that moment two of our squadrons came galloping like a storm-cloud into the Plaza and formed up in front of us but facing the federals. It was a great relief indeed to see the cavalry, but when I looked for the commander it was Tekwe who had led them. Pedro had heard my warning Blanco against entering the town without an escort, and sensing trouble ordered Tekwe to fetch all the cavalry he could find and bring them along, which he did with a dash and smartness worthy any cavalry leader in any army. Trooper Tekwe whom I had made a temporary major a month or so before, was now promoted to sergeant, but he declined the honor and walked away smiling in his Indian fashion with his friend Pedro, who also had refused promotion several times.

The surrender went off smoothly after this incident, but we were surprised because the federals were in such great numbers and much better equipped than we had anticipated. Our booty on this May 5, 1914, was: one general (Juan Solares), one colonel, one lieut. colonel, 1312 officers and men, four field guns, six machine-guns, 1600 Mauser

PLATE IX

Rebel types in northern Chihuahua, 1913-1914.

PLATE X

Yaqui Indians; wives, girl friends, camp followers. 1913-1914.

rifles, 60,000 rounds of ammunition, a number of shells for the field guns and some money. All this came into our hands practically without a shot because of the fear of an imaginary horde of Yaqui Indians. In reality we had only about 200 of them but twenty drums instead of one, a fine piece of strategem.

The Mausers and ammunition were issued to our veterans at once and their Winchesters handed to unarmed recruits. Two of the field-guns had their firing-pins damaged which indicated the federal gunners were good artillerymen.

We lost four killed and twenty-one wounded in the skirmishes created purposely to attract the federals attention while the Indians went out with their drums. Personally, I got away with a small scratch in the forearm from a federal colonel whom Pedro had the pleasure of disarming when he tried to break through our lines with ten men. This colonel was a most pleasant fellow, a professional soldier, but did not wish to fall into the hands of the Yaquis. He said, "I like my hair as it is and don't wish a haircut in the Yaqui style." When alone with him for a moment I gave him back his horse which was led by Pedro and he rode eastward. It pleased me greatly not to find him among the prisoners, and I sincerely hoped he got away. Before we parted he remarked, "I am for the land being given to the peons, but the rebel leaders are using that slogan far too much for their own aggrandizement and advantage."

When General Jager was questioned about his message to Blanco he emphatically denied having sent it. The messenger was never found and it remained a mystery, but Acosta thought it a trick sent by someone as a trap for General Blanco. If so, it might have worked had it not been for Tekwe arriving with the cavalry in the nick of time. Blanco refused to comment on the subject but he looked at me and blurted out; "As you can see, you are not the only one they wish out of the way. Please remain with us as long as you wish but stay with me at least until the revolution is over."

I had the pleasure of meeting General Solares after the surrender and he expressed his astonishment at the use of the Yaqui drums. He was a fine looking officer who reminded me strongly of my father, though Solares had a Napoleonic type of beard, instead of the van Dyke of my old man.

Francisco Murdered

When we returned to the camp, somewhat tired and weary, in the early hours of that afternoon, my servant Francisco was found dead, shot by an officer because he refused to hand over the key to my army trunk full of letters and papers. They had opened the steel trunk and gone through its contents carefully but only some letters were missing.

Pedro and Tekwe made a point of finding the malefactor who did this dastardly thing. He was found, arrested, tried, and sentenced, by Blanco himself, to be shot within thirty minutes. He was executed minutes thereafter. He may be considered lucky, for had Tekwe done what he wanted to do, the officer would have suffered an awful death.

That same evening we heard rumors that the rebels in Durango might turn against us and join forces with General Huerta, which was hard to believe. They had about 5,000 men and refused, the rumor said, to leave Durango and march on Saltillo as ordered by Carranza. It was also reported that Pancho Villa might send some troops into Durango to restore order. But if he did this, it was feared that the Durango rebels might move west into the lowlands of Sinaloa and plunder as they had done elsewhere. Such raids behind our lines would retard, if not actually halt, our advance on Guadalajara and Mexico City.

The Constitutionalists had some difficulties in keeping men from looting although it was the best disciplined army in Mexico. People in some villages did suffer and so did the upper class that remained in the haciendas or large towns when the victorious peon felt his new power as a soldier carrying a gun. Houses were robbed, women and girls outraged. It was seldom done by the real peons but by the scum let out of jails who were primed with the teachings of their so-called superiors, the charlatan pedagogues, "You are free men, do what you like!"

The people of the middle class suffered the most, as they could not, like the upper class, run before the storm. The half-drunken jail-birds, with a sprinkling of misled peons, took what they wanted, sometimes slaying those who dared to stay in their way. But it was not so everywhere.

The general character of soldiers while under certain war-strains is the same in all armies, especially when liquor is added freely. The best disciplined troops in World War I and II brought this out quite clearly and we should, therefore, perhaps, not judge the Peon-Indian soldier of Mexico too harshly.

Persistent rumors came to us almost daily of an intended intervention by the United States in Mexican affairs, but we hoped Washington would investigate and find the true conditions before deciding against us. The anti-American element among the rebels was constantly advocating joining hands with Huerta in order to make war on the States if its army moved into Mexico.

The feeling against Americans, and they insisted that I was one, was so strong that my body-guard was doubled by the alert Tekwe and they were around me constantly, all of them Yaquis, except Pedro and Jesús, both Tarahumara. This watchfulness on their part seemed to scare the would-be assassins, as it had leaked out that the sergeant found dead a few days ago was killed by one of them.

Toward the end of 1913 and early in 1914, the rebel troops under Carranza were principally made up of Sonora and Sinaloa peons and a great number of Yaqui and Mayo Indians. By the middle of May, 1914, Carranza had added several thousands of peons and quite a number of men from different tribes such as Tepehuanes, Tepecanos, Tarahumara and some Cora. However, these were not formed into individual regiments like the Yaquis and Mayos, but one did notice certain groupings in platoons and even companies.

Villa's forces consisted mostly of peons from different ranches and haciendas in Chihuahua, Durango, Coahuila, a great number of Apaches and some Tarahumaras, Tepecanos and Tepehuanes. But the latter three tribal members were usually only guides and runners. Zapata recruited his men principally from his home state of Morelos and from Guerrero. His best men were the sturdy Guerrero Indians.

These three principal armies in the revolution against Huerta were fighting more or less independently of one another as were the commanders. They had all been disappointed in Madero and his method of running the government, but they had three common objectives: I. Land and freedom for the peons and Indians; 2. To revenge Madero's foul murder; 3. To oust President Huerta and his *cientifico* clique, and in general, "Mexico for the Mexicans."

A Patrol Into the Mountains — Fighting in a Hurrican

During the surrender of Acaponeta a report was brought in by some scouts that a substantial federal cavalry force with many pack animals had been seen that noon in the foothills of the mountain region some twenty miles east of Acaponeta. This was a serious matter which had to be attended to without delay because south of us the enemy was reported in great strength and our eastern flank was wide open for anyone to pass around.

Men and horses were weary from several days of constant patrolling, maneuvering and standing about saddled, without food for man or beast. But as we were preparing to advance south, it was necessary to verify the report before leaving. We were pinched for time, so I proposed to investigate in person. Permission was granted, though reluctantly, by Blanco, who suggested that I take a regiment and try to clear the flank.

As the country in front of us was unusually rough, I took only thirteen Yaquis from Captain Sanchez' squadron, four spare horses and of course Pedro, Tekwe, Lopez and Jesus. The latter was an intelligent Tarahumara Indian who came down with us from the *barranca* country in Western Chihuahua in March. He was assigned by Pedro as my special body-guard to protect my back against foul attacks by the anti-American elements who seemed to stop at nothing to gain their ends. He was also an excellent camp cook.

We left at dawn, May 6. Captain Sanchez had orders to send a troop of thirty men to follow us an hour after departure. This troop was to stop at Cofradia, some miles across country eastward, and await orders, but at the same time to scour the country for the enemy. They were to return to Acaponeta after dark if contact with us failed.

At San Diego de Alcala, east of Acaponeta, we found that a strong federal cavalry force with a pack train had been there for a rest the day before, then had moved southward. One couldn't help wondering why this force had not come to the aid of the Acaponeta garrison on that same day, but they may, of course, have escaped from there before the cordon had completed its encirclement of the city.

We scouted in a southerly direction for awhile, then continued toward the east. After a strenuous ride, often walking and leading our horses up and down mountainous trails or no paths at all, through rivers, arroyos and ravines, we came to a small hamlet located, they said, on a tributary of the San Pedro River, not far from Sayelota, a village farther down stream. How far we had traveled was difficult to say, but as we had been on the move for ten hours, some thirty miles must have been covered although the country was rough and stony.

No one was in sight when we arrived and the adobe houses were empty. Wishing to get information as well as to meet the mountain folks, Pedro and Tekwe went out to corral them because we knew they were close as a fire was still burning in one hut. After awhile they brought in five men dressed in breechclouts and blankets. All but one carried a short bow, arrows and machetes. They were not local people but Tepehuane Indians who had come down the San Pedro River from somewhere near Buena Vista in Durango. They were a fine looking bunch of mountaineers, proud and somewhat reticent, a trait common among the people of the sierra.

While trying to make them talk with gifts of cigarettes, a fine mountain deer came out from the bush not a hundred yards away and surveyed us with a curious mien, absolutely unafraid. The temptation was great for we needed meat, but it was risky for the enemy could have been near.

As the bullet struck, Jesus jumped up and sped toward the fallen animal, grabbed it by the throat and strangled it although, I think, it was dead when he got there. Within a short space of time the Indians had it skinned, cut up and ready to be roasted on wooden spits. With this venison for dinner, many hungry guests to feed, and one horse gone lame, it was decided to camp here for the night.

Pedro had an idea these Tepehuanes thought us to be federals because we wore uniforms, but it did not take this remarkably intelligent Indian long to convince them to the contrary and I invited them all to dinner. Within a few moments a good fire was blazing and juicy pieces of venison were on the roasting-spits. The aroma made one's mouth water. The Indians did all the work under the direction of Tekwe who loved to take charge of such feasts.

While these preparations were going on an old Indian with a family of four came out from hiding in the nearby hill. These were the local inhabitants and they were asked to join us. They had not eaten anything for some time except roots and maggots and looked at the meat with real hunger in their eyes. They informed us they had not seen any federals for two days.

Before the meal started one of the Tepehuanes, evidently a headman or shaman, cut off a piece of meat and stuck it on a stick which was pushed into the ground close to the fire. He then turned to the four cardinal directions, East, South, West and North while talking in an undertone and making use of the words *Toni* (God) and *Cucuduri* (Master of the Deer) several times and then returned to his seat. We were all hungry and wanted to eat, but my Tarahumara friend Jesus jumped up and also put a piece of meat on a stick which he stuck in the ground on the East side of the fire. On each side of this stick he pushed in another, making three sticks in all. When this was done, he walked around the three sticks three times and mumbled several words, such as *Onorugame* (Father Sun), *Tata Diosi* (Father God), and once or twice the word *chomari* (deer). On the last circuit he halted and faced for a second or two each of the cardinal directions, and returned to his seat looking quite pleased. Pedro was also happy to have seen this ceremony of his people, the Tarahumara.

Each one of these ceremonies, obviously meant to be a prayer or sacrifice, was carried out in a most dignified manner and were indeed impressive in their simplicity. I also discovered for the first time that choking a deer to death is a common practice among the Tarahumara when hunting. They will hardly ever kill it with a bow and arrow but run the animal down on foot and strangle it to death with their hands. There was another incident quite noticeable by the fire. After the meal the Tepehuanes were offered water from a dipper-gourd which they refused but got up, walked to the creek close by, and drank therefrom with their hands.

The Tepehuanes were not asked any questions during the meal, but we had a long talk with them before retiring. After awhile I asked if they would like to join in the fight against Huerta with the other Indians. At first they were reticent, and almost shrank back at the thought, then changed suddenly and began to ask questions. When they found that

239

the rebels paid their men not less than one and one-half peso per day, paid daily, their attitude softened. They wanted to know if each of them would get a long-gun, meaning a carbine, and when. These wily Indians also asked for a few days pay in advance which I promised them if they returned next morning ready to go to Acaponeta. Then they left.

A few minutes after they had gone I moved my party into the woods about a mile for safety, but in spite of this precaution half of them did outpost duty throughout the night. The Tepehuanes had been misjudged, for they turned up before noon the next day, May 7, with six others and said that forty more would come from Durango and report at Acaponeta with their headman within a few days. Each Indian was given three pesos in our paper money as promised and then placed under the command of Tekwe.

As my duty was to look for federals, I wanted to investigate a certain high mesa reported by the Tepehuanes to be not far to the north before returning . We started out with two Indians as trail-blazers and advance guard, and two others protecting our rear. We were delayed by the awful terrain and the mesa seemed farther away than anticipated.

As I was considering giving up the quest and returning to a more hospitable neighborhood for the night, I noticed the sun had already begun to set and nasty-looking low-flying clouds were piling up on one another against the sierra in the east. The sight reminded me as in a flash of the cumulus clouds forming on top of Table Mountain in Cape Town, heralding one of those unpleasant southeasters that sweep over Cape of Good Hope and the flats behind. The clouds became darker and more threatening. Evidently we were in for a storm, for the heavens became black and low clouds rushed overhead like so many Valkyrie looking for those to be slain.

When I told Pedro that it looked like rain and bad weather, he said, "That is true, chief, but not only rain. We are going to have an unusual storm, a hurricane. Let us hurry and find shelter." Everything seemed affected by the sudden change in the weather. The horses showed signs of nervousness, the birds were flying hastily to and fro along the ground as if seeking shelter, several deer came out from the bush, stopped, looked and continued on their way toward some rocks quickly but as if tame.

The wind was increasing in intensity and thunder and lightning appeared all around us. Suddenly the rain came, not as ordinary rain but as if the bottom of a large lake had dropped on top of us accentuated by the driving force of the hurricane. Trees were uprooted and fell here and there, and some snapped in two with the sound of a cannon-shot.

Pedro and Jesus, who had been scouting ahead on foot, came running back at this moment and reported fresh tracks of ten horses only a minute in front of us. There was a steep and high rock formation slightly on our right front and to this the men were ordered, as it looked good for defense and gave shelter against the storm.

As we moved towards this sanctuary, a brisk rifle-fire opened up against us from that direction and two men dropped. The Sonoran troops specially trained in this kind of fighting extended automatic-

241

ally and took cover in a matter of seconds, but Tekwe with his eleven Tepehuanes without guns moved to the rear. While I was considering a retreat Tekwe crept close to me and suggested taking the Tepehuanes with their bows and arrows on a flanking move which might dislodge the enemy. I had not anticipated any assistance from these Indians but accepted it gladly and they disappeared like shadows behind bushes, trees and stones.

The storm had by this time broken into its height of fury and must have been of hurricane force, as trees were falling and some were uprooted under the pressure; the thunder rolled over us constantly as if trying to match the nerve-wracking pressure of the wind. Then the lightning struck a tree where the Indians had been standing and I feared for their safety as Hell was let loose. Word was passed around to the soldiers to keep the enemy busy in front of us, but not to advance until ordered to do so.

It was pitch dark by this time and the spooky effects of the flashes from guns not fifty yards apart intensified by the constant lightning gave one a queer feeling of the unreal. This natural phenomenon seemed to have affected at least one of my toughest men, for during one of these flashes I could see him fumbling with a rosary with its large attached crucifix which had been stolen somewhere recently, no doubt.

The enemy had kept on firing hectically without much effect for about thirty minutes. Then the firing ceased, and there was no sound except the roaring and whistling of the wind among trees. A little later Tekwe turned up and informed me that the fighting was over and invited us all to come and take shelter under the rocks. We started out leading our horses and carrying the two wounded, but it wasn't easy for the storm was still in full force and large branches of trees were flying through the air. When we got there, eight dead men were lying stretched out in a ghastly but perfect line for my inspection. Each Indian had been killed with an arrow in the back but Tekwe, the perfectionist, apologized for the two that got away.

The storm passed as quickly as it had come, and my little force reformed under a star-lit sky about an hour later. As we were wet and cold, large log-fires were started from fallen dry trees. By midnight one side of us was dry at least. The two wounded men died from internal hemorrhages during the night.

With daylight a new cheer crept into our cold bodies, especially after each had eaten a good chunk of venison and the blankets were more or less dry. Then we buried our dead according to Tekwe's conception of a Yaqui funeral, though the ceremony was cut to the minimum. We found two horses had blown into a ravine and were so badly hurt that we shot them.

In the early morning the Tepehuanes asked for the guns and ammunition they had captured and articles of clothing found on the enemy. This was granted for it was the custom of the revolution, but I advised them not to take any uniforms as they might be taken for federals and shot. The enemy horses were found saddled and tied to some bushes, but could not be claimed by the Indians as all horses automatically became the property of the army. We started back for Acaponeta and arrived there at eleven o'clock in the evening of May 8. The return journey was made a little shorter as one of the Tepehuanes knew the way, but it was awful on the horses.

To Mazatlan Front

The following morning General Blanco sprang a surprise by ordering me to report on the conditions of the cavalry forming part of the besieging forces at Mazatlan, about ninety miles to the northwest, which was in the opposite direction to our next objective, the city of Tepic, located about eighty miles to the south.

Mazatlan had been under siege by our forces for some time, but it was a futile attempt without guns of caliber large enough for the purpose. It had, nevertheless, most effectively boxed up the federals in that important seaport, although they made sorties now and again to feel us out.

When I left Blanco, Colonel Acosta followed me outside and said, "The general received an anonymous note during the night which threatened your life, hence your trip to Mazatlan for a few days. Hurry back. It will blow over." When I conveyed the reason for the trip to Pedro and Tekwe they were astounded, for a number of soldiers and non-coms had expressed to them that very morning their regrets at the foul attacks on their chief.

Not wishing to be hampered by a cumbersome escort or an unnecessarily large and unwieldy contingent as suggested by Blanco, I again chose Pedro,

Tekwe and Lopez, besides Jesus, who took care of the commissary. With one of these companions on guard one could be sure of no unpleasant surprise.

An eight boxcar train with the great luxury of a caboose was ready at the station. Instead of disconnecting the surplus cars, fifteen steers found roaming around near the yard were corralled and loaded on the train in case our men outside Mazatlan had not been issued any meat lately.

Before pulling out of the Acaponeta station I had another surprise, for a number of officers came to see me off. Men who had been hostile to me before now acted like friends and wished me a safe return. I was wondering what had made the change? Was it the capture of Acaponeta or was it Blanco's and Acosta's doing? It was a difficult and puzzling question, but I noticed with a great deal of pleasure how my Indian companions stopped what they were doing, picked up their carbines and watched carefully the group of officers as they were advancing toward me.

After watering the animals we got on our way and arrived at Castillo without any mishap at eleven o'clock in the evening. Early next morning, May 10, we moved to Los Otales and handed over the cattle to the commissary who received us with open arms, as they had not seen any meat for days. Then I inspected our outposts. I found them badly distributed, badly located and without the slightest thought of the horses or the men. They were also too far from water and the men too exposed. They could not see far enough, and in case of need the horses were too far away. These posts should have been placed farther back and on better ground, and as it was, their effectiveness as cavalry had been seriously impaired, but as we were short of men and officers they had to remain for awhile at least.

Curious to see our field guns in position I went over to the Isla de Piedra, the long island south of Mazatlan, where we had two concealed 75 mm guns, and I felt the two guns captured at Acaponeta should have been brought here. The federal gunboat "Guerrero" steamed quite close to shore and kept up a spasmodic but irritating bombardment of our positions which seemed to have a bad effect on the morale of our men.

The officers at the Mazatlan front were all talking and speculating on when General Obregon intended to attack the place. Obregon was keeping his own counsel as usual, but I could not see how a successful attack could be launched without more guns, men and ammunition. Obregon was no doubt thinking the same and biding his time, for a change in the slowly deteriorating political picture in Mexico City might sooner or later make it imperative for the federals to evacuate by sea.

During my visit to the guns, the rebel lines closed in and shortened the cordon around Mazatlan. The federals must have known or noticed the move, for their batteries opened a heavy barrage on our advance position for several hours and we lost three killed and fifteen wounded needlessly. Our men, lacking in numbers and short of ammunition, should have been moved back, not forward, but we always learned the hard way.

Upon returning to camp, a messenger was awaiting me with orders from Blanco, "Leave everything and return, urgent." The officer had arrived on an old locomotive that puffed, spattered and coughed as if in pain. It was shunted and we boarded my train which had its steam up constantly. The engineer had promised me speed if he received extra help with wood for the boiler, and we traveled at breakneck speed into Acaponeta during the early hours of May 11.

When reporting my return to Blanco, he informed me in Acosta's presence that all Americans had left Mexico and it looked like war with the United States. "This idea," Blanco continued, "is shared as well as feared by most of the senior officers, and we believe that Huerta is deliberately creating trouble with the States so as to bring together all revolutionary factions under his command against America to save his own rotten hide. Should Villa and Zapata join Huerta it will be a civil war within a civil war and chaos the result because Carranza and Obregon will never join Huerta. If Huerta succeeds in this scheme, it will be the deathblow to the hopes and dreams of millions of Indians and peons. We must, therefore, move south at once to attack and destroy Huerta's troops before the plot materializes."

Our next objective was the strategically important City of Tepic, capital of the Territory of Tepic (Hard Stone), now the State of Nayarit. The town is located on a plain at an elevation of about 3,000 feet and is surrounded by hills. The mountains are not far off. To the east is the extinct volcano Sanganuey, whose extensions reach an elevation of over 6,600 feet (2,000 meters), and beyond that is the Sierra de Nayarit. To the south it is hilly and somewhat mountainous. In the west are some plains and hills cut by arroyos as far as the Pacific Ocean. In the north the country is hilly and rough in places. Several dirt roads, good, bad and indifferent, but mostly bad, lead into the city.

The Tepic River was a small but effective watershed running by the town northward and eventually falling into the Santiago River. The climatic conditions of the city and its surroundings were reported to be somewhat damp and unhealthy, especially for visitors not accustomed to it, as the place harbored a deadly malaria. The population of the city was about 17,000.

The 1st and 2nd Cavalry Brigades, once more together, were moving cautiously south from the Santiago River feeling their way along the road to Tepic City. We had no particular orders except to clear the country of enemies and to form a protective screen for the army. This screen of scouts should really have extended from the Pacific Ocean to the mountainous regions of Sierra Nayarit but it wasn't practical at this time to do so. When we were about thirty-three miles northwest of Tepic City, Blanco received orders to drive the federals from their positions in and around it.

The column halted and Acosta and myself were called back for a conference. Blanco told us the order was unexpected but welcome, yet he knew nothing of the strength or disposition of the enemy. It was reported the day before that the federals were holding the city and the surrounding hills with a considerable force supported by several field pieces and machine guns.

Blanco suggested a sudden concentrated frontal attack at some favorable point although he did not feel happy about the idea. Acosta, the keenest of the pupils in strategy and tactics, proposed an encircling movement, but to leave an opening in the south through which the enemy could escape. I backed Acosta's idea, as our force without artillery was too small for an effective assault on a fortified position, but tried to impress upon them that it was imperative we obtain more information of the strength of the enemy as well as the terrain. To get this we should call in all the Indian scouts as well as those who knew the inside of the city.

This was done and we learned a great deal, especially from a very intelligent Huichol-Tepehuane Indian scout. He had been inside the city only a few days before and had noticed two "large guns," several machine-guns and, as he described it, had seen "twice-ten" (twenty) captains, which means that their force was about 2,000 strong.

Against this force, fortified behind walls, houses and crude trenches, we had about 2,000 men, but one-third of these would be horse-holders in case of dismounted action. We had two field-guns and six machine-guns captured at Acaponeta, but no gunners to man them. Our chance of success, therefore, was strongly against us and we could only succeed by a stratagem and even that was risky.

We talked of some means to try to mislead the enemy, perhaps a nonchalant maneuver in the open in hopes of destroying his already jittery nerves, set on edge by our recent successes and in the fall of Acaponeta only a few days ago. When I pointed out that we had used this particular stratagem too many times and therefore had only a slim chance of success with the federals in good defensive positions, Acosta turned to me a little surprised and irritated perhaps, and asked for an explanation because the proposed move had several times been introduced in lectures. My answer amused Blanco; I explained that this method was getting a little shopworn and we must, therefore, put up something new for the enemy to think about.

To get the federals out of the city quickly without losing a lot of men in a frontal attack, I suggested a ruse used in South Africa by the Boers, and also by Sun-Yat Sen in China. The idea is to create "dust-clouds" to mislead the enemy as to our strength, as one can estimate fairly accurately the strength of a force by the length of the terrifying looking dust created when a column is on the move. Blanco thought the scheme good, and fifty men were sent back toward Santiago to cut down small trees and bushes. Each man would tie his rope (reata, lasso) to a clump of bushes or a tree and drag it behind his horse, one man coming after the other, but separated so as to make as much dust as possible.

This we hoped would be accepted by the federals as reinforcements and artillery coming along the road. The men were told to start the dragging operations toward our lines a little before sunset and to make the dust-line not less than about six miles in extent and to halt at a certain place behind a hill not far from Tepic, dump their bushes and return after dark for another load which was to be dragged at eight o'clock the following morning.

At noon we had reached a point near the little town of Fortuna, about five miles northwest of Tepic. We were in plain view of the enemy scouts and the two outposts which had withdrawn from Fortuna. We had been advancing in a stretched-out kind of column-of-route formation to make a big show. Here we had the good luck to capture a careless federal cavalry scout, and we halted. He was pumped dry of everything he knew, then we loaded him up with news about ourselves: how we were "only" 5,000 strong, the advance-guard for General Obregon and his army of 20,000 coming behind us for the bombardment and assault on the city in the morning. To make the story look better we accused the federal soldier of being a spy and he was tried and sentenced to be shot before the attack in the morning. During the night, however, one of our men professing sympathy for the federals helped him to escape. That was, of course, part of our strategy.

During the early part of the afternoon each regiment took turns in maneuvering in full view of the city to work on the federals nerves. A little before sunset, a vast column of dust could be seen in the northwest. It was inspiring. Nearer and nearer it came, and, as a final flurry, the men dragged their dust-raisers in a large circle as if troops were making camp. Before dark the sky was more or less clear and the buglers and trumpeters had orders to face the city and their tattoos could be heard far and wide.

The plan to obtain the desired position for the

initial encirclement of Tepic City had to be bold and risky, for should the enemy counter-attack, we had but a few men in reserve. We gambled as well as hoped that the federal commander did not have the guts to do it.

Colonel Acosta was to circle the drained lake northeast of the town, drive back the enemy outposts and take up the most favorable position beween Tepic River and the road to Ixtlan. Colonel G., whose name I still cannot remember, was to circle westward around the town and drive the enemy outposts from the hills south of the city and occupy them; Colonel Madriga was to drive the outposts back west of the town; Captain Sanches to clear the land in the northwest and take up position between San Blas and Tepic River. Major Molna was to occupy the hills north of the town, Colonel Trujillo to clear the road from Escondida and Puga toward the city and take up position north of Tepic River; Colonel Soto to occupy the road from the town to Jalisco and prevent any reinforcement getting through from there; Captain Alamillo was to go with Acosta and take up position some distance behind him and prevent any surprise attack in his rear.

All units were to be in positions allotted them by 6 a.m. The town would be surrounded except for the road south to Compostella, which was left open as an avenue of escape for the enemy, and we sincerely hoped he would take it. On the morning of May 15 our small rebel force had completed its encircling movement after some severe skirmishes. The enemy seemed jumpy and their outposts resisted valiantly

252

but finally withdrew behind the long walls and buildings in the outskirts of the city, which gave them a perfect defensive position as we had no artillery.

At about 8:45 a.m., terrific dust clouds could be seen in the northwest. It was our men dragging bushes once more, but they looked like a large body of cavalry and guns coming along at a brisk pace. The enemy saw and wondered, no doubt, when the blow would fall, but no one had as yet tried to leave the city on the open road to the south.

The federal commander, misled by our maneuver, swallowed the bait and apparently did not consider a counter-attack feasible with our reinforcements in full view, so he missed his opportunity to beat us to the punch—we were most vulnerable. His artillery, located in the southern section of the town, did, however, begin to shell our positions in the hills in front of the guns. These hills commanded the road of their escape to Compostella and were held by Colonel G., who had orders to withdraw westward at the first sign of artillery operations against him. This he did and the exodus began.

Everything was going as we had hoped but when the guns located by the water-tank changed their target and began to shell Colonel Acosta and his men, I became a little uncertain as Acosta, although a natural and fearless cavalry leader, was also unpredictable and might make a move too soon.

The federals were now pouring out of the city at a terrific pace and everything was going fine, if it hadn't been for the guns shelling Acosta. He had waited, however, much longer than I expected when suddenly the sound of a volley was heard from Acosta's position, then another. Colonel Madriga and Trujillo and Captain Sanchez also opened fire. The engagement for the city of Tepic was in full swing.

The retreat south by the enemy was halted by the rifle fire, but those already on the road broke and became an unorganized mob falling over one another to get away. Those who were mounted galloped like mad over their own people in their eagerness to escape. Colonel G. could clearly see this mess but remained inactive with his mounted troops. Acosta was mad and charged, not at the panic stricken federals on the road, but at the guns. He and his men were superb, but they had difficulties in reaching their objective. When the rest of our troops dashed forward, the gunners turned and fled and the abandoned guns were captured by Acosta.

The retreating defenders made for the center of the city and those who had not already done so threw down their arms. General Blanco, who, through circumstances beyond his control, had been more or less inactive all morning at Fortuna, arrived and took the surrender. The booty was enormous considering the few men engaged. We captured over 500 good rifles, about 400,000 rounds of ammunition, two field-guns, four machine-guns, and more than 600 prisoners including one colonel, one lieutenant-colonel, four majors and twelve captains. More than 1,000 of the enemy escaped, but that was part of our plan as we could not have succeeded any other way. We lost twenty-two killed and ninety-one wounded of which sixty-seven were seriously hurt.

The behavior of our men toward the prisoners was not bad, at least not as bad as could be expected from half-wild Indians, half-breeds and peons, all of whom had been ill-treated, kicked and flogged indiscriminately in the past. Their conduct toward the civilian population was also good, generally speaking. There were, of course, some unpleasant incidents as in all armies which could not be condoned. But each case should be treated on its own merit.

There was an unusual case which I will give as an example. One of our men, a handsome Peon-Indian, entered the home of a well-to-do rancher on May 16 and killed the man when he resisted entry, raped his daughter and brought her to the rebel camp as his common-law wife. Her brother daringly enough came to us and asked for the return of the eighteen-year-old girl. When questioned the soldier frankly told his story; "Just before the revolution I owned a tiny ranch adjoining the large estate of the *hacendado* (the murdered man) which I worked with my brother and fifteen-year-old sister and we were very happy. But as our land wasn't large enough to support our few goats, I asked the *hacendado* to rent me a small piece of otherwise useless land on a hill for the goats to graze on. This he did, the amount for the rent was not stated, but he did say he would let me know later. He demanded as part of the rental that my sister should work at the hacienda.

"After some months my sister informed me that her master had entered her quarters and taken her by force and she was now to have a child. When I confronted the *hacendado* about the matter, he sent for the *rurales* and had me flogged, and took my home, land and goats as part payment for the unpaid land rent. Then he forced me to work for him until the balance of the debt was paid. When the peons and Indians were offered land and freedom by the revolutionaries, I joined them. The *hacendado* ruined my sister, flogged me and stole everything we owned, so I killed him. So what? I am a free man!"

Due to the seriousness of the charge against the man, as well as the army, General Blanco tried the case himself. Blanco never did like unnecessary bloodshed but willing to take the risk, asked me, the *gringo,* to decide the punishment. Two witnesses, including the brother of the girl, confirmed the seizing of the land and animals, also the birth of a child by the peon's sister. Some people may, nevertheless, be shocked at my decision: I dismissed the case and let the soldier go free. I also gave back to him his land and animals as well as the hill he rented from the *hacendado.* The brother did not seem to mind at all. The interesting side of this case was the unwillingness of the girl to leave the handsome rebel soldier. There was romance in the offing, as she refused to return home without her man. I granted him ten days leave.

There is no doubt that some of the Indians as well as peons joined the revolution because they loved the idea of a fight, but some were dragged in by friends, and some maybe by force. Others came in hate and vengeance toward a thoughtless upper class, like the soldier mentioned. Most of the peons did, however, dream and long for their homes, children, parents, their corn-patch and goats, and the various *fiestas* of their homeland.

VII

Villa against Carranza—The Benton Case

To follow more fully the events of the revolution, we are bound to look back a few months and see what happened to General Pancho Villa and what he had done.

Eight days after I left him in Juarez on November 29, he captured the city of Chihuahua on December 7, 1913, and with it a tremendous amount of military and other supplies. The fall of Chihuahua was the greatest advance so far by the rebel forces and yet the news gave Carranza and some of his generals the jitters. They seemed afraid of this Genghis Khan of northern Mexico and what he might do next, although he was fighting for the same cause and against the same enemy as they, General Victoriano Huerta.

When Villa entered the governor's palace in Chihuahua he took personal command of the relief work among the residents of the town. His first act was to reduce prices so as to permit the poor to obtain the necessary supplies. Any merchant found guilty of charging famine prices was to be shot and his stores and property confiscated.

Villa ordered all Spaniards (*Gachupines;* meaning those with spurs), some two hundred of them, to leave Chihuahua and Mexico within ten days, because they had not only helped General Huerta financially, but also joined the actual fighting against the rebels. These Spaniards (*Peninsulares:* men from the Spanish peninsula) were among the most wealthy in the Republic, and it was expected that their property would be confiscated, as they were enemies of the Madero cause, for which Villa was fighting.

Villa's drastic action was also a retaliatory measure as the federals executed a number of political and military prisoners, as well as rebel sympathizers, held in the City Prison before they left on their retreat to Ojinaga. News dispatches also informed us that generals Salvador Mercado, Pascual Orozco, Mercelo Caraveo, and Jose Unes Salazar arrived at Ojinaga, December 8, with the advance-guard of the federal force which was retreating with refugees from Chihuahua City after the battle of Tierra Blanca. These civilians who could obtain a horse, mule or burro did so, but others went on foot rather than be caught by Villa's men. The report stated that the refugees were scattered over the waterless desert for a distance of thirty miles and were suffering terribly. Only half of them ever reached Ojinaga. The others dropped in the sand and never rose again. The vultures had a feast. Many of the refugees, however, turned from the northern Camargo plains and started back to Chihuahua, preferring to risk harsh treatment by the rebels than death from thirst and exhaustion on the desert.

When General Mercado arrived in Ojinaga, he began to fortify the place immediately, for he knew Villa would not let him be in peace for long. He did the right thing, for a force of 3,000 men was within three days march of Ojinaga with orders from Villa to drive them out. They were concentrating their forces near Cuchillo Parado on the Rio Conchos, west-southwest from Presidio, Texas. La Mula Pass, southeast of Cuchillo Parado, was the point Villa's men expected to make when they advanced. The rebel scouts had already reconnoitred the country about the pass, for it commanded the best road leading to the federal positions on the Border.

We should remember that Villa had been alone for some time in the State of Chihuahua and part of Durango. He obtained his own funds by commandeering cattle, horses and other necessities for the revolution from haciendas and towns captured. In this manner he was able to raise, maintain and command his own troops without any outside aid and could therefore not see or understand why he should take orders from Carranza with headquarters far away. And yet there was an accord between them in sentiment and purpose, but it was a flimsily tied-together understanding which at first was based on revenge for the murder of President Madero, followed by the idea of ousting all *cientificos* from the government and giving the land to the Peon-Indians.

Villa had done most of the fighting during the time Carranza was clinging to the Pacific Coast and doing nothing, from Villa's point of view. Carranza and Obregon were actually fighting hard and advancing southward while training troops so they would be prepared for the heavy fighting to come. Carranza should under ordinary circumstances have informed Villa, but he did not seem to dare to show his comparatively weak position, which created a misunderstanding never to be overcome.

However, had Villa not done what he did, the federals could easily have captured the States of Chihuahua and Durango and the iron heel of dictator Huerta would have been on Carranza's stiff and unyielding neck. The federals could have attacked Carranza from every point of the compass, by land and sea. That would have been the end of both Carranza and Obregon.

We know that Villa started his career as a bandit and struggled against the government in the spirit of revenge for the wrongs done him personally and his family. The violence, hate and desire for revenge which poured out from time to time from his tortured soul since childhood, one can understand, for it was an idiosyncrasy, but his real weakness was a combination of violence, ignorance and hate.

Many of Villa's most depraved actions seemed to have originated in the mind of his close friend and body-guard Rodolfo Fierro. While under this influence he did the wrong thing always. He became violent and reverted to what he really was at heart, a bandit.

But Villa said what he had to say with a forcefulness which did not suit Carranza and Obregon. He was too resolute for them, and yet he was often in need of good judgment and in want of decision. Above all, he lacked control over his own will and temper. Very few of his closest friends knew that the agonizing recollections of his mother, sister and home, were distorted memories which made him do outrageous things, that placed him in a light of a lesser and even of a degenerate fiber.

Wherever he went his troops were successful, but there was also unnecessary killing of prisoners, looting and raping, in which respect his men did not stand alone, as Zapata's men often did the same. One can hardly blame Villa, Zapata and others for what they did, as they were the natural products sprung from the seeds fallen from the putrid social structural growth started by the *gachupines* and the hierarchy after the Conquest.

Carranza, a former *hacendado,* was too much of the old school of Mexican intellectuals to weigh or even consider the possibility that Pancho Villa, the illiterate peon-mestizo, could possibly become a threat to his position as First Chief of the Constitutionalist Army and Party.

But as time went on Carranza became unsure of his position and realizing that something must be done besides giving vague, petty and seemingly unnecessary orders, he started to send Villa supplies. This paid good dividends. When Villa received the provisions, such as coal for his locomotives and money printed by Carranza, he in turn realized that a central directorate might be a good thing, and assented without demur, as long as Carranza did not meddle in the domestic affairs of his region or with his troops.

It was difficult, of course, for Carranza to carry on the revolution as First Chief without giving some orders which Villa would often as not ignore, answer in the negative, or ridicule as weak or asinine. This attitude naturally hurt the old man's dignity, but it was also bad for the discipline of the army. And thus it came about that Carranza, half afraid that Villa might declare his independence and carry on by himself, like Zapata and others, left Culiacan with his staff on February 15, 1914, for Chihuahua to help Pancho Villa. The real reason was, they said, not so much to help as to keep an eye on Villa and try to keep his excesses under control.

Carranza did what he thought best but in the end he became incensed with Villa, who had sent him an insolent reply to an order. The probable truth of the matter was that Carranza and Obregon looked with disfavor and alarm at Villa's growing popularity among the Mexicans as well as his favor with the American government, and had sent him some restraining as well as undiplomatic order, entirely out of keeping with such a powerful and stormy-petrel general as Villa. The answer was insubordinate, for Villa told them to mind their own business and leave the fighting to soldiers. Carranza wanted to act at once, but Obregon advised him to bide his time.

Later, the First Chief having a score to settle with Villa, proposed a meeting between them to talk matters over. What Carranza really wanted was to show this peon-upstart who was the head of the army. They met and Pancho Villa, always willing to show off, put up such a great review of troops that it staggered Carranza. He was so impressed that he appointed the peon-upstart, who he had come to punish, to be the Commander-in-Chief of the Army of the North instead.

Villa read the old man like an open book, but not wishing to hinder the revolutionary effort, recognized Carranza as the First Chief, which he had never done before. Villa, however, told Carranza in no uncertain words, "You run the office but do not give my troops any orders as I command my own army and will tolerate no interference." It was an insult, but Villa, rough as he was, might not have meant it to be. Carranza said nothing as he understood the man better by this time.

These two did, however, agree to fight Huerta until victory was won; to improve the conditions of the poor; to distribute land and give financial aid to the Peon-Indians; to do away with all abuses by the rich and the clergy; to remove the hitherto dictatoriral army and replace it by the Constitutionalist Army; and to punish all Catholic priests found guilty of giving moral or physical support to Huerta.

The old man was undoubtedly an astute politician full of cunning as well as wisdom, but he seemed to have lacked plain common horse-sense when dealing with Pancho Villa. Carranza played his cards with skill, but sometimes he reverted to type and acted like the domineering *hacendado* that he seemed to have been. He thought that his diplomacy and agreement to some of the demands had lulled Villa into a yes-man, when in reality his many subterfuges were making Villa, previously loyal in his way, into an opponent more difficult than ever to control.

When Villa became an army commander he could not handle the situation as well as before, although he learned a little the hard way, losing a lot of men and animals in doing so. Then Villa had the good fortune to receive Felipe Angeles, the ablest general in Mexico, who, disappointed in Carranza, left him and came to Villa. Had it not been for Angeles, Villa's army may have fallen apart by its unorganized guerrilla bands, as they lacked discipline and leaders trained in military science. Angeles came because he wanted the revolution to go on unhampered by jealousies and petty politics. He did not approve of Carranza constantly trying to put Villa in his place without the know-how.

Although Villa admired Angeles and learned a lot from him, he often ignored his advice. He did, however, keep on winning battles by the sheer weight of his charging *dorados,* even without adequate supports, reserves or formation. Thus, ignoring Angeles' advice was the weak link in Villa's armor, and caused his defeat later by Obregon, who was big enough to learn at least a few of the fundamental principles in the science of war.

Those who influenced Villa in the right direction were Abraham Gonzalez, Francisco Madero, and Jose Maria Maytorena. Later he met George Carothers and General Angeles. The first three infused the early revolutionary ferment with great success, but failed to inject the necessary calming influences into his somewhat inflammable nature. Angeles tried to give him what none of the others could, which was order, discipline and a good artillery. He failed in the first, was less than half successful in the second, but built up for him a well trained artillery brigade.

One of Carranza's provocative actions, which stimulated the ill-feeling, was his constant lack of consideration for Villa on important matters such as top-level conferences to decide Mexico's fate. He could easily have considered him to some extent, for after all, Villa commanded an army of his own which was as large as Carranza's and the territory under Villa's influence was about the same as his. Carranza should undoubtedly have considered him if for no other reason than harmony within the revolutionary camp. As far as the writer knows, there was no intended insubordination on Villa's part, but defiance and hate was created by the old man's attitude and lack of understanding of his leading general.

Carranza was stubborn and kept on regardless and perhaps was sincere in his desire to do the right thing. But eventually he overreached himself, purposely or otherwise, and pushed Villa too far, forcing him into a situation from which there could be only one outcome—a break. It appears as if Carranza became apprehensive, if not actually afraid, of Villa's intentions and, backed by Obregon, he tried to stop Villa from getting to Mexico City before them.

Villa, feeling the slur of being side-tracked by the First Chief and realizing that he was a marked man, began to object forcefully. Carranza, now sure of himself, thought the time ripe to halt and break up the "Villa coterie of cutthroats," which he once called them, and wired each general under Villa asking them on what side he would stand in case of trouble. Their answer was not a pleasant one for Carranza, it said, "We will side by the Commander of the Army of the North." Carranza, strangely enough, did not believe this telegram and declared it a forgery.

Villa, independent of spirit as well as action, made a sudden unauthorized attack on Torreon and captured it after heavy fighting on April 2, 1914.

Most of the federal troops escaped by retreating. When he entered the city, it was in flames and the inhabitants starving. After feeding the population by commandeering the food from hoarders, he followed Huerta's forces and attacked them at San Pedro de las Colonias and drove them eastward to Saltillo.

Carranza, somewhat irritated and perhaps a little afraid of Villa's eleutheromania, threatened him with a court-martial and the removal of his command. But at the same time, he ordered him to take the strong federal position of Saltillo. There were nasty rumors this had been done by Carranza in the hope that Villa would fail. Villa did attack with great success and captured a tremendous amount of guns and ammunition which strengthened his independence greatly.

About this time a Carranza force was fighting a losing battle against strong federal concentrations in Zacatecas. Evidently in a desperate mood, Carranza ordered Villa to send a force with artillery to their assistance. Villa proceeded into Zacatecas with a force almost ten times larger than requested, and the federals, caught unaware, were driven out.

This success alarmed instead of pleased Carranza as he now feared more than ever the strength and intentions of Villa, who seemed to be ominously endangering his and Obregon's plans for the future. He again threatened Villa with disciplinary actions for disobedience of orders, but Obregon, not wishing an open break at this time, struggled against it. Villa, being somewhat well informed through his espionage system in the Carranza camp, knew his days were numbered as commander of the northern army, and began his final preparations to march on the capital and to reach there ahead of the other two.

Carranza's threats naturally annoyed Pancho Villa and being in a bad mood he broke away from Carranza's camarilla in June by resigning his appointment as Commander-in-Chief of the Northern Army. This force which had been raised by Villa remained loyal to him, and not one unit went over to Carranza's side.

The root of the trouble seems to have been, not Carranza's constant suspicion of Villa's intentions as much as his own downright jealousy of Villa's military successes, in which Obregon might have shared Carranza's views. Villa, on the other hand, disliked the do-nothing-but-interfering *hacendado* and his condescending attitude as the First Chief.

Carranza, apparently disturbed at the turn of events, answered Villa's declaration of independence by cutting off his coal supply. This was an unexpected blow to Villa as his trains were standing on the tracks ready to move south, which was not desirable in Carranza's scheme of events.

Villa had a good director of transportation, but he failed his chief by not having any coal in reserve. Villa's trains were halted successfully and were barely able to get back to Chihuahua City to reorganize. He was temporarily isolated in the north, but he controlled the railroad in that direction up to the U.S. border. The Constitutionalist Army was now split into two enemy camps for the control of Mexico, and everyone knew it was only a question of time when Villa would move against Carranza.

Although Villa knew that his views, sentiments, injudicious violence and disregard of public opinion were accumulating against him in America as well as among some of his Mexican friends and supporters, he could not grasp the seriousness of the consequences. He would not or could not restrain his own actions or those very near him, such as his body-guard, Rodolfo Fierro.

The Benton Case

To comprehend more fully the many difficulties facing Villa, we must look back a little into the events at the beginning of 1914. Ever since I had left him, Villa had carried on his campaign in Chihuahua and done wonderful work in the field against the federal army. At the same time he had irritated people unnecessarily with his rough and tempestuous behavior, and thereby excited the opposition against himself to a greater intensity among the upper class Mexicans, Americans and, last but not least, the Church.

Carranza, probably meaning well, cautioned him repeatedly, which only annoyed Villa as he did not trust Carranza's good intentions. His American friend George Carothers, who was President Wilson's agent in Mexico, did the same and so did General Angeles, but one might as well try to whisper into the ear of a charging bull-ape.

Instead of putting his house in order, Villa went his own way, but after a while he became intermittently morose. During the course of this saturnine state of reasoning, he made fatal errors, but the crowning glory of his almost child-like stupidity for revenge was the Benton execution. Before we go into the famous "Benton Case," it may be necessary to mention a few of the more important events in Mexico at that time, as they could easily have put Villa's iron nerve on edge and to some extent influence his actions. Reports had come in that Torreon had fallen to the federals once more, and that Ojinaga was well fortified by his old enemy, General Mercado, after his tragic desert march in November 1913 from Chihuahua.

It was generally understood that Villa was anxious to march on Mexico City to forestall Carranza and Obregon, just as much as the other two were straining all hands to be there before Villa. He was still subjected to orders from Carranza which disturbed and bothered him, as he thought them petty and irrelevant to the fighting at hand. He could not, however, advance without first taking care of the federals at Ojinaga and Torreon. He had sent troops against Ojinaga, but all attacks had been stubbornly thrown back and his generals Torribio, Ortega and Madero stood there helpless.

Villa, restless over the stale-mate and other matters, moved quickly to the far away Ojinaga and took over the command himself. After a few rearrangements of the disposition of his troops, he attacked and so strong was his personality that in less than half a day he drove the federals over the Rio Grande for internment by the United States.

Villa hastened back to Chihuahua to prepare for Torreon and his cherished march on the capital. He needed money, lots of it, for ammunition, clothing and many other necessities which forced him to confiscate almost everything belonging to Luis Terrazes and others owning millions of acres of land and lots of cattle. These were sold in the United States, but it was not enough, so he demanded 1,000 head of cattle from each hacienda not yet confiscated by the rebels.

The Mexicans paid, but a Britisher named William C. Benton objected. This man, married to a Mexican lady, had obtained a large amount of land by purchase in time of famine and had also annexed, it was reported, still larger areas by the aid of some crooked *cientifico* in the government under Diaz. Benton was somewhat too hot-headed for his own good. He had a grievance, no doubt, but he was a poor judge of men and could not control himself.

On or about February 16, 1914, Benton demanded an interview with Villa, but was told to wait till next day. Benton, spoiled by years of successful bullying of peons and Mexican cowboys, lost his temper and forced his way into Villa's headquarters. When told to get out, he called Pancho Villa, "A damned cattle-rustling thief," and reached for his gun, but Villa's body-guard grabbed Benton before he could shoot and held him. Villa's guns were on a table far out of his reach.

He was arrested, of course, and, do what they could, nothing would change Villa's mind. Benton had to pay for his insult. He was sentenced to death. Even Villa's close friend, Carothers, could not do a thing. The power of the British Empire, the threatening might of the United States, nothing could save Benton. A firing-squad ended his life at Samalayucca, a place on the railroad about twenty-five miles north of Juarez.

Had Benton not drawn his gun on an unarmed man, the story might have ended differently. He was also an outright fool to call a man like Pancho

Villa a "cattle-rustling thief," for it is said the greater the truth, the greater the libel. There were several reports going around which might illustrate what kind of man Benton had been. A rumor stated that he was engaged by Villa to sell the commandeered cattle in the United States, cattle belonging to Benton's closest Mexican friends, and he made a good thing out of it. There was a row as to how much commission should or should not have been deducted for his underhand work, for Villa considered the rebels should have received more. There was another story which did not go down well in the United States: Benton, a Britisher, is supposed to have made some rotten remarks about American women in the Foreign Club in Chihuahua and was given a punch on the nose in front of everybody by an American newspaperman.

Before the Benton incident, Villa was the favorite Mexican general in the eyes of the United States Foreign Office, which Carothers had probably a lot to do with. The Benton execution produced such impetus to the already existing public resentment against Villa in America, that he was doomed to failure eventually. Washington officially changed its opinion and Carranza became their choice to fill the gilded chair in Palacio Nacional.

Benton made a presumptuous and foolhardy mistake and paid for it; Villa made an even greater error, and suffered tremendously for it later. One can't help thinking, however, that Benton asked for it by doing what he did. Had Villa's guns been within the usual reach, Benton would have been shot the second he reached for his, and no one would have said much about it. Reports have it that Villa did not actually order the execution; it was precipitated by Rodolfo Fierro, who was afraid that Villa might change his mind and pardon Benton.

It seemed peculiar to everyone at the time that the United States, the upper class Mexicans and the Mexican hierarchy, having a choice of two men, preferred the illiterate ex-peon-bandit Pancho Villa to the intellectual ex-senator, Venustiano Carranza, for the presidency. One cannot help thinking that this preference for Villa was due to the fact that he, being incapable of handling internal and foreign affairs himself, would be forced to leave these matters in the hands of others, who might be less scrupulous than he. Carranza, being capable, did things for himself and could therefore not so easily be reached or influenced by concession hunters and other selfish interests who, like vultures, preyed villainously on the natural resources of Mexico.

Villa's success was built on violence. It was his violence at Torreon, Juarez, Tierra Blanca, Chihuahua, Ojinaga and many other places that eliminated Huerta's forces, before Carranza and Obregon were organized, and without this violence—as bad as it was —the peons and Indians would probably still be in bondage and slavery.

If we intend to sit in judgment on Pancho Villa's crimes or his morality, we are bound in the spirit of fair play also to consider the good he did for the poor, his victories over the tyrant oppressors of the people, the benevolent influences he had over a multitude of oppressed peons to whom he gave New Hope.

The plethora of books, articles and movies on Pancho Villa's life have produced an almost nauseating dyspepsia within those who knew him. Everything written about him is, it seems, from hearsay; rumors as his political enemies made him out to be. The writer is not making excuses in Villa's behalf, for he was bad in many ways from an American point of view.

There was a boyish impulsiveness and simplicity about Villa which appealed to one, but Carranza and Obregon saw nothing but a violent barbarian in him. To some people, Villa will never appeal, but he did, nevertheless, as much as any other man to free the Peon-Indian from the iniquitous peonage system of slavery.

To understand Pancho Villa we should take full cognizance of the tragic events of his early life— the unconventionality or abnormality of his upbring- ing—for just as the young peon-bandit was, so was the general of the army.

VIII

*In Huichol Indian country—Yaqui guard killed with an
arrow—We hunt killer—A broken hunting knife
—We return to Tepic by a ruse*

Two days after the fall of Tepic City, General
Blanco summoned Acosta and me to what we thought
was the usual noon conference. He told us that two
Tepecano Indians had come to our camp that morning from the mountain regions in the northeast and
reported that the advance-guard of a considerable
cavalry force was moving southward from Valpa-
raiso in Zacatecas.

We had hardly any maps except a small scale
one which included the whole of Mexico. From this
it appeared as if the enemy was making for the
northern section of the State of Jalisco, which is a
narrow 120 mile long strip of mountainous territory
running north, looking like a sore thumb on the
map, jammed in between Tepic, Durango and Zacatecas.

Blanco had orders to clear that country as much
as possible of the enemy, get information of his

movements and bring in supplies for the army. He was now, however, in a quandary what to do, because of the distance and the inaccessible nature of the country between us and the enemy, who might also be the Durango revolutionaries that rebelled against Carranza.

Our next objective was Guadalajara, some 150 miles to the southeast. Blanco was afraid the enemy intended to reinforce that garrison or try to get at our left flank and to our rear. While interrogating these Indians further, it was discovered they had seen about 300 mounted men, but admitted they could have been either the main body or the advance-guard of a larger force. One of them, evidently a headman or shaman, thought it an advance-guard as they had no scouts or rear-guard, which was typical of the federal army.

Acosta asked Blanco what he proposed to do, but Blanco side-tracked the question by turning to me for an opinion. When I suggested sending a messenger to Generol Obregon for instructions, Blanco winced a little, shook his head and said, "No, we must decide here and now what to do, and as we cannot rely on the information from these strange Indians, one of you will take a regiment and reconnoitre in that direction, and if need be, as far as Zacatecas. When finished, return south and rejoin the main column somewhere near the Tepic and Jalisco Border."

Blanco then looked at me with his attractive grin and added, "You have been attacked and accused by some of being a *gringo*. It might be a good thing for you to get away for a while. Take over the expedition. There is good hunting in the sierra for it is full of game and, apparently, federals." As I was always fond of getting out with an independent command, I accepted the mission which looked interesting; besides, I was getting a little tired of the constant accusations, by some, of being a foreign agent.

To get the necessary information of the country ahead, Pedro and Tekwe were sent to bring in the Tepehuanes who joined us during the patrol on May 6 east of Acaponeta. From two of these we learned they had been in the northern sections of Jalisco (Where the land is sandy) located not far south of their homeland in Durango, and that the mountainous region through which we had to pass was difficult. It would be unwise to take a large number of horses; they thought fifty at the most but that twenty might be better. Scarcity of water and grass at this time of the year was a great factor against a large number of animals, so the fewer the better.

I asked Blanco to reduce the force to twenty men as it was silly to try to take a regiment into the inaccessible mountains, against the advice of friendly Indians who knew the sierra so well. This worried him, and he suggested that Captain Sanches take charge of the expedition; but by this time I had begun to relish the idea of seeing a new and strange part of the country, as well as do a little hunting, and he was persuaded, although he insisted on at least half a squadron. He also proposed that twenty or more Winchester carbines, with fifty rounds per gun, be carried on spare horses to arm friendly Indians. He had heard that the Cora and the western Tepehuane Indians would make good material for soldiers under their own chiefs, especially "If you promise them absolute control over their own land, affairs and religion."

After a lot of dickering, we started out from Tepic City. My little force consisted of 53 men, 12 spare remounts, 10 days rations for the men and two days rations for the horses. I also managed to talk the general out of carrying the cumbersome extra guns and ammunition as the pack animals would hamper our mobility.

We moved eastward on an old road, which had seen better days, and passed north of the imposing volcano Sanganuey rising some 2,000 meters above the sea. When near the volcano, Acosta, who had come along to arrange some system of intercommunication between us, left and returned to the city, but he was just about dying to come along with us.

The guides had strict orders to avoid populated places, especially haciendas, along the line of march as the owners were usually in sympathy with the federals and may have had some means of contacting them. We rode past San Luis, which seemed deserted, and then on by a trail to Alica where stood a few abandoned houses. The Santiago River, which is about thirty miles east of the City of Tepic, at this point is also called "Alica River" and seemed to go under the name of Rio de Lerma in another part. We crossed with some difficulties, and as two horses went lame among the rocks, we camped for the night near a place called Aguapan, where there was some grass for the horses.

Pedro and Tekwe had, at my request, chosen two Tepehuanes, one Cora and one Huichol, as guides and interpreters. The Huichol was one of the few volunteers among us from that tribe which is not anywhere near as warlike as their neighbors, the Cora, who are few in number. He came from somewhere in the high sierra where his father had a ranch near a place called Ocota. This Huichol recommended that only ten horses be taken into the high mountains and warned that the rainy season would start within a month and make traveling in the sierra practically impossible, especially with a lot of horses.

At dawn the following morning we freed the lame horses to graze on their own and picked up a very old trail which led us higher and higher, but up and down, into the mountains and eventually through a virgin oak forest. That day was not so very difficult, except that the men had to ride and walk in Indian file all day which made our party stretch out for almost a mile from front to rear along the trail. This was most inconvenient, as communication to the rear was difficult except by calling from man to man.

We had not seen a human soul for two days and the country was silent as a grave. We had been moving eastward and came across some grassland here and there, but it was dry stuff, even for hungry horses. At one place we saw a small lake far below us at the bottom of the pine forest, and it looked a likely place for deer. We had seen deer several times during the trip, but I did not use the gun for fear it might alarm the men coming up behind.

We camped in an open place in the forest that night where there was a clear spring of good water, but so small that the horses had to stand in line waiting their turn to drink. Alongside the spring were five old and rotten arrows stuck in the ground. The Huichol guide asked me to let them remain as they were "prayers to the Goddess of the Southern Clouds" placed there by one of his people.

Three large deer were shot as we camped and all had a generous portion of venison for the evening meal with plenty left over for the morning. There was, however, an argument between the Huichol, Cora and my Pedro as to how the animal should have been killed and treated before skinning. I was forced to stop it as the men were tired and hungry. To my great relief they went to work on the animals without further protest. It was quite chilly. I was already regretting having brought so many men and was seriously contemplating sending thirty of them back next morning.

The trail we had been traveling over seemed abandoned or unused for a long time as it was overgrown and not visible in places; in fact there was no trail at all for long stretches when machetes had to be used to get through. It appeared to me that the Huichol, however good a scout, could hardly have guided us through had it not been for the old trail-blazing marks to be seen here and there constantly pointed out by Pedro. It wasn't so bad in the forest itself, but difficult in the open places where the underbrush had taken over.

The whole territory seemed deserted and we met only two half-starved Indians in four days, and these we brought back with us for safety. They were of the Huichol tribe and I was surprised they did not object to being detained; in fact they seemed quite content after getting a square meal. On the fourth or fifth day we began to go down more often than up, and eventually we reached an Indian village on the side of a slope not far from a river. The Huichol guide, who was known to us as Jose, informed me this was Guadalupe Ocotan, a Huichol village, and that the river was the Chapalagana. The place was very run-down looking, especially the temple and the god-houses.

Jose was quite happy to be among his own people and met two old friends in the pueblo. His home near Ocota, he informed me, was in the northeast, and it would take two or three days to get there with all the horses as the arroyos were dry.

When the scouts returned that night, they reported no enemy in sight nor had the people in the village heard of any federals for a long time. Jose, although a Huichol himself, did not seem to take much cognizance of these statements because the answers came, he said, from intimidated persons, people who were afraid, and he asked me to send for the headman of the village.

The man came at once and informed me that he had only heard of some troops being in Mezquitic (Among the mezquite trees), a town outside the Huichol territory, about seventy or eighty miles to the north. He also volunteered the information that one of the tribe had returned from a pueblo in the south, two days before, and had not heard of any soldiers.

Early next morning Pedro got orders to pick two runners to scout southward for about fifteen miles. He promptly volunteered to go with a Huichol he had met in the village the night before and they started out at a good gait, dressed in native garb, before 7 a.m.

That morning was taken up with caring for the horses, as some fetlocks had been cut on the sharp stones and the stumps of the cleared underbrush; they also had a well earned rest. Placing Tekwe in charge of the men, and with patrols out south and east, I took Jose as an interpreter and visited several homes in the village in the hope of getting some information of the enemy, however, meager. It was surprising how little these people knew or cared of the world outside their tribe, but they seemed to know a great deal about tribal history, and the gods.

Jose surprised me several times because he knew more than any one in Ocotan. Then I found that his father, a famous singing-shaman, had for years been training his son in the lore of the tribe with the idea and hope that he would step aside some day in favor of the election of Jose, as the singing-shaman of the community.

When we returned to the broken down Huichol temple in which we lived, Jose, to whom I had taken a great liking, told me that the trail in the sierra to the north could not be traversed by fifty mounted men at the same time without grave risks, as the paths were often too steep and difficult even for a mule or burro. The grass on the high mesa was now very dry, and corn as food for horses was out of the question, as that commodity was scarce. The little left among the people was carefully hidden in storehouses or caves. He also pointed out that water was there, but the rivers and streams were dry except for waterholes here and there in the deep sections of the rivers, and these were difficult to reach by horses as the river banks were steep. Then he added that the sierra had many wonderful springs of water and that many were inside almost inaccessible caves high in the mountains and were holy to his people.

From what Jose had said it was apparent that no federal cavalry force of any consequence could traverse the Sierra Madre from the north and threaten our flank. It was therefore more important for us to pay attention toward the east, and I decided to move some of the men nearer to Jose's home at Ocota where he promised me many of his people as scouts, men he knew and could trust. As we had to wait for Pedro's return, I began to make a few notes on the legends of the Huichols, with Jose as my able assistant, and I got so deeply interested that it was night before I noticed it.

Pedro and his Huichol companion returned from their scouting trip about eight o'clock in the evening after reaching a place called Huajimi. He looked a little tired, but the Huichol scout, although considered a good runner, was all in, and no wonder; they had run more than thirty miles over rough country. Jose, who had been talking to the scout, said his countryman had never traveled with a man like Pedro before: "He ran up and down steep inclines, jumped like a squirrel from stone to stone in the difficult deep arroyos and never stopped to rest." Pedro apologized in a way for taking so long, but it was due to not having used his legs for running of late, and they were a little stiff from days in the saddle.

The most important information brought back by

Pedro was the rumor that troops had been at Bolaños but had moved eastward to Tlaltenango and that a small force, probably a company, was at the town of Juchipila. The latter place was about sixty miles east of us as the crow flies, but they had a fairly good road from there south into Guadalajara. When he had finished, Pedro, the proud full-blooded Indian, added as an afterthought that the people in Huajimi were mostly half-breed Mexicans who did not belong to any particular tribe, and he wasn't sure if he could believe anything they said.

The following morning I picked twelve men including Pedro, Jose, one Tepehuane and the Cora to move to Ocota with me. The rest were to remain at Guadalupe Ocotan under Tekwe, who was given Pedro's friend, the Huichol runner, as a guide because he spoke some Spanish. Tekwe was visibly upset by the order and begged me to let him come along, and Pedro pleaded for him for they had become inseparable.

I looked at Tekwe, and as I am not entirely unconscious of premonitions, and usually follow a hunch, I cancelled the order and decided to send forty men back to Tepic City immediately. They left during the morning of May 24, returning over the same route they had come, as the trail was now wide open and easy to follow. I let them take the spare horses, except those for the pack-saddles to carry the fifteen Winchester carbines and ammunition taken from some of those returning. A Yaqui sergeant was in charge of the party, and with him I sent a note to General Blanco telling him what we had heard and of my intentions of arming some of the Indians; that we would scout eastward, and return south via Ixtlan in the southeastern part of the Tepic Territory, where I would try to contact him.

Some of the Yaquis grumbled at losing their guns, but Tekwe explained they would get new ones in Tepic and they departed. We moved out at noon and were guided in a much winding and round-about trail down into a wide and deep gorge with a dry river bed. Water could be seen in small pools here and there but far away and difficult of access, and I felt contented at having sent the men back to Tepic.

I found the route more difficult than anticipated, and decided we would be forced to camp on the mesa that night far from water. It didn't really matter much as Jose had insisted on carrying water to the horses from a small pool in a gorge two hours before halting. We were off again at dawn, traveling along a mesa but, in spite of the fairly good trail, the going was slow as we scouted as far east as practicable to the amusement of the four Huichol Indians that had joined us for the trip. They did not seem to understand the reason why.

On a rise we came upon a large heap of stones where Jose and Pedro dismounted and were joined by the Huichols. They walked to the heap, then each threw a stone and a stick or some grass on it, mumbled something, then mounted and rode on. Pedro reminded me that I had seen similar heaps in his country, in western Chihuahua, and that each stone was a kind of prayer for good health and good luck, by the thrower, for the journey ahead.

We made camp that night in a deep gorge alongside another dry river bed so water had to be carried from a water hole for the horses. We were off again by dawn the following morning and soon reached a number of houses; the largest one, proudly pointed out by Jose, was a Huichol temple with its adjoining god-houses.

We stayed only long enough to see the headman and then continued to a locality called Taquitzata (The silk of the corn is falling) by Jose, but he added with some scorn, "The Mexicans call this sacred place Ratontita." Although Ratontita was only some three to four miles away, it took us more than an hour to get there, due to the necessary scouting. We found it to be another Huichol temple with its god-houses and a number of small Indian farms scattered nearby, the whole giving a somewhat peaceful impression.

Jose, who had not been home for six months, was asking for news of his family as our next camping place was his home. It was not far, but one had to descend into a deep gorge and then up again before reaching the mesa on which Ocota stands. The distance may have been eight miles, but it took us several hours as we had to wait for the scouts to get ahead. We reached there about five o'clock in the afternoon with two horses lame.

Ocota or Ocotsari (Where there is resinous pine wood), as Jose called the place, is principally one of several religious centers of the Huichol tribe and had the usual temple with a number of god-houses. Spread out on the pleasantly rolling mesa were also a number of small farms with avocado trees growing here and there close by.

Our scouts had aroused the curiosity of the inhabitants and many came out to see the "rebels." Jose's father, a fine old boy, was surprised and much pleased to find his son as interpreter-guide to the *jefe* of the soldiers and made immediate arrangements for me to be housed in the temple. I thought it peculiar that I was not invited into one of the ranch houses, but learned later that the Huichols are against strangers sleeping in their houses for fear they might fool around with their women.

During the first evening at Ocota, Pedro and Jose obtained the four best runners in the place as scouts, and at daybreak two of them started out together in a northeasterly direction toward Mezquitic with orders to look around, then return to report. The other two went east and southeast with orders to make for Bolaños and Chimaltitan, when one should return and report, but the other to continue to Tlaltenango (better known as Sanchez Roman), find out what he could, then return at top speed to Ocota. Each man was promised twenty pesos when he returned — each got five pesos in advance.

Jose's father was the best informed man in Ocota and he confirmed the rumor that a large mounted force had been in Mezquitic some time ago, but had moved and were now in the neighborhood of Tlaltenango.

As we needed meat, Pedro and Tekwe went northwestward with two local Indians to get a deer and to scout, as we were ten or twelve miles east of the Chapalagana River in country which could easily harbor an enemy.

Jose and his father spent the early part of the morning trying to persuade me to issue the fifteen guns to his men in the community of Ocota. About twenty men were presented as trusted men, and I picked six; the rest did not appeal to me as responsible enough. When I informed Jose and his father that the remainder would be selected from other settlements, it started a strong remonstrance against the idea. They advised me forcefully to confine the recruiting to their community only; outside men could not be mixed with theirs as it would invite trouble. The old man said, "If you pick men from two or more settlements, they will soon quarrel and break up into several parties, each group being members of their own community under their own recognized leader."

As I did not wish to pick any more "musketeers" before Pedro and Tekwe had interrogated each thoroughly, I let the matter rest until their return. I was rather disappointed for it was evident how loosely the social structure of these Indians was held together. Each community was a complete little state, with its own government and headman, and having very little truck with outsiders except, perhaps, for such small commercial enterprises that may exist, and pilgrimages to ancient and distant holy places located outside their mountainous homeland.

When I changed the subject, and asked about their legends and gods, both father and son seemed eager to talk, but it was noticeable how they became silent when one of their tribesmen approached. The day passed pleasantly, for the old shaman was a veritable storehouse of information.

There was grass on the slopes, but it was too dry and hard to do the horses any good. As I wanted to preserve the remaining horse-rations, two mounted men, leading a pack-horse, were sent about six miles to San Sebastian in the hope of obtaining corn. They came back with only half a bushel and informed me there was corn there but they refused to sell.

Jose persuaded his father to sell about a bushel of corn, but that was all he would part with. As an after-thought, he said he would exchange corn for some guns and ammunition, which cheered me, for it meant he had corn on hand, but instead of trading, I doubled the guard on my little arsenal although I knew the Huichols would think twice before tackling my Yaquis.

Midnight came and yet no sign of the hunters. One of the scouts sent north that morning came back and reported meeting some of his countrymen returning from Mezquitic. These men who came from San Sebastian told him that the federals left Mezquitic four days ago and had moved southward. On hearing this he returned at once to give me the important information, and held out his hand for the rest of his pay.

This was the third rumor of the enemy in that direction, but there seemed to be too much vagueness as to when they had left and where they had gone. On questioning him further the man was positive that no troops were within a day's march of Ocota, but from what he had heard he thought the federals had gone into Zacatecas on the road to Colotlan.

As I had already begun to realize that a Huichol is very adept at stretching out a flimsy uncertainty into a solid fact when it is convenient or to his advantage, I sent Jose to arouse the men at 2 a.m., with orders to eat and be ready to march at dawn. When we were about to leave for San Sebastian to interview the Indians who had been in the north, Pedro came running toward us and reported having killed two deer, but he had also come upon fresh spoors of twenty men traveling westward. He and Tekwe had followed their tracks for some distance and then returned to where the Huichols and the game was, hence the delay. As my little force was on the alert and we needed meat, two pack horses were sent with Pedro to hasten the removal of the deer to Ocota. The horses were watered in the meantime and Jose's father sent for, but he denied having heard a word of any troops in the neighborhood and I was inclined to believe him.

After talking with Pedro and Tekwe about Jose and his father's remarks, they did not seem at all surprised. They talked to the six men, discarded one but picked two others, which made it seven guns for the Ocota area. They all agreed to come to us when called, but no guns were given them.

After a generous piece of roasted venison had been enjoyed by everyone, we moved cautiously toward San Sebastian about noon on May 28. What was left of the animal was given to Jose's family, but we carried the other buck on a pack horse for the morrow. The trail went through some pine woods along rising ground toward San Sebastian and then down again to the village located near a practically dry creek where water was standing in small pools in places. Before entering the place the scouts had carefully searched the surrounding country and some of the better houses, most of which were in bad need of repair.

The headman, who had been warned of our coming by the scouts, came out to greet us and kindly offered the temple for me as my headquarters. The Huichols who had been to Mezquitic were interviewed and they confirmed what the scout had said. They denied having any knowledge of troops passing through San Sebastian during the last few days, which was verified by the leading shaman and the *gobernador*.

Tekwe, who did not believe a word of the villagers, suggested that we take and hold at least two of the leading men as hostages for our own safety. Pedro, his best friend, advised caution, as these people, although not of fighting stock, could make it very nasty for us if aroused and suggested we wait until the return of the scouts. As this was more in harmony with my own thoughts, I decided not to act and the two warriors went off remonstrating about who was right.

Early that evening the one and only child of the chief fell sick with pains in her stomach. "She was dying," the shaman reported. The leading shaman was sent for, but the child got worse. Pedro, whom I considered the best shaman-doctor in Mexico, came to me with a glint in his eye and suggested that I "cure" the Indian girl, and thereby get the goodwill of the headman and the people, all of whom seemed to dislike White men. The idea was good but dangerous because the Huichol shaman might object and cause trouble. Pedro brushed my fears aside and asked me to give her some of my "magical white powder." The only medicine with me was some bicarbonate of soda.

Before going into the house of the sick girl, Pedro gave me a lesson in the art of shamanism. He advised me not to dispense the magical powder without some outward show of power and great knowledge, or the people standing around would consider me a novice and even the child might not believe in me, which would be bad.

Thus primed what to do and feeling like a fakir, I went into the house and found the poor girl in awful pain. As she was too young to be pregnant, I was afraid it might be appendicitis which could lead to complications difficult to handle. While looking at the girl from the doorway Pedro said something to the shaman that was forceful enough, for he stepped to one side without a word when I came forward.

Pushing my fears aside, I solemnly and ceremoniously mixed the bicarbonate of soda in a gourd with some water in front of everybody while murmuring words with mystical intent. Then when everything was ready, I raised the "powerful medicine" towards the East, South, West, North, Above and let a few precious drops fall to the ground, which is Below in the six world-directions. During this ceremony, I noticed all those present watch me intently as if fascinated, and the girl had stopped complaining of her pains.

When I handed the patient the gourd, she grasped at it eagerly and drained the contents. Then another theatrical kind of inspiration came over me, probably animated by their entranced faces, for I grabbed a large burning stick from the fire, extinguished the flame and then passed the smoking stick up and down over the body of the girl and finished by making a Cross of Smoke over her as I had seen it done by shamans among the Tarahumara only a few months before. When I did this a distinct gasp of astonishment could be heard from the otherwise so stoic Indians. Even Pedro was deeply impressed when I turned and made crosses of smoke over the heads, and on each side of, all those present.

As there was nothing else to do, I left the house with Pedro who, visibly moved by the performance, touched my arm and said *"Jefe,* you are a great healer." A short distance from the house stood the local shaman who had been somewhat rudely pushed aside because Pedro proclaimed me such a great medicine man.

He was watching me intently with a scowl I thought, and I had a hunch to make peace with him before it was too late and told Pedro to invite him over. Pedro sensed the idea, for he was quite respectful and begged him to come, which he did although he looked scared. Telling the others to move aside, Jose interpreted my instructions to the shaman. They were, "The girl is not well yet but you can finish the cure. Go inside and in front of everybody wipe off with a finger a drop of the sap to be found at the end of the pine wood on the fire and smear this over the navel of the girl — then leave her."

This he did with quite a flourish worthy of his profession. By the time he had finished, the bicarbonate of soda had done its work, the girl felt better and got up to the great joy of her parents. The shaman was reinstated in the good-graces of the community for it was his magic, of course, that had done the trick, but I had made a new friend.

Yaqui guard killed with an arrow

When we returned to the temple, it was late and the men were asleep alongside their guns, close to the small pile of Winchesters and ammunition. Just inside the entrance, which was dark and door-less, stood a young Yaqui on guard. As I had not slept for over forty-eight hours, I lay down on my laurels as a shaman-healer about midnight. The sleep must have been deep and heavy because I woke up with a start. It was dark outside, but I could distinguish the men rushing out through the doorway, and extending around the building — not a word was spoken — not a sound anywhere.

As I had lain down fully dressed, it took only seconds to pick up my guns and follow. Tekwe, who was outside directing the men, informed me that the Yaqui guard had been dropped by an arrow. Leaving Pedro to take charge of the wounded man and two men to guard the guns, it did not take long for the remaining Yaquis to search the neighborhood as dawn broke. They returned empty-handed and in an ugly frame of mind.

When I examined the wounded man, I found the arrow had penetrated his chest two or three inches above the heart. Pedro wanted to push it through rather than pull it back as he couldn't tell what kind of tip it had. When the arrow came out through the back, we found it had a very blunt wooden point. The man was now bleeding profusely and there was nothing we could do except try to impede the flow. He managed to tell how he spotted four men on his right outside and leaned forward to have a better look. When the arrow struck from the left, he rolled over and called Tekwe lying close to him. That was all the man could tell before he departed to the Happy Hunting Grounds a few minutes later.

It was now daylight and the very hostile Yaquis searched the village. It would not have taken much opposition to start a massacre. The area around the temple was also scanned carefully, but the place had been walked over by many people the day before, so no particular clue could be determined. Pedro and Tekwe, who had taken a larger circle than the rest, came upon tracks of six men leading toward the village from the west, and spoors of six running men traveling northwest.

This almost cleared the local people of all blame. The headman thought it was done deliberately to discredit the people of San Sebastian, but Tekwe was sure they were after the guns. To punish the intruders, I demanded from the headman ten Huichol trackers, armed with bows and arrows, to come with us. These he provided willingly. After detailing two Yaquis and the Cora scout to guard the guns and horses, I promised the Huichols a rifle and twenty-five rounds of ammunition for each of the six, dead or alive. When hearing this, the Yaquis grunted their approval. The Huichols became eager for the man-hunt and started at once at a fast pace, but Tekwe and Pedro were always far ahead.

I was in good physical condition, and had been considered a good long-distance runner in the past, but had to exert all my reserves to keep up with these Indians. We had been following the spoors running and jig-jagging for some distance when we came to the edge of a mesa, where we could look down for thousands of feet, it seemed, into an enormous gorge. As we needed a rest, cover was taken alongside some large boulders close to a crevice leading to the very edge of the *barranca*. About three or more miles across this enormous sundering breach of the earth was another mesa, where, Jose told me, stood the sacred Huichol temple of Santa Catarina.

Pedro returned shortly after we had halted and advised vigilance as the enemy must be close by, for it had slackened its pace, evidently thinking no one was on its trail. We were on a tree-less part of a mesa, infinitely removed, it seemed, from the outside world. I stood there entranced at the magnificent scenery — mountains towering over mountains in the north, the long, deep and wide chasm, the mesa — and then I looked at my Huichol companions with their bows and arrows. I began to speculate with intent curiosity why I was there and wondered if I had any right to chase these half-wild Indians and kill them in their own country. I also figured it was foolish as we might easily run into a trap.

In the middle of my reverie Tekwe came back and reported the enemy had joined eight others and then entered the underbrush of the gorge about two miles west of us. The Yaquis got up eager to follow and get revenge, but the Huichol shaman held up his hand to speak and said, "The gorge has many caves to hide in. Your guns are of no advantage down there in the thick bush as you cannot see for more than a few yards ahead. Their bows and arrows are therefore more effective. Besides they can get above us and roll large stones on our heads and start a landslide. No, we should not enter that gorge," he advised.

I was disappointed at his attitude and at the same time somewhat relieved for the place reminded me of the forbidden looking gorges we fought in during the Zulu Rebellion, only this one was worse. As there was nothing else we could do with unwilling Huichols on our hands, we started on the return journey to San Sebastian. On the way I questioned Pedro how near we were to the tracks of the twenty men he had found a few days before, and as he thought it was only about an hour away, we changed our direction to have a look.

The Yaquis got orders to shoot a deer or two for the pot as we needed food, but not before noon. One of them shot an animal almost at once after starting and much too soon for safety. When Tekwe reprimanded the young brave for his indiscretion, he received an insubordinate but understandable reply: "My brother was shot last night and we are returning empty-handed because these frightened coyotes refuse to fight. I had to kill something."

After having a good piece of steak, we all felt refreshed, and the men were alerted to look for old spoors as well as fresh ones. The Huichols moved foward in extended order toward the south with the Yaquis coming up behind but in close formation. Hunting for old tracks slowed down our progress considerably, which suited me as my right shoe was chafing me badly.

By one o'clock in the afternoon it was obvious that we could not do what we had to and return to San Sebastian that night. One of the Huichols and a Yaqui were therefore dispatched to the village for food, water, a pack animal and my saddle horse. They were to meet us at a point agreed on not later than one hour after dark and before if possible.

At about two o'clock the right wing of the Huichols picked up the old trail which led us westward along high and wooded ridges and a small mesa. Another hour and the spoors turned northward, and we were getting near the place where we were that morning, close to the gorge. The Huichols halted and signaled they wanted to say something, and the shaman came back and impressed upon me most emphatically not to go any farther because we had no water or food, and added, "Let us return to San Sebastian. Give us the guns and we will come here tomorrow and draw them out from the gorge." Tekwe thought the suggestion childish, as the men we were after would be far away by the morning. This talk by the Huichols was only a subterfuge and a means of getting the guns.

The Huichols were evidently not to be relied upon in case of a fight, and I conveyed my thoughts to my trusted friends, Pedro and Tekwe, who had come to the same conclusion, for they shook their heads incredulously as well as in disgust. The Huichols were, therefore, brought in from the flanks and all of us moved on to the agreed meeting place, which turned out to be a sheltered spot under a ridge, in sight of a peculiar rock formation that looked like two stone towers at a distance. We reached the place about 6 p.m., and two Yaquis went to hunt deer. The rest started fires going, but many of them ran out to bring in the game after hearing three shots. It didn't take long before pieces of venison were turning over the fires on newly cut roasting spits.

The Huichols, who sat around their own fire, had some ceremonies connected with the deer, but when the shaman wanted to dig an earth-oven to cook the meat on hot stones according to their custom, they complained of being hungry and roasted the meat on sticks instead, like the Yaquis. The supplies came as the meat was ready and everybody was happy for our empty bottles were refilled.

When we prepared for our safety, the Huichols were given the choice of supplying the outlying pickets or do camp and horse-guard. They chose to do the pickets, no doubt because of their fear of the Yaquis, who had difficulties in controlling their inner feelings toward them. It was agreed that one man be placed at each of the four cardinal points and remain awake until relieved by the other man, who was to sleep close to the man on look out. The Yaquis took over the camp-guard, but they did not trust these Huichol outposts, for each one of them was not only cleaning his gun but also sharpening his evil looking knife.

Having slept but little of late, and being tired after hours of running in the high altitude, I lay down in the shelter of a large rock where Pedro had put my saddle and must have been asleep before hitting the ground. Tekwe woke me up about one o'clock and whispered that something was wrong and that every Yaqui had been alerted. Then he told how he had visited the Huichol outposts at midnight and couldn't find them. They had all gone some distance around the escarpment to the east and made a large fire. Further, there were five more in their party now than before. Jose, who had remained with me, was visibly shocked at the incredible behavior of his countrymen.

While Tekwe and three braves went to scout for a mile or so westward, the remainder of the rations were placed on the pack-horse including a whole deer, and my horse was saddled. When the scouts returned, we moved quietly to the new position picked by Tekwe, who can see at night as well as any cat or owl. As it was a good defensive position and easy to evacuate in case of need, we sat down for a strategy palaver, which all the Yaquis were allowed to attend.

The scout sent to watch the other camp came back at this moment with the information that the Huichols had left and gone eastward, which could only mean to San Sebastian. Tekwe, always keen to strike an enemy before he has settled down, proposed that we move on San Sebastian as the Huichols might be after the spare guns and our reserve ammunition. It was logical reasoning, but it meant two hours traveling and every one was tired. Jose, whom I trusted in spite of what his people had done, thought traveling over the rough ground in the dark would be slow and proposed that we rest and start out at dawn.

Pedro thought the same, and as one of the Yaquis was fumbling with a broken sandal that must be repaired, I overruled Tekwe and decided to stay and eat, but move at daybreak. It was interesting to note that several of the Indians preferred to rest rather than eat—they were tired.

A *broken hunting knife*

For many years it has been a constant practice of mine to carry a long and heavy hunting knife stuck inside my right legging as an emergency weapon while hunting. Moreover, in Mexico, Tekwe had often made me practice throwing this knife at different objects, and under his expert tutelage I had become more or less proficient at the sport. As luck would have it during this night I was sleeping on my left side when something heavy fell on top of me. Grasping for the knife, I swung the hand back of me with all force, and it struck something hard and with it came a deep groan. As I did not wish to give up the knife which had stuck, I gave it a severe wrench with a bending motion and it was free. When I rolled away from the limp burden, I found Tekwe standing there, knife in hand, ready to pounce on the Indian who had disturbed my rest. He told me how he woke hearing something and got up as the man fell on me. Apparently the darkness had deceived the man, or he fell on me by an accident, but his knife was buried deep in my saddlebags used as a pillow about six inches from my neck which gave me the seconds needed to get rid of him.

301

With daylight it was obvious that my knife had struck and buried itself in the backbone and killed the man instantly. When the knife was wrenched free with a violent twist to one side, it broke about an inch from the point. It was eventually resharpened at the point and has been kept for the last forty-four years as an emblem of good luck.

We return to Tepic by a ruse

After breakfast the most choice pieces of the deer were cut away and placed with the dead man on the pack horse. Jose did not recognize the man, but Tekwe thought it was one of the men rejected for a gun two days before in Ocota, and he was, therefore, brought along for identification. The men were told not to use their firearms for hunting on the return journey, but if they wanted meat to help themselves from the carcass left behind. Almost everyone cut a piece for his next meal.

We re-entered San Sebastian before noon on June 1, and found the Huichol scouts had returned. The one sent farthest east reported a company of infantry at Chimaltitan. He had not gone as far at Tlaltenango because it was reported the federal regiment stationed there was shanghaiing peons and Indians to work for them and sometimes into the army. There was also a rumor among the people that the federal troops in that area were to move eastward and some southward soon.

After getting this important information, I turned my attention to local matters, for the chief and the leading men of the place stood waiting, seemingly much afraid. Apparently the Yaquis, in a spirit of revenge, had told them some tall stories of my anger at the killing of the Yaqui, and the attempted assassination, and that the village would no doubt be put to the torch.

This I did not know, but it must have looked dark to them when I made every one in the village walk past the dead man, but no one recognized him, of course. He was buried immediately. When asked why they left their outposts and deserted us during the night, the Huichols frankly admitted being afraid of the Yaquis as they had threatened to slit their throats. Tekwe knew nothing of this but two of his men admitted saying something of that kind to frighten the dirty coyotes for shooting one of them. Tekwe admitted, however, it was lucky that the Huichols left during the night for the tension among his men was running high, and it would not have taken much to have started a fight.

As the scouts from Jose's village had done a good job, they were paid as agreed, and I put them down as likely men for a gun each. They were asked to remain with us for a while as more scouting had to be done. The Yaquis were alerted to the fact that we needed these men later and to leave them alone, which they did.

That afternoon was spent resting and taking care of ourselves, horses and equipment, as we had to move soon. During the evening my newly acquired friend, the local shaman, mentioned that the horses looked like "starved goats," but the grass would be green soon after the rains. "But," he added, "if you must leave, don't go through the high Sierra, go east toward Bolaños, then south." Although we were almost ready to leave, his remarks spurred my efforts, besides putting ideas into my head, for I decided to get rid of the guns by issuing them to the Indians at once.

My plan of how to get out of the sierra and at the same time get information of the enemy, and do some good for the rebel cause, was a little vague even to myself, but something had to be done. A messenger was therefore sent to Jose's father in Ocota with instructions to come with seven men to get their guns at sunrise the following morning and be ready to go on a few days march. Then I unfolded my seemingly risky and almost crazy plan to Pedro and Tekwe.

The idea was to arm fifteen Huichols with the spare guns and march them on Bolaños or Chimaltitan. About ten or more miles ahead of these "soldiers" would be a party of five unarmed Huichols traveling as "traders" to spread rumors everywhere that a large rebel force had crossed the sierra from Tepic and was now marching eastward to encircle the federal troops in northern Jalisco and Zacatecas.

The remainder of us, my own men, would come not far behind the Huichols with guns to support them when necessary. But should the federals give ground, we would take the old road to the south and the Huichols could return home with their guns. Should, however, the federals be inclined to dispute our right of way, we would not try to force our way through but retrace our steps and try to return by the same trail on which we came.

Pedro thought the scheme might work if the Huichols were not told the whole plan, but Tekwe was sure the Huichols would run away at first opportunity, especially when they went outside of their own territory. I also informed them of my decision not to discipline the Huichols for the killing of the Yaquis, as we could not prove who did it. Besides, we needed their friendship and cooperation to succeed, not only against the federals, but in our own escape. Both of them were quite pleased at the prospect of getting away from the local Indians and complained they were thieves, as many small but important articles belonging to our men had mysteriously disappeared. Even Jose, one of their own tribe, was robbed of his flint-lighter, Tekwe said.

The following morning, Jose's father was at the temple before dawn with his men. When I told him part of the plan, he shook his head and said it was too risky for his people in case we failed. But, he continued, if you place the Yaquis in front, we will follow them, but we must be given the rifles before starting.

Personally I did not care much for this unexpected turn of events, as I already had realized that the weak link in our armor was the unreliableness of the Huichols. If I let them march behind the Yaquis, there was grave danger of them running back home with their guns at the first shot or even before. Tekwe thought the same and pointed out possibility of treachery, and that it would not be right to make the Yaquis face the federals with scared Huichols armed with guns behind them. "I suppose you know," Tekwe added, "that we look upon these cowards as enemies after the murder of the other night."

As this confirmed my own views, I dismissed Jose's father and sent for the headman of San

Sebastian and told him of the plan. He was more reasonable, probably from fear or perhaps thought it would be a cunning move to obtain the guns. At any rate he was willing to supply the men on the condition that all the carbines be given to his men. If so, he would also supply the "traders" traveling ahead to spread the news of the advancing and marauding Rebel Army. The shaman doctor who had been displaced by me a few days before had come with the chief and now asked if he could take charge of the "traders," which was granted for he was obviously a capable and respected man among his own people.

To clinch the deal I gave the shaman and the headman a Winchester each with some ammunition. Jose's father, who was outside, was also given a gun and ammunition to soothe his disappointment, which pleased his son. As too many persons had by this time learned of our plan, it was imperative to start at the earliest moment before the scheme could be conveyed to the federals. There was also the grave danger that the fast approaching rainy season would be upon us which would make traveling through forests of the sierra very difficult, in fact impossible.

The five "traders" were given a short briefing on what to say, especially about our great number, mobility, and the fact that federal soldiers were absconding and joining the rebels in vast numbers everywhere. Then the shaman in charge was given fifty federal pesos to "trade" with and off they went. Now the guns and ammunition were issued and the Huichols acted like little children with a new toy. I did not wish to be handicapped with all the packhorses, so two of them were given away: one was given to Jose, who promptly handed it over to his father; the other to the son of the shaman of the "traders" already gone. The kid led the horse away proud as he could be. These were in reality princely gifts to these Indians and every one was content.

Four hours after the "traders" had been sent ahead to propagate rumors, the armed Huichols started out ahead of the Yaquis. The distance to Bolaños as the crow flies was about eighteen miles, but the trail seemed twice that distance. At one place, after descending and climbing various elevations, going down it seemed more often than up, we struck a very rough part where the shaman of the Huichols came back. He suggested the Yaquis be sent ahead of them, as his men were restless and did not relish the idea of being captured by the federals while armed with guns on the trail leading to Bolaños only an hour or so ahead.

Jose, who did the interpreting, was obviously ashamed of his countrymen and asked me to give them orders to continue. Tekwe thought otherwise and suggested they be permitted to drop behind, as they might run ahead and inform the federals, which would be worse than if they ran away back home. Then I realized that Jose's father knew his people well, for he had anticipated this very thing and deliberately forfeited the rifles rather than disgrace his son and their village.

The Huichols stepped aside and we passed. Tekwe asked permission to place two of his men behind them so as to prevent a stampede back to their homeland. One of the men was the brother of the

Yaqui killed with an arrow by the Huichols, Tekwe said, and he petted his rifle significantly.

A while later we reached a river after a steep and difficult descent where we hid and took care of the horses. Jose and our Cora scout were sent on in native garb to have a look around. They returned a few hours later and reported no federals in sight. They had gone to Bolaños and found that our "trader" friends had been there and gone on to Chimaltitan, leaving terrible tales behind them of our behavior and how a great Rebel Army was approaching.

They had also managed to purchase a large quantity of tamales and wanted help to bring them to us, so the men had a good meal that night. But we had trouble in our rear which was discovered when the man returned whom Tekwe had sent with tamales for his two men. He told us there was serious trouble among the coyotes (Huichols) who wished to return home but didn't dare to because of the Yaqui rear-guard. After translating this, Tekwe added, "They are twelve against two," and spat contemptuously on the ground.

As I was rather tired of this constant wrangling with the Huichols and being perhaps a little afraid of them becoming a greater burden, I told Tekwe to send for his two men and let the other Indians go. A little later we heard two shots, and when the Yaquis returned, both of them carried two carbines. The one explained that he had seen his dead brother's gun in the hands of a "coyote," and it made him mad and took it from him, as well as the gun from the man who tried to stop him. The Yaqui seemed quite pleased because his brother had been revenged from his point of view.

After giving Jose and the Cora scout a good rest, they returned to Bolaños to see if it was feasible for us to by-pass the village in the daytime without being too conspicuous and if not, how to do it at night, but above all get news of the federals. It was late in the afternoon when they departed, and we were down to the last of the reserve rations which were issued to men and horses. Morning came and there was no sign of rain, which I accepted as a good omen for the rains were due. The boys returned at noon and told us that a troop of federal cavalry had come from Chimaltitan while they were in a *cantina*. The federals talked a lot and mentioned that Tepic had fallen to the rebels who were now marching on Guadalajara, and that a large rebel force had crossed the Sierra del Nayarit to attack the federals in Chimaltitan who stood ready to move out.

Jose did not dare, he said, to order any tamales in front of the federal soldiers but managed to purchase some corn meal in a bag. Hearing this Pedro went out and picked two handfuls of leaves from a certain bush, crushed them between two stones, and mixed them with the water when making the corn-meal-dough. The dough was made into cakes by patting them between the hands, then baked by the fire. These small but rather thick tortillas tasted quite good, but we were hungry of course.

Our bellies were full with corn meal and water, but I was in a dilemma for there was nothing left to eat for man or beast. As something had to be done and I needed a lead or inspiration, Jose was asked to relate once more what the federals had said. When he had finished there seemed to be no doubt that the federals were under a nervous strain because of the "large" rebel force that had crossed the sierra, that their morale was at low ebb and their fighting spirit lacking.

It became quite obvious to me that hesitation and delay on our part would be fatal, and I decided to take advantage of the situation and try to bluff my way through by making a bold move against the federals. The idea was conveyed to all hands, and as no other suggestions came forth, we moved from the shelter of the river on to the road. The Cora scout was sent ahead to the village to "demand" food and shelter for "300 men," the advance-guard of the rebel army.

The Huichol shaman must have done his work well as the federal cavalry patrol evacuated the place immediately after sighting us and galloped off, with us after them. We halted at the south side of the village, fired a few shots for good measure, and then looked around for some corn for the horses and about two days ration of corn meal for the men. The people were friendly enough after receiving federal money for everything taken. Several of them told of the discontentment among the federal soldiers and that many desertions had taken place.

With the horses fed and several days' ration issued to the men, our next objective was Chimaltitan. To mislead the headman of Bolaños, he and the people were told that the rebel army had halted for awhile to allow the federals to retreat, as we did not wish to fight in the streets. They were all grateful.

Tekwe and Jose rode toward Chimaltitan about four o'clock in the afternoon and did not meet a single federal. All the local natives told the same story, "The regiment left the pueblo an hour ago and moved eastward into Zacatecas." When we entered the town, we found ten boxes of ammunition left behind from lack of transportation. As it didn't fit our carbines, the Yaquis had a certain amount of fun destroying the whole lot, and then we moved south.

Before we left, the shaman in charge of our "traders" turned up and told how one of his men had been taken prisoner by the federals, and requested that they too come with us, as they were afraid of what the federals might get out of their man by torture. I was forced to turn down the request as I was apprehensive of what the Yaquis might do to them, but gave him the last pack horse, now useless to us, and a handful of Carranza paper money as a present for a job well done. He returned home quite content.

Pedro had secured a guide, and we moved on in haste as I was afraid that the captured Huichol might tell everything about us to the federal commander. The guide was good and friendly to our cause. He informed us how the federals had moved east, instead of south, and that we had a good chance of getting to Tepic if we kept from the main routes. He thought that it would take us four to five days.

It took us six days to reach Plan de Barrancas because the rains came. In spite of the discomfort of boggy infested trails and roads, flooded creeks and rivers, the rain proved a blessing as it kept the federals in the villages or at least confined them to the main roads. But not far from Hostotipaquillo, about seventeen miles east of our destination, our forward scout advised us of a small federal cavalry patrol coming our way. As we could not move away from them, we took cover but remained mounted, as I wanted to avoid a clash at this time.

It didn't take long before twenty federals came in full view, and we could have wiped them out to the man as they had no scout or advance-guard. The Yaquis had been told of my intentions, and we moved out in the open, hoping they would turn and gallop off, but the unexpected happened. Our presence surprised the officer for he hesitated, then gave orders to dismount and deploy as if on a parade ground. Our ragged and tattered appearance had perhaps startled him, and his indecision brought about his undoing.

We had avoided the enemy for days as our only chance of getting through. We had sneaked away hungry and wet like thieves in the night several times to avoid a fight, but as this gallant young man insisted on combat, the signal was given. The Yaquis slid off their mounts automatically and were in among the bushes before the federals had dismounted. It was a one-sided skirmish which lasted only a minute or two. Finding themselves outflanked, the federals mounted and galloped toward the Santiago River, leaving two dead, one wounded and the officer a prisoner. He had turned to pick up a wounded man, but was pulled off his horse when he passed one of the Yaquis.

He was a handsome young blade and smart looking but was upset, naturally, and he kept on stroking his fine crop of hair, which made me ask if he was nervous. His reply was amusing even to the Yaquis when he sheepishly said, "I was told the

Yaquis, like the Apaches, were fond of collecting war trophies in the line of scalps." The wounded man had been treated by Pedro and was declared fit to walk and, as we could hardly bring these men along or shoot them, they were told to go back to their regiment. Before leaving they received some "important" information about the rebels. I told him how two large rebel forces were marching on Jalisco from Tepic, and that we were a scouting patrol of the left wing of the army. Little did I know that I had hit the nail on the head, for two columns were actually advancing, but this I did not know until a day or so later.

The morning following our arrival at Plan de Barrancas we moved to Cacalutan, a short distance in the west, but Pedro and Tekwe continued southward to Ixtlan to try and contact the cavalry. Pedro returned at noon and reported meeting two rebel scouts operating fom Ixtlan on foot. They reported that General Blanco was somewhere near Ixtlan and that General Obregon was moving his infantry up close behind the cavalry. Tekwe had continued on to report our whereabouts and safe return. He turned up the next morning and reported talking to Acosta and delivering all we knew of the enemy. The trail he had taken from Ixtlan was very bad, and he suggested we move along the trail south of Nochitiltic River, then across the mountain to Jomulco.

We reached Ixtlan or Iztlan (Where there is obsidian) a day later, and it was a pleasure to see Acosta and also to get a change of clothing and something to eat, as corn meal and water, day after day, is a tiresome dish. We couldn't shoot anything for the pot for fear of being discovered, as the country east and southeast of the Huichol territory swarmed with federals. They may have been irresolute at times, because of jumpy nerves, and lackadaisical in their pursuit of us, but they were there and we could have lost more than our scalps if caught.

Blanco and Acosta kept on asking questions of the Indians in the sierra, their feelings toward us and would they make good soldiers. I advised them not to waste any more time on the Huichols, but did recommend them as excellent trackers and scouts, but suspicious by nature.

When I visited our outposts around Ixtlan, I came on an almost level plain on which stood hundreds of mounds, some of them fifteen to twenty feet high. It seemed to be a grave yard of a lost people, but there was no time to investigate as we were on the move.

IX

Our stay in Ixtlan, after our return from Huichol country, was short-lived as the push on Guadalajara was about to be launched. It was, therefore, never understood why the cavalry was pulled back to Ahuacatlan (Where there are aguacates). It was a gloomy kind of place, but we soon moved eastward again in two columns — one toward Magdalena, the other on San Marcos. Both places were in the State of Jalisco and occupied after a number of skirmishes.

General Blanco, with the 1st Brigade at Magdalena, moved forward and captured Tequila. Acosta and I, with the 2nd Brigade, took Ahualulco (Surrounded by hills). We met stiff resistance at both these important towns. The defense did not, however, seem coordinated as it lacked intercommunication as well as spirit. The federals had to give ground and we followed cautiously at their heels, for they were in considerable numbers.

We returned to the captured town, and found that our scouts had located the enemy at Grendain, a place east of Tala, and estimated his strength at about 4,000 men, eighteen field-guns and a number of machine-guns. At La Venta, west of Guadalajara, there was another federal force of about 4,000 men, with eleven field-guns and a great number of machine-guns.

Due to the comparatively close proximity of the enemy, and being somewhat uncertain as to the discipline of the newly formed 3rd Brigade which had been brought up, I took Pedro, Tekwe and Lopez as my aides and left for Teuchitlan to make a surprise round of the outposts early in the morning of June 1. We had a squadron at Hacienda Refugio, and there to my horror, the outpost, all members of the 3rd Brigade, were having a *fiesta* and were dancing to the tune of a guitar at 12 noon. Their carbines were carelessly stacked against a wall some distance away from the *patio* on which they were dancing with some women. They had no outposts and the vedettes had moved in from their advance position to take part in the fun.

There was nothing else to do but to remove the captain in command and appoint the first lieutenant in his place. When we went out to place the new pickets, we ran into an enemy squadron coming along the road without scouts or advance-guard. Pedro, who had been running on foot a few hundred yards ahead, spotted them and gave the pre-arranged danger signal.

316

The enemy was taken by surprise when we opened fire. They dismounted in good order and opened fire in our direction, but it was erratic and ineffective as we were under good cover. Pedro, sitting alone behind a knoll, also out of sight, did a fine thing when he opened fire on the enemy flank at a range not exceeding fifty yards. The federals, thinking themselves in an ambush, mounted in haste, leaving several killed and wounded behind. We suffered no casualties, but I wondered what would have happened to the hundred rebels, dancing a mile behind, if we hadn't come along that morning, or if Pedro had not opened fire from his lone position. Our little party of seven might quite easily have been lost.

After this lucky skirmish the men were posted and we continued the round. Eventually we came to Tala, where there should have been an outpost and two outlying pickets, but there wasn't a soul in sight, and a strong force of the enemy was within six miles. As we were tired and the horses all in, I decided to take a chance and remain there for the night. This might have been foolish perhaps, but one gets a little indifferent when dead tired.

Pedro and Tekwe, always careful, arranged for a very inconspicuous little hut in the middle of a row of houses in the outskirts of the village. The horses were placed in another hut-like structure in the rear of us and given something to eat. Lopez obtained a large bowl of brown beans (*frijoles*) as if by magic, from out of nowhere, and then went to stay with the horses. Pedro went out and came back with some clothes into which he changed. When he was finished, he looked like a local Peon-Indian and not at all like the proud scout that he was. Then we all laid down for a much needed rest.

I woke up with a start at about midnight. Voices could be heard through the half open door, and then a great number of mounted men came past with a battery of guns and limbers. Pedro could be seen dimly outside talking to an officer. He came in a few minutes later, leaving the door carelessly half ajar but said nothing until the troops had passed. Then he closed the door and began to mimic his meeting with the federals. He bowed to me in a servile kind of manner and spoke in a meek tone, "No, Sir, I have not seen any of the ruthless, murderous rebels and if your Excellency will take the road to the left, it will lead to good water for a camp." He had directed them toward our main column, but the officer went in the opposite direction which had been anticipated by this wily Indian. There never was a more cunning and intelligent scout and friend than Pedro, the Tarahumara shaman-doctor.

It had been my intention to ride south from Tala to Ahuizculco early on June 22 as we had some troops there, but I changed the direction to visit Hacienda Buenavista, where Captain Cordines had a squadron, not far from the La Vega railroad siding, some twelve miles southeast of Ahualulco. Tekwe was sent to Colonel Acosta with a report on what we had seen so far.

I had contemplated remaining at La Vega for an extended reconnaissance, but left the place suddenly without any reason, a hunch perhaps, and proceeded to my headquarters at Teuchitlan, two to three hours ride to the north. After about thirty minutes on the way we heard the tooting and grinding of brakes of railroad cars and moved up under cover of a hill to have a look. There to my amazement stood nine long trains full of federal soldiers on the tracks. They had no advance-guard, rear or flank-guard and no scouts, which was lucky for us. The trains had stopped in front of us, and some cars were not 500 yards from our position.

After a careful scrutiny I estimated the enemy strength to be about 6,000 men, and counted fourteen field-guns on flat-cars. As the federals were making hasty preparations for disembarking some horses, I signalled to Pedro and Lopez to move away to our mounts. Then I noticed a man walking towards us carrying something on his shoulder. It looked like a tripod and I presumed he was a signaler. When he was about 200 yards away, Lopez could not resist the temptation and took a pot-shot at the man, and he fell. As this was more than I had bargained for, we rushed to our horses and left the area as fast as they could carry us.

The strong federal force in this locality worried me not a little for it had cut off our outposts at Refugio, Ahuizculco and Buenavista, but this was not too late to remedy if we could get back to the division in time. The ride back to Teuchitlan was not so easy, for the enemy had gotten off the train and fanned out in all directions. We had remained too long on the hill watching them, and the shot which bowled over the signaler, no doubt, accelerated their movements.

We returned late and found to our discomfort that the town had been abandoned and Blanco had moved out and bivouacked a few miles away. After feeding man and beast from what we could find, the three of us continued to the rebel camp without any trouble. Tekwe, always thoughtful, had a fine Indian stew waiting for us.

The camp was soon full of activity. Extra scouts were sent out and the outposts doubled. An Indian scout was also sent to each of the outposts telling them to hold on if surrounded, but to pull back if they could, and that assistance would be sent if possible.

Due to faulty intelligence and poor reconnaissance by some of the new scouts, our outposts, scattered far and wide, became sitting-ducks for a vigilant enemy between them and us. As speed was necessary, I took the 2nd Cavalry and moved out early in the morning of June 23 to try to extricate those who might be left alive.

When we approached Hacienda Refugio, a sharp musketry fire was heard, and we soon learned that the little force was surrounded by a federal regiment. We had 100 men inside. The hacienda was well built and easy to defend, but I knew that our men were short of ammunition. Pedro and Tekwe who had been out scouting, returned and reported that the federals did not bother one side of the building but kept on attacking the other three sides. This seemed very strange as it appeared as if the federals wanted our men to escape, which seemed fantastic. The thought became so fixed in my mind, however, that I sent a camouflaged Indian scout into the hacienda with orders for them to try and come out that way. This was done because I did not wish to force the issue by attacking the federals, as we had two more outposts to relieve. After awhile it was almost funny to see our men galloping out, one man after another, while the federals kept on firing as if their lives depended on it on the other three sides. It was a most ridiculous situation unless, of course, the federal commander had a soft spot for us.

Every man got away except for the four dead left in the building. When we closed in to protect the flanks of our escaping men, my horse, a present from Blanco, was wounded badly and had to be shot. Due to this incident, which halted our advance for a minute, we discovered an officer and twelve federal soldiers sitting in hiding behind a wall and captured all of them without a shot. While interrogating the young subaltern, he told me, among other things, that the federals had a civilian foreigner among them. He had questioned several officers if they had heard of a *gringo* serving with the rebels.

As I was the only foreigner besides Major Kloss, who was a German and never referred to as a *gringo,* I naturally became curious, but we had work to do. Since the federals attacking the outpost seemed friendly and did not pick a quarrel over our intrusive action, which would have riled many a commander, I decided to send the thirteen prisoners back to the federals. Before doing so I gave the officer a piece of paper with my name on it for the foreigner in their midst. The men were taken to the other side of the hacienda and there, carrying a white flag for safety, we let them go when in sight of their comrades. By doing this I felt we had evened the score a little bit at least. Pedro grunted an approval of the action, and Tekwe said, "We have saved twelve cartridges as we could not have taken these dismounted men with us." We lost eight killed and some wounded at this place, but it was the most friendly encounter with the federals during the entire war.

As there was no time to spare, we continued to Buenavista, where the enemy had our men surrounded. The federals were so busy trying to dislodge our patrol that it was easy to dismount and move up close. Our attack in their rear was sudden and unexpected, and they broke away immediately. When the 1st Squadron, which had remained mounted, charged their flank, it knocked them off balance and it became a rout. They left forty-six dead and twenty-eight wounded behind.

We had another outpost of eighty men to relieve at Ahuizculco, which a local scout had reported was under siege by some 200 federals. Time was becoming a serious factor as the place was about ten miles away, and the outpost was short of ammunition and food and might be forced to surrender. The scout, I was told, was a very reliable man, and as there wasn't time for my own scouts, we pushed on, dismounted and moved in for the attack with one squadron in reserve. When we closed in, it became obvious that the enemy was in much greater numbers than reported. They had nearer 2,000 than 200 men.

We were hurled back by well placed troops and caught in a strong enfilade fire which was most uncomfortable. I signaled the retreat, and in the melee which ensued I lost another horse, but managed, with the aid of Tekwe, to pick up a frightened riderless animal.

We were forced to withdraw and reform our scattered men and horses, worn out by constant traveling and too little to eat. During the pause thus created, Pedro brought a blindfolded man dressed as a peon who had requested to see the gringo *jefe*. The man, obviously a soldier dressed as a servant surprised me when he handed over a note on which was written:

"Dear Thord-Gray: The rebel cause is doomed, come over to the federal side before it is too late, I will guarantee your safety. Bradstock."

In chapter one I mention having met this man in the German Club in Shanghai October 1913, when he and von Trotta practically goaded me into coming to Mexico by their derogatory remarks about the rebels. He also made me a bet that the revolution would be over and lost before my putting feet on Mexican soil. This note confirmed my previous suspicion that he was a British agent, as an American would hardly be able to join the federals while the U.S. Army was occupying Veracruz.

As this message from the federal lines could easily be misconstrued, I told Pedro and Tekwe of its contents. Pedro was much upset and asked, "What do you intend to do?" Tekwe wanted to shoot the man before he could see how weak our men were. When questioned, the messenger was quite open and said the federals were convinced the rebels had been pushed into flight, and the federals were about ready to eat. Hearing this, I answered my companions by ordering the messenger under a Yaqui guard and the entire force into skirmishing lines and counter-attacked suddenly.

The move was most effective for it took them by surprise. Not only did our outpost manage to break through, but the federals, not knowing our weakness, withdrew toward the outskirts of the town. We, glad to get a rest, turned and bivouacked a few miles away to lick our wounds, but no fires were allowed. Our total losses in freeing the three outposts were forty-six killed, 112 wounded and thirty-three missing, but we were lucky to get out at all.

One of our patrols returned that evening from south of Buenavista bringing a mule wagon with twenty federal rifles and about 2,000 rounds of ammunition, found under the altar of a small church. It is necessary to explain perhaps that the rebels were methodically searching every church for hidden guns, and we found rifles by the thousands, machine-guns and vast quantities of ammunition hidden in crypts, under and behind altars, intended to kill Peons and Indians, because they asked for land. This antagonized the people and had a great deal to do with the confiscation of much of the Church properties later, as well as the demand for the separation of Church and State.

At three o'clock in the morning of June 24, the scouts reported a federal force of about 1,800 men with six field guns moving in our direction. We saddled and moved away toward Teuchitlan, but the well mounted enemy caught up with our tired mounts and forced us into a defensive action. To preserve our ammunition, the men got orders to fire only when the federals came very close.

The fight lasted for about three hours. They pushed us to the limit. Then there was a sudden lull in the fighting. We were in a tight place, and it seemed inevitable that the federals would attack again, as we were practically at their mercy. Then, to my surprise, eight federals came out in the open carrying a white flag. As only a moment previously, I had noticed federal troops movements on both our flanks, and fearing a trick so often used by the federals in the past, I was about to give warning when the men, remembering the hundreds of their comrades dead for accepting such surrender in the past, opened fire, and not one federal escaped.

Shortly after this unpleasant incident, the federals withdrew without any apparent reason other than the two feeble counter-attacks we had made, or perhaps, because of the good marksmanship of the veterans of the 2nd Cavalry. When they departed, I thought it another trick, but was glad to see them go and took advantage of the peculiar situation by pulling the men out in the opposite direction as fast as we could. It was a distressing looking hejira of exhausted men that marched by me, some of them dismounted carrying their wounded, tired, hungry and thirsty, but not a word of complaint — it was a fine bunch of men.

A local peon rebel sympathizer guided us through a difficult terrain to a safe place away from roads and paths some miles from Teuchitlan. There was an uncomfortable, damp, cold wind from the north, but fires could not be allowed. It was unlikely though that the federals would try to follow us for the place was easily defended. Besides, government troops hardly ever left the main roads and the comforts of a town or village.

We had been almost at the mercy of the federals, but their commander did not have the guts to follow up his success, and as good cavalry leaders are born with the gift of daring in the pursuit, we thanked our lucky stars that this commander was not one of them. Our casualties in this fight were fourteen killed, twenty-two wounded, and forty horses put out of action. I felt deeply the loss of my Tarahumara friend, Jesus, who dropped when a shell fragment hit him in the back as he was handing me a water bottle. His last words were those of sound advice, "Hurry, *Jefe,* I know the color of this blood, I can't live long. Get out of here quickly." These words, I think, hastened my retreat to a safer place after he died a few seconds later.

Pedro volunteered to run as a messenger to Blanco with the latest information on the enemy. In my note I urgently requested two regiments to be sent to San Ignacio Refugio by four o'clock next morning, and to be prepared to take back the badly mauled 2nd Regiment for rest and replacement.

Colonel Acosta, acting division commander, came with reinforcements during the morning of June 25, and it was a pleasure to see him and the supplies. We did not get all that was asked for but almost. He brought the first regiment of the 2nd Brigade and 200 replacements for the 2nd Regiment, also 300 remounts and some ammunition in a mule-wagon. No Red Cross supplies of any kind, except a box of bandages, but he brought several mule-carts for the wounded and enough medicaments to treat them.

It was a pleasure to watch Acosta's bright and eager face when told of the engagement of the day before. He was itching to come with us to Teuchitlan, which I had orders to take before nightfall. As the 2nd Regiment had to be reorganized, new men placed in different squadrons, and many promotions made, we moved to a more suitable place to carry out this work and let the men rest a few hours.

PLATE XI

Rebels by train, 1913-1914.

PLATE XII

Execution of spies and traitors.

The column moved early in the afternoon toward Teuchitlan, some six miles distant and defended, we understood, by about 600 federals. Just after we had reached a place called La Labor, our scouts and advance-guard contacted enemy outposts of some strength, who seemed inclined to dispute our right-of-way and opened fire. Being well placed and under good cover, they managed to do some damage; we lost a number of men in a matter of minutes.

Our flanking movement, which had been under way for some time, completed their maneuvers and the outpost of twenty-five men was annihilated. Then we continued carefully and came without opposition to within sight of Teuchitlan. The scouts combed the town and reported they could not see any federals. Two squadrons were dismounted and went on a house to house search; they came across some scared people, but no federals.

As this looked unnatural and much like a trap, especially as the people were afraid to answer questions, we occupied the southeastern edge, near the fork of two creeks, with two squadrons as a second reserve. A double line of scouts were sent out, followed by echelons of squadrons of the 1st regiment; then came two squadrons in reserve to support our far flung flanks.

We moved north and northwestward. When about three miles out of town we ran into a substantial federal force, which evidently was waiting to surprise us in the town itself after dark. We did not attack at once but fanned out for the encircling movement. It was rough going, and the enemy held their ground stubbornly until the "Dragon's Wings" were closing in on their flanks; then they left in a hurry but in good order, with, however, twenty-four dead and eighty-one wounded in the field. We lost comparatively few as the nature of the ground was in our favor — thirteen killed and twenty-nine wounded.

We returned to Teuchitlan for something to eat, leaving a squadron as an outpost where the enemy had camped and left some food before evacuating the place in a hurry. Later the brigade bivouacked in a safer place outside of the town. During the questioning of a captured officer, he intimated it had been common talk among the federals for some time of the strange and sudden appearance of military strategy in the midst of rebel guerrilla tactics.

It was a good thing we did not remain in Teuchitlan during the night of June 25, as the enemy, heavily reinforced, began an encircling movement of the town. As it happened, it would not have made much difference for the men were aroused at 3 a.m., to be ready to march at 4:30 a.m. We moved out silently and escaped the federal trap, but had to fight a rear-guard action against a vastly superior force which pushed us unmercifully all day in a deplorable downpour of rain. Men and horses were dead beat, for it was necessary to return to guerrilla tactics to hold our own, but the spirit of the men was high.

After hours of fighting it dawned upon me that this was not the usual local matter but a final attempt by the federals to destroy the rebel army. The enemy was wonderfully equipped with machine-guns and an unlimited amount of ammunition supply. They also seemed better led than before, and appeared to have had a spiritual awakening, reborn, so to speak, to its former glory. Further, we were outnumbered four to one, and I began to wonder what was happening to Blanco and Obregon.

Many of our men were lost on June 26, but we hoped some were stragglers and might turn up later; there were sixty missing, besides the twenty-nine killed and sixty-one wounded. I'm not quite sure who should be blamed for this debacle, although from my point of view, they should not have ordered a short-manned brigade to deal with an Army Corps. When reviewing these men, and talking with many of them after making camp, most seemed in good spirits and had no complaints except that many of them wanted to make fires which could not be permitted, although we were camped by Hacienda de la Var.

The retreat from Hacienda de la Var

Late during the night of June 26, orders came from Blanco, at Hacienda La Cruz, to move early next morning and to avoid clashes with the enemy as Constitutionalists were concentrating all forces for a counter-attack. We broke camp in utter darkness long before dawn June 27, and reached Hacienda La Cruz in the pouring rain. The federals harrassed us a great deal by following close on our heels and inflicting much damage, but I couldn't help admiring the federal commander for his resourcefulness.

Men and horses were tired and weary, and several men in the 2nd regiment showed signs of mental, as well as physical, fatigue. This regiment should have been relieved two days ago at San Ignacio Refugio for several days rest since some were in bad shape and needed to be watched carefully. Some actually had reached the limit of their endurance and reaction was setting in. I was afraid these otherwise normally fearless men might become puling and sickly in reasoning. Under such conditions a man might throw down his rifle, run or surrender because of fear which is not really his, or from the need of sleep and food.

This was the condition of some of our men, and they were alienating others into discontentment and fear. This deplorable plight I had seen several times among the federal soldiers, but never before among our own. The 1st Regiment was in good shape and could have held the enemy back at several points, but I had orders to avoid all fighting if possible. It was, nevertheless, necessary to visit Hacienda Carmen, although a risky and long way around, to inform our troops of the enemy strength and our concentration for a counter-move. Our force lost nineteen killed, eight wounded and twenty-one missing during the retreat from Hacienda de la Var.

We left Hacienda La Cruz, June 28, after a good twenty-four hours rest for men and animals. Our destination was the town of Ameca, located south of Ahualulco, where we were supposed to be gathering a force of several brigades for a rear-attack on the enemy.

Not many miles from our starting point we sighted a considerable federal force, about a brigade, moving westward. As the enemy seemed to be intruding on our area, I took up position a few miles south of the village Santa Cruz, which halted their column. It was almost ludicrous for they looked at us for an hour and then returned eastward from whence they came. I could do nothing, for my orders were to avoid a fight. Due to this incident, and because the federals did not seem to wish to force a passage westward during daylight, we bivouacked for the night about four miles south of Santa Cruz to discourage them, I hoped, from attempting a westward movement at night. We arrived at Ameca in the morning of June 29 after a restful night, and found it one of the largest towns in the State of Jalisco.

The enemy, located some ten miles east of Ameca, had not changed position except for occupying Hacienda Buenavista. As I was not quite sure of some of our new scouts, I took a squadron for reconnaissance eastward, and was forced into quite a tussle with a large federal patrol, which was too inquisitive for my liking. It was driven off, but only after I had received aid from one of our other patrols.

Blanco, Acosta and I had a happy reunion which was celebrated with a bottle of good Burgundy produced by the chief. I was quite surprised and disappointed at the conference that followed because there was no definite plan of action and so no orders. There was talk of moving forward over a mountain trail for a rear-attack on the federals, but there was nothing comprehensible as to our next move, and I had a feeling we were detained purposely by G.H.Q., for some unknown reason. While sitting there I remembered the resourceful federal commander who had chased me into Hacienda La Cruz only a few days before, and I wondered if we had lost the initiative and were actually on the defensive.

The indecision of the high command almost made

me nervous, and since we were inviting disaster by sitting still, and not knowing what the enemy was up to, I suggested a reconnaissance in force eastward to show our colors, and offered to take it. Blanco seemed quite keen on the idea, and was apparently relieved, for he told me to take any and all troops required.

Thus it came about that I, with the 1st and 2nd Cavalry, moved out of camp to try and clear the neighborhood of inquisitive scouts and enemy patrols. Everything went well, but just before noon of July 6, we had a set-to with a strong federal force at a hacienda. We managed to beat them back after several hours of severe fighting, but it was a poor victory as we lost forty-two killed and many wounded. The enemy left eighteen dead behind, and we captured twenty-two prisoners. From one of the two officers taken prisoner we learned that the federal brigade we had tussled with had been sent to feel out our strength, so our losses were not wholly in vain.

It was quite late that afternoon when General Blanco arrived with a brigade and made a surprise visit. He presented me with a set of shoulder-tabs, with two stars on each, being that of a lieutenant-colonel, and apologized for the rank not being that of a full colonel.

A jaunt into Guadalajara

When we parted for the night, Blanco told us he had orders to "keep out of or away from Guadalajara, to operate some distance south of the city, and drive the enemy out of Hacienda Castillo." The cat was out of the bag. We had been detained by

Obregon — or perhaps Serrano — who did not wish Blanco to capture the second largest city in Mexico. He wanted the honor for himself, of course.

The following morning we were bivouacked about ten miles southwest of Guadalajara, and Acosta and I were discussing Obregon's instructions for Blanco to stay out of the city. Pedro had just returned from a visit inside the town and reported that the federals were relying on their forces, now moved to Orendain, some ten miles west of Guadalajara, to keep the rebels at bay. They were, nevertheless, ready to pull out at the first sign of a general advance by the rebel scum. At this point, Acosta, who had an adventuresome soul, looked at me with a grin from ear to ear, and I presumedly did the same, for then and there we decided to have a look at Guadalajara.

Pedro informed us of the terrain, the roads into the city, and where the outpost had been that day. As a kind of excuse within ourselves, we both agreed that scouting with a strong patrol might well lead to some valuable information of the enemy, and with a squadron of the 2nd Regiment we moved toward Guadalajara with four mounted scouts ahead. Nearing the city, Pedro dismounted and ran ahead, as was his habit when on a dangerous mission. He was dressed as a local peon, and turned now and again to signal "danger," or to summon us by gesture to come on.

We had been advancing carefully, but before we realized it we were inside Guadalajara without meeting a federal soldier. We had changed our formation inside the city into column of fours with an advance-guard of four men, but these men were behind Pedro. Everything was going smoothly when we ran into a federal patrol of about twenty men, who turned and galloped off at the sight of us. We halted, of course, to investigate as we did not wish to be caught inside the city, but as the enemy seemed to be scared, we remained, when suddenly trumpets and bugles began to sound the alarm ahead of us.

Acosta nodded to me and we were turning around to gallop away, when Pedro came running with the information that the garrison was evacuating the town in haste. They had taken our squadron as the advance-guard of the rebel army, and were retreating eastward. It was then decided to show our strength and we began to march the squadron up one street, and down another, but leaving the center of the town severely alone. People, the common people, were running ahead and alongside us shouting: "The Carranzistas are here!" We also noticed that among them were some extremely pretty girls and very good looking young women, which made the trip rather pleasant.

The situation was incredible, almost ludicrous. Pedro and Tekwe went ahead toward the center of the city when we found the enemy had left, and we after them. In less than an hour after frightening the federal patrol, we had shown ourselves all over the western section of the city in a display of open contempt for the federals. When almost in the center of the town we remembered Obregon's order, "Stay out of Guadalajara!" As we had seen enough, we turned southward immediately and were soon in the open southwest of San Pedro, and the fun was over.

Acosta couldn't hold it back and told Blanco of our escapade, and he being a good sport, admitted he would have done the same if given the chance, but added, "I presume you realize you have given Serrano a good excuse to act against all of us if this leaks out!"

The following day, which was July 8, while we were jockeying for positions not far from Hacienda Castillo we received news that Obregon had attacked the federals at Orendain, driven them eastward, and had occupied the city of Guadalajara with a division that afternoon. It was the capital of the State of Jalisco, with a population of about 118,000.

The Hacienda Castillo fight

Our advance-guard met the federals at Hacienda Castillo, some two hours ride southeast of Guadalajara. Blanco dismounted the newly formed 3rd Brigade, mostly made up of Jalisco men, and sent them forward to dislodge the enemy. Before they left, I begged Blanco to send a regiment around each flank of the place, but for once he was stubborn or perhaps he believed the federals to be on the run after the fall of Guadalajara.

The 3rd Brigade moved forward in three waves, in good order, and came quite close to the hacienda defenses without much or any opposition. Blanco, Acosta and myself were on a ridge watching the advance which was now less than 200 yards from the enemy lines, and not a shot had been fired. The silence was unnatural as well as foreboding, and I did not like it at all. Then some one shouted "The

335

federals are surrendering," and there, sure enough, was a large white flag plainly seen waving from the hacienda in front of the rebel lines. Blanco got up from his prone position and gave me a good slap on the shoulder with the remark, "You and your flank movements." For some reason, which was never explained, our men halted automatically as if by an order and there they stood, when Hell was let loose.

A dozen machine-guns and some 2,000 riflemen opened up and several field-guns let go with grape-shot at a range not much more than a hundred yards; the second line was about a hundred yards behind the first. The brigade reeled like a drunken man under the impact, turned, and ran in disorder for any place of shelter,

The federal commander seemed to know less about us than we of them, for when the brigade broke in flight, he counter-attacked with an infantry regiment. He must have had cold feet as he soon recalled them behind the walls of their defenses, which was our good luck.

Seeing the debacle, Blanco, who was a little confused, turned to us, and we ordered the 1st Brigade forward to hold the enemy while the 3rd Brigade got out. The 1st was made up of many Yaqui veterans from Sonora and Sinaloa, and we knew every man and their families and trusted them. Acosta took the 1st Regiment, and I the 2nd. The 3rd Regiment was to remain saddled but hidden behind a ridge to await orders. We advanced quickly through the broken and retreating ranks of the 3rd Brigade, and found much comfort in seeing a number of them turn, and come forward with us. The artillery gave us quite a dusting, but somehow their shrapnel seemed ineffective as they burst too high, and there were many duds.

Acosta moved his men to the right in a flanking move, and I did the same on the left as arranged, and found some cover about 500 feet from the hacienda, where we regrouped. We got a signal through to one another, and the two regiments advanced simultaneously into the open for the final assault. Acosta charged in splendid style and no regiment of the Guards could have done better. The 2nd Regiment, more in the open on the left, tried an extended flank movement but failed, due to the terrain and lack of inter-communication.

As luck would have it, the enemy seemed in a jumpy mood, as we could see some of them leaving their positions and moving to the rear, as well as from the hacienda, more or less in disorder. Therefore, I gave up any further attempt at a flank movement and went straight into their defenses. Some grape-shot came against us, which was most unpleasant, but instead of raking the ground in front of us most of them went high. As we came closer to the hacienda defenses, most of the federals were leaving, but some hung on. When we made the final dash, the federals broke and scattered widely in full retreat. They seemed to dissolve into nothing in their haste to escape.

When inside, I met Acosta, and he could not refrain from giving me a Mexican *abrazo* in sheer joy of the success. The charge from two sides was sudden, determined and unexpected by the federal commander. He had seen the failure of the 3rd Brigade, and was caught inside the hacienda, having a drink with some staff officers, not knowing what was going on outside, but celebrating the repulse of the rebels. The commander and those with him were all killed, for no one could save them. Two of his companions, later found to be colonels, saw us enter and tried to escape to the roof of the fortress-like building, but were dropped before getting far.

The federal casualties came to: two generals (Jose M. Mior, and Pena, both killed); three colonels, three lieutenant colonels, six majors, thirty-seven officers of other ranks, and 320 men—all killed. We took 340 prisoners. We lost 112 killed and over 200 wounded. Part of our booty consisted of: five field-guns, four machine-guns (eight machine-guns got away), over 300 rifles, large quantities of ammunition, and 400,000 pesos in silver and federal notes.

The great number of killed in proportion to those wounded may have been due to the close range in the final assault. The great difference in the casualties between the attacking force and the defenders came about when the federals began to evacuate, and were knocked down like nine-pins, and, no doubt, some of those remaining were not allowed to surrender in the heat of the moment. The high patriotic spirit of our men had a great deal to do with the success when, again, the federal soldiers were imbued with defeatism. If not, the three thousand federals would never have been driven from their strong position, throwing away their rifles, abandoning their field-guns and officers because of two dismounted cavalry regiments, less than a third of their strength, and without artillery support.

Here was a wonderful chance for the cavalry, and I have never ceased wondering why General

Blanco did not order the 3rd regiment into the fray, as he must have seen everything from his position. Why he refused to outflank the enemy was also beyond my comprehension, when it was not only safe and easy, but the obvious thing to do. Blanco was a fine and brave soldier, but he wasn't himself that day.

Before Acosta and I were about to leave the hacienda, a peon informed us of a concealed room in which some people were hiding. He led us to a large room with some old tapestry hanging on the walls. Pushing one of these aside, he exposed a well-hidden door leading to a very narrow but well furnished room. Here we found, not high federal officers as expected, but three women: one of them was a most stunning looking young woman about twenty-two years of age, the oldest was her aunt, a nice looking old girl, the third a Mexican girl, evidently their companion.

When interrogated we found that the girl and her aunt were of a German-French mixture. They said they could not get back to Mexico City because of the revolution. When this was all over, Acosta said, "They are all yours, Gray, do what you can for them," and moved on. As the men with me had not eaten anything for some time, and the hacienda was stocked with food for men and animals, I invited the ladies to eat with me. Before I left the place, an hour later, we had become quite friendly, and the ladies had a permit to enter Guadalajara. Leaving a small escort for the ladies, I was on my way, but wondering why these people had not moved on to Mexico City long before our attack which might, however, have been unexpected by the federals.

A good haul

Immediately after the wounded had been attended to and the men had eaten, we fanned out as usual with a great number of mounted men to mop up stray federals that might attempt to reform. At one point we noticed a buckboard-type of covered wagon drawn by four fine horses coming towards us. When the driver spotted us as rebels, he swerved around and galloped away as if possessed by the Devil himself and we, the "Devils", after him.

Thinking that someone of importance was inside the carriage, I called to a Colonel Zanches to send a troop after us in case of need, and the chase was on. It was interesting and fun, but it took us an hour to pull him up, and then we discovered, not a high ranking general, but something much better, as it contained six boxes packed with silver pesos and Federal Bank Notes.

The ten of us had gone too far eastward, however, and were suddenly hemmed in from two sides by strong enemy patrols. The driver was knocked off his seat by Tekwe, who took up the reins and began to drive, as he probably had never driven before, back toward Hacienda Castillo. Our horses, as well as those with the wagon, were tired, and when the enemy was about to close in for the kill, a squadron of the 2nd Regiment appeared. The federals, not knowing how many more were coming, turned and galloped away. When the loot was counted, it came to 750,000 pesos in silver and bank notes. After taking care of the dead, wounded and prisoners, the division marched into the town of San Pedro, about three miles south of Guadalajara, during the evening of July 9, for a much needed rest.

Evidently the routing of the federals at Hacienda Castillo, and the wonderul work done by Obregon's columns during the last few days, seemed to have cleared the State of Jalisco from any real or serious opposition by the enemy, for a time at least.

The Cavalry enter Guadalajara

The 1st Cavalry Division moved into Guadalajara during the morning of July 10 for a rest and found, to its surprise, the decent billets were arranged for in advance, the rebel army was improving. It was also pleasing to see how the common man in the street was in sympathy with the revolutionaries, for hundreds of them were standing about that evening trying and hoping to join our ranks.

During dinner that night, Acosta brought a clipping from some American newspaper which lambasted the rebels terrifically for what it called, "unnecessary destruction of the Mexican railroads," but there had been much such criticism from the same quarter. We did, of course, tear up the railroad tracks, burn, and blow up bridges, but only as a military necessity or, on occasion, to save ourselves from being hung in the nearest tree.

In the early part of 1914 we were often caught on one side of a river armed with bows, arrows, machetes and pointed hardwood sticks as spears, and were forced to destroy the bridge to survive and to halt, if only temporarily, the well equipped federal force against us. However, as soon as we received guns and ammunition, this practice was discontinued, but the federals, now scared, destroyed the railroads and constantly so to stop our advance. They were poor sports and would not admit their work of destruction and placed the onus of their acts on the shoulders of the rebels, which falsehoods were often published in the American press.

During this second phase of the campaign, the rebels naturally did what they had been taught and outflanked the federals whenever possible, disrupted the tracks and blew up culverts behind them. But this was done only to halt their retreat and to facilitate the destruction of the enemy as a potential force. Critics should remember that the destruction of enemy communications is one of the chief objectives of a commander whenever possible.

The first serious opposition we ran up against in Guadalajara was the Mexican Church, as the clergy were against us and instructed the people to have nothing whatsoever to do with the Constitutionalists. The priests forbade their followers to swear allegiance to the rebel cause, but if they had already done so, they could, without punishment in the hereafter, repudiate such an oath.

The clergy suffered sometimes during our advance, not because they were priests, but because they interfered in the revolution by joining the forces against us and encouraged others to do the same. Some small units of Huerta's army seemed to have been made up exclusively of priests, actively fighting the freedom movement of the people—and all agrarianism.

X

A one-sided fight—Fighting around Mezcala, Ocotlan, San Jose, Poncitlan, La Barca, Tanhuato, Yurecuaro, Mirandilla, La Piedad, Irapuato, Hacienda Temaxcatio, Salamanca, Celaya, Queretaro, Coachite, San Juan Del Rio, and Tula

During the morning of July 12 some friendly natives reported a federal regiment at the south end of Lake Sayula (Where there are flies), some sixty or so miles to the south, and it was decided to push them back before they could interfere with our foraging parties now scouring the country. As the 3rd Brigade was made up mostly of green recruits from Tepic and Jalisco, I proposed to take one of the regiments to investigate, which would also serve as a training exercise for men and officers. Blanco agreed, and I also took Pedro, Tekwe and six Yaquis with me as a matter of course.

We reached Jocotepec on the western shores of Lake Chapala by what seemed to be rather winding trails and roads. As the lake looked fine for men and horses, we bivouacked close to it, but had not off-saddled before a trader from the town nearby came to peddle some fine looking serapes and sold them all. Pedro and his scouts went ahead to investigate beyond Zacoalco (Besieged: Shut-in) and returned during the late evening.

We moved early next morning. Pedro went with the scouts, and Tekwe with the advance-guard, to guide these rather green recruits in what to do. Just outside Zacoalco we met several of our carts coming from the south loaded with supplies. Their escort had not seen any federals. Tekwe was waiting for us at Uetiltique, a small place on the west side of Lake Sayula and, having seen no enemies, continued to scout around the Lake as far as Atoyac (Where there is an arroyo) and would return from there.

When we had camped on the south edge of Sayula, the town was put out of bounds, and the officers sent me a deputation requesting the withdrawal of the restrictions. This was refused, of course, and as an example the pickets and patrols around the camp were doubled, for this was war as well as a field exercise which these newly baked officers foolishly thought did not apply to them. When Pedro returned with the scouts, he reported seeing a number of officers in a *cantina* drinking heavily.

We were inside enemy territory and as discipline had to be brought home to these officers, the camp was aroused just after midnight. Eight officers were missing so we moved our camp to Los Puertes, on the east side of the Lake, with eight horses carrying empty saddles.

Two scouts returned at daybreak and reported a troop of enemy cavalry at Guzman, a good size town about twenty miles south of us. None of the absentee officers had turned up, so I decided to rest the horses until after the noon meal. Scouts were sent over the Sierra del Tigre, a local ridge, to observe enemy movements. At one o'clock in the afternoon two tired and bedraggled looking officers walked into camp and were placed under open arrest.

We were ready to move on Guzman at 2 p.m., when the scouts reported the federals had been reinforced by a squadron at Guzman. As we could not get behind the enemy without long marches and delay, we rode directly on the place by the road south.

My regiment was made up mostly of cowboys, who made good scouts, but they were bad at relaying information and always most inaccurate in estimating numbers of men at a distance. We moved out and I kept Pedro and Tekwe, with his Yaquis, with me for the time being. The column was halted on top of the Tiger Mountain divide, to investigate the terrain in front of us and get news from the scouts. Soon thereafter one of them came at top speed and reported that a federal squadron was coming along the road only about three or four miles away.

We were in a good location, put it lacked water, so we moved forward quickly to a position north of Lake Zapotlan (Where there are zapote trees), dismounted and took cover. The federals came along the road with no scouts and their advance-guard not fifty yards ahead of the main body, which was not a squadron, as reported by the scout, it was a regiment.

Our men, extended in a half-moon formation due to the nature of the ground, had orders to hold their fire until the front ranks of the enemy were within a hundred yards. The men did well. When they opened fire, it looked like wholesale murder. In their confusion, some of the enemy dismounted and tried to escape but were shot down before leaving the road. The rest turned and galloped back toward Guzman in a disorderly rout.

When it was all over, we counted ninety-one enemy dead, among them a lieutenant-colonel and two majors. We captured sixty-two wounded, among which were a colonel and three captains, besides sixty-nine wounded horses with saddles. As the federals did not have a chance to fire more than a few rounds, we suffered no casualties, which made this fight stand out as the most one-sided I have ever been in.

We returned to Sayula late that night with the wounded prisoners. The dead had been left, as we had no tools to bury them with. However, a messenger was sent to request the people at San Sebastian to do so, but the coyotes from Tiger Mountain had, no doubt, a fill that night.

As officers and men had done well, we camped in the same place as the previous night but without many restrictions. We left at daybreak for Atoyac and found six very dejected officers. They had obtained an ox-cart and followed us to Los Puertes and, finding us gone, continued to Atoyac. They were placed under open arrest, but I withdrew the charges against the two officers who had rejoined us by walking seven miles.

With the mission completed, I was keen to return to Guadalajara before the push on Mexico City had begun in earnest, and we started out at once. Due to the poor condition of the horses and extensive scouting eastward, we didn't get there before the following day, July 17.

Before the regiment was marched back to its brigade, I sent for the six officers under arrest. The insubordination was gone, and they were a sorrowful looking bunch standing there with just enough swagger left to be attractive. They were very young, and this was their first experience of war, so I dismissed the case and they left in jubilant spirit. I considered the trip well worth-while, if only for the sake of these young blades who had learned a lesson. They all expected a court-martial, which would have meant dismissal from the service or worse, and they were so keen to remain.

Acosta took me to dinner that night and treated me to some of the famous Guadalajara beer. During dinner he informed me of Gen. Huerta's resignation from the presidency on July 15; that he had appointed Francisco S. Carbajal provisional president, and then left the country with some of his generals.

After a few days training of new troops in Guadalajara, Acosta and I, with the 1st Brigade plus two squadrons, left the city in the afternoon of July 23 with orders to clear the road, and the town of La Barca, of the enemy. The place was located southeast of Guadalajara on the Lerma River, east of Lake Chapala. The 2nd Brigade was to follow, as our support, in about six hours time.

We met persistent and unexpected opposition by large patrols upon reaching the approaches of Mezcala, a town on the north shores of the lake. We had done over thirty miles, fought six severe skirmishes, and as the men and horses needed a rest we bivouacked at Mezcala late that evening. Our casualties were heavy as compared to the ten dead federals found along the road.

In a building, which we searched for spies, I noticed several fine looking jars, nicely decorated— they were all of Tarasco make. After a few hours rest, the federals forced us to move, and we found it difficult to get to Poncitlan due to the terrain and the stiff resistance, but we managed to reach Ocotlan before dawn July 24. Here we had the pleasure of surprising a federal outpost of 100 men fast asleep and obviously under the influence of *tequila* or other liquor. Two of the men escaped and galloped eastward to La Barca on the border of Michoacan (Country where people have fish).

In an attempt to prevent the enemy digging in and getting too firmly entrenched, we made a forced march on La Barca, but again met stiff resistance here and there, especially at San Jose. When we reached La Barca, we found to our surprise that it had been evacuated only shortly before and there was only a rear-guard remaining, which moved on after a skirmish. The people told us they had all gone to La Piedad, a town in Michoacan. We were most grateful to find La Barca abandoned, for the men were all tired and hungry, not to mention the poor horses. Our casualties during the day were heavy and many horses were killed.

A dispatch came that evening from General Blanco telling us to proceed to La Piedad and clear it of the enemy. In the order Blanco said, "There will not be much opposition," which turned out to be poor intelligence work on our side.

We remained in La Barca for several hours that night and were grateful for a square meal of good tortillas and excellent tamales. We broke camp at dawn on July 25 and moved toward Tanhuato, a town about half way to La Piedad.

It was almost a disaster at Tanhuato. The captain commanding the squadron of the advance-guard and scouts had evidently become careless, for he entered the town without the usual line of scouts and was ambushed in the center of the place. As luck would have it, I was riding with the leading squadron of the regiment behind the advance-guard. When we heard the firing, I extended into three waves, each of squadron strength, and entered the town.

When we reached the place where the advance-guard had been, it looked like a slaughter-house. In the confusion of the melee, I heard a thud, my horse sagged on his knees and fell before I could dismount. As gallant as any man could be, Tekwe, seeing what had happened, dashed up, dismounted and offered me his horse. About that moment Acosta came galloping with a squadron and as he pulled up alongside to help me, he was hit in the left arm.

When reinforcements arrived, the federal trumpets sounded the retreat, and firing ceased almost at once. A few minutes later we could see them galloping eastward. With our men scattered all over the town, and a whole squadron dead or dying in the street, we could not pursue. In fact, I was happy to see them go, as this could have been a major disaster for the 1st Brigade if the federals had had the guts to hold on to their perfect position.

They had cleverly concealed a regiment behind walls and in houses and had opened a deadly fire from only twenty feet away on the advance-guard which was riding through town in close formation —without scouts. The captain in command was one of the first to fall, which was best for him. He was a childhood friend of General Blanco, with whom he used to go hunting as a boy. Hence the promotion. The enemy left only a few dead behind a wall. When Acosta's arm was bandaged, I found it to be only a flesh wound and it looked clean.

We buried our dead, but left those badly wounded in a house and moved on to Yurecuaro, a short distance away to the northeast. We bivouacked on the south side of the town, but not before several skirmishes had taken place and the federals driven in the direction of La Piedad. In so doing they left many dead and wounded behind them in the field. We lost a number of men which made it a bad day for the 1st Regiment: we had lost ninety-two killed and sixty-one wounded, most of them seriously.

An urgent dispatch was sent Blanco requesting 150 men for replacement, remounts, ammunition, and some Red Cross supplies. We broke camp before dawn on July 26 and left Yurecuaro at a fast but cautious pace toward Mirandillas, a town about half way to La Piedad. Two squadrons were sent as far as Verduzco, where they were to turn east in the direction of Pandillo for a flanking as well as rear maneuver against Mirandillas.

About five miles west of our objective, the advance patrol cut off and captured an enemy outpost. Ordinarily, they would probably have not been allowed to surrender, but our men had strict orders to bring in prisoners for information. Not one of the three captured men responded to questioning, and they seemed to be devoid of any knowledge of military value, so were sent back with their guard for detention and further questioning later. After awhile the officer in charge of the troop informed me that one of the prisoners had offered to join the rebel ranks and at the same time had interrogated him on our strength, etc.

As many thousands of federal soldiers had come over to us in this manner, this was nothing unusual, but the officer added, "This man is dressed as a peon-soldier, but I think he is an officer in disguise." As we were short of men, we decided to try counter-espionage or a ruse. The officer was sent back with instructions to accept him in our service but also to drop careless hints of our strength, doubling our numbers and adding that two brigades were in reserve not far behind, then send him out with a patrol.

Acosta and I talked with the soldier, and there seemed to be no doubt that he was an officer, probably of field rank, who had precipitated his own capture. He tried to act dumb, almost dull-witted, but he made a slip eventually. When asked how many men the federals had at La Piedad he answered, "I do not know, but our column was four kilometers long while marching in close formation." This was no answer for a peon, and it was lucky for him that we needed his services and let him go on patrol. Shortly thereafter he disappeared and was last seen galloping to the federal lines. I am sure he thought us naive and simple creatures, and we may have been, but he served our purpose.

We met stiff resistance at Mirandillas, and a great deal of house to house fighting took place, besides encountering two nasty barricades constructed of carts and furniture in the street. The

351

enemy retreated suddenly from the center of the town without any apparent reason, as they were holding their own, and so we suspected a ruse. We managed with some difficulty to hold back our men, as I wanted to gain time for our two flanking squadrons to show up, and also to investigate the sudden withdrawal, we began a thorough house search.

When the federals noticed the great dust clouds created by the squadrons advancing on their rear-flank, they must have taken them for a much larger body of men, because they evacuated the town in such a hurry that they failed to notify forty men concealed inside houses that commanded a clear view up and down the street on which we would have come in the pursuit. When the men discovered this well arranged trap, and remembering the ambush at Tanhuato the day before, they shot every federal concealed inside the houses. Besides these, we found many dead federals in the streets and in the barricades and twenty-one wounded. We lost heavily. A great number of our horses were put out of action, but we found sixty-five good federal horses and saddles in a corral which made up for our losses.

After taking care of the dead and wounded at Mirandillas, every available man was rushed to La Piedad to prevent the enemy reforming. Before nightfall we faced the town from the west and the south. We had no artillery for a siege, and what was almost as bad, we could not even guess the strength of the federals inside the town. The captured prisoners thought they had a cavalry brigade, but were not certain. We had not seen a rancher all day, and as the country seemed to be empty of people, we figured they had gone into hiding.

When we arrived, we made a bluff demonstration of strength by maneuvering different units around for an hour in full view of the federals, then withdrew a few miles for a well earned rest. Long before dawn on July 27, we began our dismounted movements toward the La Piedad defenses. We could not surround the enemy, due to the Lerma River running east and north of the town; besides, we wanted them to have an avenue of escape as we were short-handed with scouts and patrols scattered in different directions, and one quarter of our men tied up as horse-holders. Acosta and I were usually optimistic before an operation of this kind, but this morning neither of us could look forward to it with any pleasure.

Severe street fighting began, as soon as the strong and well placed outposts had been driven back. There were some unpleasant looking barricades to overcome, and the corner to corner fighting was tough. The federals defended every place with an unusual tenacity, and when the outcome of the fight was in doubt, we doubled our efforts, in sheer desperation, and pushed on somewhat foolishly perhaps, but it paid.

The enemy, apparently convinced that we were vastly superior in numbers, began to give ground faster. At the end of seven hours of continuous house to house fighting, the federal bugles sounded and the firing tapered off. They rushed for their horses, well hidden behind some houses, and galloped off looking more like an undisciplined old type of Boer Commando than a brigade of regulars.

We did not try to pursue; we couldn't, because we had only two squadrons in readiness as the rest had dismounted and advanced on foot. We should never have been sent on this mission without guns and with at least two brigades.

When we tried to reform our ranks, many of the men were so tired they had fallen asleep where they had been standing when the federals left. Although tired, Acosta and I were forced to take turns scouting the road leading to Irapuato because we were never more vulnerable than at this moment. The enemy left a great number of dead and wounded behind in the streets and inside of houses. How many of these were not allowed to surrender no one will ever know. We lost over a squadron. The federals put up a good scrap, but when seriously opposed their hearts were not really in the game.

The booty was poor and did not justify our losses, as the suffering of the wounded was awful, and we had no medical supplies nor a doctor. Several of the wounded asked to be put out of their misery, and I was later told three of them were.

That evening we received 200 replacements and 200 remounts. In a wagon driven by eight mules we found some ammunition, but the Red Cross supplies found in the same wagon were not sufficient to dress our day's casualties. Acosta did not seem disturbed over his wound which was healing nicely.

Men and horses got a well earned rest that night and the following morning. We were all cheered up by the arrival of the 2nd and 3rd Cavalry Brigades just before we moved away from La Piedad. Gen. Blanco came immediately after his troops with some medical supplies, but still not half enough even for the severely wounded. He had, however, brought all he had.

I tried every trick in the bag to relieve the suffering of these staunch young men, and let Indian shamans and even witch-doctors go to work as it seemed all wrong to let them die by the dozen from lack of medical aid. We made "salt water" for washing of wounds, and it seemed better than the chewed tobacco juice which the Indians used. They also blew tobacco smoke on the wound, especially those shamans from Sonora and Sinaloa. They believed tobacco smoke to be very powerful medicine.

My friend Pedro, the Tarahumara shaman-doctor, was of inestimable value among the sick. Some of his cures, especially his herb cures, were excellent; they must have been for the men got better. Whenever he went out scouting, he invariably brought back bundles of medicinal herbs. For example, in the warmer places he picked a plant of the Spurge Family (genus *Ricinus*). He wrapped some of the leaves mixed with fat inside some other larger leaves and cooked them in hot ashes. The salve thus produced he rubbed on festered sores. His seemingly most effective medicine as an astringent for the cleaning of wounds came from a plant of the Composite Family (genus *Cacalia*). The plant is pounded to a mash, mixed with water and applied to the wound. Pedro also used the roots of this plant as a purgative, a cure which he strongly believed in for almost all sickness. He pounded or ground the roots of this plant into a fine pulp, mixed it with water, strained it and gave potions thereof. This remarkable shaman-doctor performed five major operations with his hunting knife and without any medicaments. One man survived, but the others would have died anyhow.

We left La Piedad before noon on July 28, leaving the wounded behind with a squadron. The 2nd Regiment formed the advance-guard, and as we had a great number of fresh remounts, we traveled fast and camped for the night a few miles southwest of Irapuato at nine o'clock that evening. As the 2nd was my own regiment, I went with them to clear the road for the division coming close behind.

Our advances, which we actually expected to be held up at every point of vantage, was comparatively peaceful, marred only by a few skirmishes in the mountain paths and when entering Penjamo, a town in the southwestern parts of the State of Guanajuato (Place of frogs), where four men were wounded. Information from the local ranchero indicated the enemy to be of division strength inside Irapuato, which some of us did not believe as the resistance along the road had not been more than from a regiment, at the most a brigade. The town was of good size with a population of about 21,000.

At 2 a.m., the following day, a squadron was sent some distance east of Irapuato, to clear the area of federal outposts and patrols. When this was done, they were to take up position and wait for orders. Should, however, the enemy evacuate the city in disorder, they were to charge and disperse them. Another squadron was sent west of the city with similar orders.

The 1st and 2nd Brigade moved forward and reached the outskirts at dawn, without much opposition. When the advance-guard met stiff resistance, the two brigades dismounted and attacked at daybreak. We found the federals well under cover of houses and inside buildings. Three large barricades blocked the streets in the south.

The defenders held their ground tenaciously and contested every inch of ground. They yielded here and there, but we were thrown back elsewhere. We managed to reach the barricades, but it was now obvious that we would lose a lot of men without obtaining our objective. Blanco, being stalled completely, agreed to a flanking move, which he had previously pushed aside as unnecessary.

The 2nd Regiment was in reserve and standing saddled and ready to move. One squadron was sent west of the city to reinforce the one already there, with orders to demonstrate their presence in front of the enemy, disarm all patrols and outposts and return the men to the federal lines without harm but stuffed with information as to our great strength. Leaving one squadron behind, I took the remaining three squadrons and traveled fast east of the town in an encircling movement. This I found was not an easy operation as we were forced to make a longer sweep than anticipated over the stony ground of Sierra de Guanajuato, which seemed to extend southeast of the town and included a stony river to cross.

When we came down to more level ground, my Indian hunters from Sonora and Sinaloa, making up the scouts and advance-guard, soon captured the city-bred federal outposts. They also corralled two strong mounted patrols who foolishly had off-saddled and were resting.

As we were near our objective, I had to act fast. The prisoners were sent back to the federal lines in Irapuato on foot and carrying a white flag. They had been informed of our great strength, each squadron became a regiment, and that the city would be surrounded momentarily. Pedro told them that we were not at war with the people but with the *cientificos,* and that the Peon-Indians would be given land when the war was over. He also advised them to tell their comrades to throw down their guns and march north to Guanajuato. Thus fully primed, the eighty-two prisoners stood aghast when told to walk back to the city, for they had been told by their officers how the rebels mutilated and hung every federal captured. Only one hesitated and said to his companion, "We will all be shot in the back," but he left with the rest.

We watched them go and remained for awhile after they had reached the city. While sitting there trying to form a definite plan, I recalled how the Yaqui drums made the federals surrender at Acaponeta only a few months before, and I had a hunch to try a similar trick with trumpets and bugles. The squadron trumpeters, including my own, were sent to several points some distance apart, and as near the enemy as was practicable, with orders to face the city and blaze away a few different blasts as if a brigade was maneuvering, then to return to their units.

When they began trumpeting, it looked silly, but it was too late for regrets, and I had to carry on the bluff — win or lose.

As it was necessary to give the federals time for reflection, we waited awhile, during which time the men had a chance to eat what they had. As part of this strategy of nerves, Pedro had been sent to the west of the city, with orders for them to do as we had done with trumpets to show our strength,

PLATE XIII

The Price of Liberty.

The rebel soldiers hung like scarecrows along the country-side in 1913-1914.

and to send all prisoners captured back to Irapuato. Further, they were to refrain from any attacks on the federals without orders regardless of what happened. I gave the last order as I was afraid my men might advance too soon and frighten the federals back into Irapuato, which might easily ruin our chances of success. A Yaqui galloper was sent to General Blanco giving him my somewhat flimsy plan, and asking him to renew the attack from the south as soon as possible.

When ready, the trumpeters sounded a few more calls and then "dismount." Ten minutes later, "advance" was sounded and we moved into the open in full view of the enemy positions. We had come forward in close formation on purpose, but now trumpets sounded "Extended order," a maneuver which the boys did in splendid style while moving slowly toward the city.

The first thing that surprised me was that the federals seemed to ignore our presence, and I felt we might be walking into a trap. Tekwe, who was walking by my side, pointed to the north side of the town, and there a mass of people were emerging, moving northward, struggling and pushing one another.

Apparently the federals had some green and badly trained recruits, or they had been pressed into the service against their will, as it was incredible that soldiers would leave their excellent positions under cover and retreat after successfully holding us in check for the whole day. My men were immediately brought back to their horses and, leading their animals, were moved closer to the road of the fleeing enemy.

Many of the men that we could see on the road had discarded their rifles. This was a peculiar situation as we couldn't handle a large number of prisoners and still remain an efficient fighting unit so we sat down and waited, glad indeed to see them go. After about a thousand had gone past, some new units came into view. They kept their formation better, but pushed and crowded those in front of them in a nervous manner. As most of these carried guns, we mounted to the tune of bugles and trumpets, as demoralizing agents, and rode into view. When "Charge" was sounded, the discipline that might have been there vanished. The federals broke in panic; it was the complete disintegration of the forces defending Irapuato. After riding through their ranks a few times, we reformed and the blood-stained 2nd Cavalry led away. To continue would have been butchery.

It puzzled me, for I could not understand why the federals left their positions so soon. Later in the evening, however, a captured major informed us what had taken place: "A trusted scout reported several thousands of Carranzistas in the east moving toward our rear. Then came the cavalry patrols you had captured, who returned with news of your vast numbers. On top of that was a report from the west of a rebel brigade closing in on the city. As a great number of men had thrown down their guns and left for the north, the commander had no choice but to order evacuation before it was too late. With this order their morale broke and all rushed for the road, your cavalry did the rest."

The moral value of envelopment could never be more clearly demonstrated than here, likewise the demoralizing effect by bluff-maneuvers, for we had only about 350 men but they thought us to be a division. The enemy left sixty-two dead inside the city and among them was the parish priest of Irapuato. On the road north of the town were found ninety-one dead, but eight of these had been knocked down from behind and trampled to death by their comrades while trying to avoid the charging 2nd Regiment. Among the seventy-four wounded federals found in the streets and along the road were two priests of the Carmelite Order, who had fought as volunteers against us.

Our booty came to 460 rifles, mostly thrown down by fleeing men, 40,000 rounds of ammunition, and 205 horses and saddles. The small amount of rifle ammunition might well have been another good reason for the retreat. The commander must have known this and should have retreated north during that morning and thus saved himself a disastrous and irreparable defeat. I never did find out what happened to the federal commander, but he might have taken off his tunic and escaped with the rest. We lost eighty-one killed and ninety-one wounded.

We tried hard not to take prisoners on the north end of Irapuato and let all who wanted to escape do so, but Acosta, at the south end, captured 412 federals and among them a most charming young woman who acted as a Red Cross nurse among the federals. She offered to help our men and was immediately placed in charge of all wounded. She dined with Acosta and myself that night, of course, and it was a treat to talk to someone from the outside. She informed us, among other things, that war had or was about to break out in Europe.

The 2nd Brigade was on its way by 2 a.m., July 31, to take up position north of Temaxcatio to prevent the enemy escaping in that direction. We estimated the federals to be about 2,000 to 3,000 strong. The road from Irapuato, which crosses the river west of Temaxcatio, was well guarded and made it necessary for us to take the rocky paths crossing the southern extensions of Sierra de Codorniges, a strenuous and difficult journey for horses at any time, especially at night. The distance traveled could hardly have been eleven miles but it took five hours.

The 1st Brigade moved from Irapuato before dawn the same day and advanced cautiously when they reached the hills. Both Pedro and Tekwe had been out scouting this area all night and reported there were abundant opportunities for concealment ideal for an ambush. At the river, which is not far from the village of Temaxcatio, we met formidable resistance, and it became necessary to send strong parties north and south of them. Fearing being trapped, the federals eventually retreated and joined their main body in the village.

By 7 a.m. we had Temaxcatio completely surrounded except for the road leading south to the somewhat large town of Salamanca, which was left open on purpose, as we could not afford the men necessary to guard and care for a large number of prisoners. Being short of men, it was better for us to wear down the morale of the enemy and whittle him down physically by constant pursuit.

When we attacked, it was from two sides simultaneously, but it was tough going for several hours. As we broke through the outer defenses, the enemy began to pour out along the road south to Salamanca.

It was an unpleasant spectacle, horrible in every sense, for it was a massacre and nothing could stop it. Many of the federals threw down their rifles and joined those crowding the road and were shot down as fast as our men could load their guns. The men doing this damage were of the right wing of the 1st Brigade which now had their revenge for the slaughter inflicted on them a few days before at Tanhuato.

The enemy lost 225 killed and over 100 wounded were among the 804 prisoners captured against our own wishes. We lost sixty-nine killed and eighty-six wounded. The booty consisted of six machine-guns, 1,002 rifles, 70,000 rounds of ammunition in boxes, and almost that amount in the pouches and bandoleers carried by the dead and prisoners. We also received 220 horses and saddles besides some most welcome meat rations and corn-meal, enough to give our men a really good meal.

General Obregon arrived with some troops that evening after the scrap, but the maneuvering of his troops had undoubtedly contributed greatly to our success. He sent for Acosta and me, and we wondered what it was all about, as we needed rest more than anything. Obregon questioned us on the fight quite carefully, complimented both of us, and then presented me with a pair of shoulder-tabs with three silver stars on each, the insignia of a colonel. Blanco was not present as he was confined to bed with fever and had remained behind in Irapuato all day, thus being cared for by the good looking Red Cross nurse.

Before we left, Obregon thought it expedient to order the 1st and 2nd Brigades to move south and occupy the town of Salamanca that night. The moving of troops at night was of my own volition for I had preached the advantages of such maneuvers ever since arriving in Mexico. But this was a little different. The enemy had been put to flight, but to order very tired horses and men over a strange road to assault a large town at night, without first having ascertained at least some information of the enemy strength and disposition was quite risky. My views were respectfully submitted, and I suggested that the area be scouted during the night and we attack before dawn. Colonel Serrano, standing beside Obregon, seemed to object to my suggestion; Obregon became hesitant but was persuaded by Serrano. It was decided we move without delay. It should perhaps be mentioned that Mexican officers did not as a rule like to move at night, except when they were in an embarrassing predicament and wished to escape from something, and Serrano was later notorious for being so inclined. Before leaving that night, the wounded were transferred to a building for transportation to Irapuato the next day.

As soon as we returned to our bivouac after our visit with Oregon, four of our best Tarahumara scouts under Pedro were sent along the road to Salamanca with orders to send a man back with information each time they saw anything unusual. These men ran the twenty-two miles there and back in less than three hours, each carrying a carbine, ammunition and a blanket. This did not seem to bother them at all except for the one who had a very sore foot caused by running barefooted when a sandal broke and could not be mended. They had not seen an enemy.

Acosta agreed with me this was almost a foolish undertaking, and slowed down the pace soon after we left. We were barely crawling along the road when Pedro returned some fifteen minutes before the others and told us that the road was clear. We could not see twenty paces ahead, but increased our speed and then it began to rain. We met some unexpected resistance when entering the town and on the east and south sides, after passing through. It was unpleasant in the dark for a few moments as they were in hiding. Then the federals, evidently shaky from the day before, gave ground and it was all over. We lost four wounded.

General Obregon and staff arrived in the Salamanca camp in the afternoon of August 1. He must have been in a hurry, as he ordered the already misused 1st and 2nd Cavalry Brigades to move on Celaya that night and to take possession of the town in the morning. We broke camp after a hurried meal and started out toward the city, which had a population of about 23,000, and was located some twenty-five or more miles to the east.

Acosta took the 1st Brigade, on the northern route, through Salitre, and I the 2nd Brigade over the southern road through El Guaje, which skirts the railroad here and there. We arranged to meet just south of Teneria, a few miles west of Celaya. If this was not possible, I was to move south and try to occupy Molina, a place not far from the Laja River. Acosta would remain around Lemus, a few miles west of Teneria, until contact was made between us.

Everything went according to plan, and we made a double assault on Selaya, August 2, from the northwest and the southeast . There was opposition, but

365

the federals seemed to have lost their punch as well as nerve, for they evacuated the town after an hour's fight, and retreated eastward toward the City of Queretaro. Acosta and I made our headquarters in a house next door to the Hotel Jardin.

We all had a short but much needed rest during the morning of August 3, when Blanco arrived looking very fit and expressing regrets at not being present at the Obregon conference. I tried to draw him out in regard to Serrano. He avoided the subject, but said, "Serrano is now more than ever the power behind the throne, and he likes me about as much as he likes you; we must not lower our guard."

We received orders to leave Celaya at 4 p.m., August 3, and marched east on the City of Queretaro. We were told there might be stiff opposition as it was an important strategical point. We entered the city at 4 a.m. the following morning without much serious resistance, except for a severe skirmish or two.

It appeared as if our forced march took the federals by surprise, as they expected our column to be held up along the road. There were several good skirmishes during the evening and the night before and should have held us back quite seriously at Coachiti, located in the fork of two rivers, not far from the state boundary on the Guanajuato side. Instead they fought half-heartedly for a minute or two, then ran to a new position. They were not alert, and were easily dealt with.

As an example; there was a substantial number of men, nearly a hundred, lying in ambush waiting for us, when our scouts caught them all "asleep," and not one of them knew what happened. It was over in a jiffy. There seemed to be no inter-communication between the enemy outposts and their main-body, and most certainly not between them and the commander in Queretaro. There was no doubt that the backbone of the federal army was all but broken, their spirit was lukewarm, they fought without enthusiasm, and preferred to abandon good positions rather than stand firm, when they had a very good chance to hold us back. This was noticeable when taking Queretaro, as we had only seven men wounded while capturing this politically and strategically important place.

The 1st Brigade received orders to move on San Juan del Rio in the afternoon of August 4, with Colonel Acosta in command. He asked me to come along as his chief-of-staff and second in command. Our objective was located about thirty miles southeast of Queretaro, and we reached there at eight o'clock the following morning. There was some resistance along the road, a few skirmishes, but only one of a serious nature, as there was no pep in anything the federals did. They shot and ran what seemed a hundred times, when they could have held us up seriously. A captured federal officer informed us that he had heard there was a war going on in Europe, but wasn't quite sure. After a rest we continued to an hacienda, the name of which I never knew, but it was located some distance east of San Juan del Rio. We lost a few men while dislodging the federals from the place.

The 1st Cavalry Brigade, still the screen, advance-guard and spear-head of Obregon's army, left the hacienda camp during the evening of August 5, with orders to occupy the City of Tula, in the southwestern parts of the State of Hidalgo. As the success of our mission rested entirely on the element of surprise, all fresh and good horses of the division were issued to the brigade, and we moved on at a killing pace.

When we contacted the enemy, he was in retreat, but we pushed his patrols so hard that they got mixed with their own rear-guard, and that group was forced into the main body, as it could not move fast enough. It was a rugged country and our only chance was to push on and give them no rest or chance to reform. Suddenly the federals gave up trying to defend themselves and moved away from us in disorder as fast as their mounts could carry them.

We entered the city during the evening of August 6, after a strenuous night and day ride of about fifty miles and fighting several skirmishes. There were no signs of the federals in or around Tula when we entered. The towns-people informed us that the federals had come galloping madly through the town in panic an hour before our arrival.

We lost a number of men in this scramble for Tula. The federals, being in a hurry to save their scalps, left their dead and wounded where they fell. We had a detachment following us to take care of our casualties, but most of the enemy wounded could not be treated until two days later, and many died from exposure and lack of care.

Tula was the ancient capital of the Toltec Empire which was defeated and subdued by the Chichimec Indians about the time of the Battle of Hastings. The streets and gardens of this lovely and peaceful town were practically littered with ancient sculptures in volcanic stone and many terracotta figurines. The place was a veritable treasure house of Toltec remains, and I estimated the larger pieces, some of them very large, to be over one thousand in numbers, and the figurines could easily have been over ten thousand.

I purchased quite a number of large sculptures and hundreds of lesser ones, but since I could not take them with me, they were placed in the custody of a few families to await my return. Seven years elapsed, however, before returning, but all my things were intact except for a few which could not be found because the people had died. This archaeological collection of several hundred pieces was later given to Dr. Erland Nordenskiold for the Ethnographical Museum in Gothenburg, Sweden.

XI

*The occupation of Teoloyucan—General Iturbide—
Obregon before the capital—The diplomatic
corps and Obregon—Sir Lionel Carden—A jaunt
into Mexico City and a skirmish—We reconnoi-
ter the capital and meet a Zapata regiment—
Obregon enters the capital—The British legation*

In the afternoon of August 7, the 1st Cavalry
Brigade received orders to move at once and occupy
the small railroad station of Teoloyucan, some twenty
odd miles north of Mexico City. We were informed
that the federals were at Cuatitlan, about eight miles
south of our objective, and that they had outposts
and patrols reaching almost into Teoloyucan. The
main force of the enemy was reported to be at Bar-
rientos, some few miles south of Cuatitlan, with reserves at Atzcapotzalco, the northern section of the
Capital.

We left Tula that evening and it was an unpleasant ride through the night as many unusual
precautions had to be taken, and many usual ones
discarded. The enemy, estimated to be more than

ten times our strength, was somewhere in front of us. The fear of a desperate last stand, or an ambush on a large scale, was constantly with us.

Only once during the night did it look shaky. We had been traveling fast for several hours when, suddenly, about 2 a.m., a startling volley was heard close to our right flank. The darkness, the terrain, and the necessity for speed had ruined the disposition of our flank-guards, and made concealment and surprise attack by an enemy quite easy.

We halted and deployed scouts with a squadron behind them. Only a few shots were exchanged after the first volley, when it was discovered the enemy was nothing but a squadron serving with General Pablo Gonzalez, who had bivouacked for the night, and taking us for the enemy, had opened fire. Fortunately only a few men were wounded. Otherwise, nothing startling occurred except for a few shots exchanged between our scouts and an enemy patrol.

We reached Teoloyucan at 6 a.m., August 8, all tired but in good shape. About an hour after us came Brigadier General Coss with a most terrible, disorganized-looking mob, called a brigade. They looked like bandits, but were good guerrilla fighters.

While scouting toward the capital, during the forenoon of our arrival at Teoloyucan, Pedro and Tekwe met a man in civilian clothes who demanded to be taken before the general in command. They blindfolded and brought the man to camp just before noon and, as General Blanco was absent and we did not recognize Brigadier General Coss as the man in authority, he was received by Acosta and myself.

He presented himself as General Eduardo M. Iturbide, governor of the federal district. In much contracted form Iturbide said: "I have been placed in command of the Metropolitan Police and they have kept order as far as possible within the capital with the arms taken from the armory. The city is nevertheless looted here and there by the underground elements. This started when it became known that the president had decamped. Some vendettas and other kinds of murder have taken place when people resist the plunderers. There are thousands of starving people in the capital who need help, and troops are needed to stop further sacking of the city by bandit gangs. I have come here for the purpose of getting food for the starving."

When Iturbide had finished, he was invited to have lunch with us, and we found him a real fellow, most interesting, and he had guts. Blanco turned up before we had finished, and was most willing to help. He had, however, strict orders not to enter the capital before Obregon's arrival and was forced to decline. Nevertheless, we received valuable information about the federals. Iturbide wasn't sure, but thought most of the federals had moved southeast and south of the capital. When asked how many they were, he did not hesitate to say that it was difficult to estimate due to the many absconders, sometimes as many as a battalion per day.

Our visitor reiterated that he did not know the strength of the federal forces, and we were inclined to believe him with certain reservations, for after all we could hardly expect him to be a traitor to his own side—he wasn't that kind of man. As there was nothing else for Iturbide to do, and we did not wish him to see too much, he was again blindfolded and escorted back to the city. When he left, Acosta advised him to return after Obregon's arrival. After Iturbide had gone, a report came in estimating the federals to be about 25,000 strong, but a captured officer thought the total remaining force was about 35,000.

On the afternoon of Iturbide's visit, Pedro informed us he had found a hand-car in a shed at the railroad depot. Acosta almost shouted for joy, and we agreed on a scouting trip toward the capital. It did not take us long before we were on the way with Pedro, Tekwe, and three men working the crank bars. We were moving at a fast pace, and before knowing it we had entered Tlalnepantla, where there were a few people about who seemed nervous as they did not know if we were federals or rebels. They must have taken us for the former when we continued to Atzcapotzalco. Here we entered a *cantina* for refreshment and information and found that the federals, although moving southward, were not a mile away—we thought it prudent to go no further. We also realized it was getting late, and as we had to receive the remainder of the division, we returned in a hurry.

We got back to Teoloyucan after dark and found our troops already there. Blanco, like a chained lion, wanted to know where we had been. He calmed down when told of the scouting on a hand-car. A rascal himself, he was sure we had been up to something besides scouting and was a bit sore about being left behind. He was contented when informed that we had not seen a federal soldier on the way.

Generals Jesus Carranza, Pablo Gonzalez, and some others arrived at 11 a.m., August 9, with about 2,000 men. Gonzalez, who was one of the favorites of Venustiano Carranza, sent for me in the afternoon and askel if I would join him as his chief-of-staff with the rank of brigadier. After thanking him for the compliment, my answer was, "You had better speak to General Blanco as I am with him." At this moment several officers came in and the meeting was postponed.

Some members of the Diplomatic Corps sent a messenger to Obregon expressing their desire to call on him before any protracted siege of the city began. They proposed to be in Teoloyucan at 3 p.m., August 9. Obregon had not yet arrived, but permission was granted.

As Carranza's forces were some distance away, Blanco felt that we should make a bluff show of strength to mislead any inquisitive diplomat who might be in sympathy with the enemy; as we had only about 6,000 men, as against almost five times that number of federals, in and about the city. The 1st Cavalry Brigade was chosen to do this, which was a kind of a feather in its cap.

Saddles were wiped off the best way we could, horses groomed in the cowboy style, and the men made to look their best, which did not really mean much as they had been on a stiff campaign for almost a year without supplies. At three o'clock the brigade stood ready to mount; we were still standing there at four and at five, but there wasn't a sign of the diplomats. The troops were dismissed at six, after waiting for three hours.

This request for an audience and not keeping the appointment made a poor impression on everyone. Someone expressed the thought that the breaking of the arranged meeting was done deliberately to put the peon-bandit-rebels in their place. If this was so, they made the mistake of their lives because their stupid action boomeranged later, especially against the British, who made the arrangement—the very people I had been bragging about to the rebels.

A messenger arrived late that night with a peculiar apology to Obregon. There had been "a mistake," but they would be there August 11. The apology did not go down very well as we were sure their action had been meant as a deliberate insult.

An interesting question came up. What foreign power was most against us? Everyone knew how the British government had backed Huerta and lent large sums to Mexico for arms and ammunition to kill off the rebels. On the other hand, nobody worked harder for the establishment of General Huerta than the American Ambassador, Henry Lane Wilson, so it was a fifty-fifty question between these two governments. Yet the United States had landed troops on Mexican soil in opposition to Huerta, and were still holding the city of Veracruz and the territory around it—by force.

General Obregon arrived during the morning of August 10, with his staff and about 1,000 men as a body-guard.

The following day came the diplomats, including those from France, Guatemala, and Sir Lionel Carden of Great Britain. In their party was also Gen. Iturbide, accompanied by two men. There was a short, but distinctly cold, reception for the visitors before getting to business. The diplomats seemed embarrassed at our indifference to their presence, and there was not the usual parade or review, not even a guard of honor. There wasn't the slightest sign of cordiality from Obregon, but it was obvious that he was enjoying their perplexity.

There seemed to be no doubt that the diplomats had agreed before coming how to handle these "rebels." They intended to make the "bandits" wait until they were grovelling in abject humility and reverence before their august presence.

Iturbide pleaded his case to Obregon in a straightforward manner. His execution was a foregone conclusion in the minds of most present, but Obregon, obviously touched by the sincerity and pluck of the man for walking willingly into a lion's den, revoked the order. I felt proud of Obregon that day, because I had been afraid of what Serrano might do to this fine man.

Sir Lionel Carden

Although I did not take part in the negotiations, I attended with Blanco at his request. When I was introduced to Sir Lionel he made some remark about knowing my name and asked, "You are not a Mexican, are you?" When informed of my affiliations with the British Army, he remembered the name and told me there was a cablegram at the legation for me. He also gave me the first official information that a war was going on in Europe.

The conference between the diplomats and Obregon became bogged down at the very start because of the supercilious and condescending mannerism displayed by some of the visitors—which was plain stupidity. They soon had to pay for their foolishness. Shortly thereafter the diplomats were floundering helplessly in the quicksand of embarrassment, when Obregon became abrupt and told them plainly to mind their own business.

During the impass thus created, Sir Lionel, who must have known he was in disfavor, made another indiscreet move when he came over to my side and opened up with a barrage of questions of delicate military nature. Each question was a slur as well as an insult to my loyalty to the rebel cause, to the uniform I was wearing, and to my integrity. Among other interrogations, Sir Lionel said: "You are a British officer, and it is your duty to help me with infomation. Tell me, how many men has Obregon? Where is Carranza, and how many men has he? How many field-guns have you? Do you intend to shell the capital and when?

Needless to say I was aghast at the presumption of the man, but realized I had to keep my temper and play a part however unpleasant. Hesitating for just a moment I answered with the most deliberate distortions of facts and outright falsifications. I said: "Sir Lionel, what I am about to tell you must not be mentioned to a soul as it might get me shot as a traitor. We have 20,000 men within two miles of here, 10,000 more will arrive tomorrow morning, and Carranza with 18,000 men will arrive at a place five miles from here during the night. We have six batteries. As far as I know the city will most certainly suffer from shell fire if the federals do not get out immediately."

To clarify my remarks it should be mentioned, perhaps, that we had only about 6,000 men with us. Obregon's troops and those of Carranza did not exceed 18,000 all told, and they were two days march or more away. We had only eight batteries altogether and only one battery with us. The troops of Pancho Villa were not included or considered as one of us, as he was on his own far in the north. The British Minister looked seriously at me and then spurted out, "There is no hope for the federal troops. I will try and get them out of the capital tomorrow."

As I was too monopolized by Sir Lionel I did not have the opportunity to talk to any one else after the introductions, except to Captain Harry Hopkins, a former commander in the U. S. Navy. He seemed to be a free-lance but must have been in an advisory capacity to somebody or he could not have been present. He was extremely well informed, a good fellow, and we became friends for life. When the diplomats left, their heads were bent, and they did not strut as they had on their arrival.

The cavalry under General Blanco broke camp the day after the visit of the diplomats and left Teoloyucan at dawn and moved toward Atzcapotzalco, which was south of us and closer to Mexico City. We moved carefully with the 1st Brigade extended in four waves, each of a regiment in strength. Two brigades followed in column of route, and another but rather poorly manned brigade came with the headquarter staff. We met some resistance and spasmodic firing took place between our advance guard and the enemy patrols, but this petered out and ceased entirely when they found us disinclined to be detained.

That night in Atzcapolzalco the staff was informed by Blanco that he had orders to investigate and clear the approaches into the capital on the morrow. Our civilian scouts, including Pedro and Tekwe, had reported the center of the city as being devoid of federal troops, but there was considerable military activity east and southeast of the city. This explained why the enemy outposts and patrols moved eastward, instead of south through the town, when dislodged by us during the day. We knew, of course, the federal commander had orders from Obregon to get out of the capital to save it from an artillery bombardment, but Sir Lionel may also have had something to do with this rapid withdrawal, as he had said so after hearing my exaggerated account of our strength.

When we heard of the next day's orders, Acosta and I went into one of our usual huddles and talked about Mexico City, which we had done quite often before. Neither of us had been there and were simply itching to have a look, for this was the site of the ancient City of Tenochtitlan, the capital of the fabulous Aztec Empire. Besides, we knew that the city was famous for its interesting nightspots, and we had been away from civilization for some time and instinctively agreed to go in for a peep at least, come what may, that very night.

We were young and foolish enough not to consider our action indiscreet or out of order. We would scout, and as we were adequately endowed with sufficient imagination and ego to conceive that our unauthorized mission could be of some importance to our future military operations, off we went. Peculiarly enough our escapade that night did have a strong bearing on future operations. We did not tell Blanco of our intentions, for he had orders not to enter the city, as the temptation for a frolic might be too difficult for him to resist. General Obregon's order seemed peculiar, however, for the city had not been cleared at all, so it was pretty obvious that Obregon wanted to march in as the conquering hero before anyone else—why not?

We considered taking the hand-car which had come with us but decided on horses, each taking a man for the animals. I took Pedro, who ran on foot 200 yards or so ahead, armed with a revolver, bowie-knife and his sling from which he never seemed to part. Tekwe, to his disgust, was left behind to take care of our things and the spare mounts. Acosta and his mounted man carried holstered cavalry carbines and revolvers like myself.

Pedro traveled fast and when he stopped to investigate, we did the same. At Tacuba we ran into three fully armed soldiers who told us they were scouting for Obregon, which we knew was a lie. Pedro maintained they belonged to General Coss and were on their way into town for a spree. As we could not hold them without returning to camp, we let them go.

At Popotla we seriously considered returning to the division for in front of us stood twenty armed soldiers under a sergeant. Apparently they had not seen or heard Pedro, who had returned to warn us. Seeing us in doubt, Pedro suggested that he return and speak to the sergeant, as they were not federals.

I was a little against the idea, as these were days of trigger-happy soldiers, and I did not wish to lose my inseparable companion, friend and teacher in the Tarahumara language, wood craft, and the lore of his tribe.

It was already nine o'clock at night, and there was something about the appearance and general bearing of these men which indicated they were not ordinary soldiers. As a prompt decision was necessary, we let Pedro go and he walked boldly up to the party and was soon in conversation. He returned after about five minutes and revealed that it was a party of Guerrera Indians, in other words Zapatistas, who were on a reconnaissance patrol. They had reached their objective and were considering returning south-westward around the city, whence they came, when they heard our horses. Pedro told them of our presence, but they already knew of three men on horseback, and where they were hidden, and invited us to come forward to be recognized.

We had lost almost half an hour and both of us thought it foolish to ride up to twenty armed Zapatistas who, after all, were anything but friendly with the Carranzistas, as they had been working against us on Pancho Villa's side for some time. However, we had to find out if there was a strong Zapatista force behind these men and decided, on Pedro's advice, to meet them.

They were friendly enough, but interrogated us thoroughly for they took us for federal officers at first due to the cut of our uniforms. The man in charge was Sergeant Juan Herrera, an Indian, who seemed a very level-headed man. He told us his patrol was operating from a Guerrero regiment now located around Tecamachalco, some ten miles southeast of the capital. The patrol had come dismounted because the absence of sound made observation more easy.

Like most people of wild mountain regions, these Indians were incommunicative but displayed no animosity, in fact became quite friendly when two packs of cigarettes were passed around. When told of our scouting mission, we found they had met several federal scouts during the day, all of whom had been dealt with in the usual way. These Zapatistas wanted to come with us into the city as they had only seen the outskirts, and thus our night-prowling of four became one of twenty-five, as we could hardly say no.

As soon as we entered the main part of the city, the Guerreros changed their formation into Indian file, on both sides of the street, with about ten yards separating each man. It seemed like a self-acting maneuver for no words of command were given. It was most difficult to see any one of them, and we felt most conspicuous riding in the middle of the street with these ghost-like Indians shuffling along silently on both sides, in front and in rear, without the slightest sound. If this was a trap, we were most certainly right in it, and could never escape. Pedro was far ahead as usual, and he too had vanished into the night.

Just after Acosta had said something about "This is no fun — let's go back," the Indians ahead halted and those in the rear closed ranks. The sergeant then informed us he wanted to take another direction to rejoin his regiment. We parted after the usual leave taking and the four of us stood once more alone. I am sure all of us, even Pedro, felt a great relief. The street was empty and too quiet; it gave you a feeling of a ghost town, so we hurried on for the return to camp.

As we made a turn to the left around a street corner we heard a shout, and then rifle fire, not far behind us. We should have hastened away and gone home, but as we thought our Guerrero friends might be in trouble we turned and rushed toward the shooting. When we rounded a corner, we found them caught between two enemy patrols but, crouching in doorways, giving a good account of themselves. The federals between us and the trapped Guerreros could be seen silhouetted during the firing and numbered about twelve men. We could not see how many were on the other side of our friends. As the bullets were zipping wildly past us, we dismounted around the corner, and three of us came forward into position behind some pillars in front of a big house and opened fire on the federals, not twenty yards distant. Our attack was such a surprise that they broke and ran past us not four yards away. We fired from the hip and couldn't miss, but one escaped. The federals on the other side also turned and ran, as they probably thought us in great numbers.

The reunion with the Guerreros was brief but warm. They lost four killed in five minutes or less of fighting, but the federals left sixteen dead and dying in the street. The wounded were so badly hurt that nothing could be done for them. Besides, this was now a most unhealthy spot to remain in. We broke up almost at once and reached camp at two o'clock in the morning, more by luck than good judgment. As we parted it was agreed not to mention the incident to Blanco and, as an extra goodnight Acosta said, "That wasn't much of a night club party you gave me!"

We reconnoiter the Capital and meet a Zapata regiment

At four o'clock in the afternoon of August 13, we sent a number of intelligence men and women dressed as peons into the capital to get information. At five o'clock several waves of mounted scouts followed them. At six, the 1st Cavalry Brigade under Acosta, accompanied by Blanco and me, moved forward for a reconnaissance in force. Each regiment was allotted a section of the northern part of the city and each squadron a specific street. Two squadrons from the 3rd Brigade came up close behind each of our flanks. The 2nd Brigade stood saddled and in readiness in case of trouble. General Coss was to take care of our rear, although he was too far back for any practical use. The whole idea of this move was to find out if the enemy had really evacuated the place or not. We searched only a few of the most likely looking houses and moved on, taking dynamiters with us to blow up any building harboring armed federals.

The irony of fate brought us past the place of our skirmish during the night before. The bodies were still on the ground and their presence puzzled

Blanco a great deal for there were only federal soldiers. "This is very strange," he said and continued, "Why, it looks like a massacre," to which we agreed of course. The Guerreros had, thank goodness, carried their dead with them and we did not volunteer any information of the affair. The civilians in the adjoining houses were made to come out to remove the dead, but could give no account as to the fighting except that it took place in the middle of the night and stopped suddenly.

Blanco had orders to send a brigade to clear the northern half of the city, but we found this difficult without also moving eastward; we had strict orders to avoid this eastern district as well as the area around the National Palace. When Chapultepec (Hill of the grasshoppers) came into sight, our troops were pulled in and reorganized into their former units. Blanco took one of the flanking squadrons and returned northward. Acosta and I with two squadrons moved eastward, then north and did not see a federal soldier all day. But there were a great number of very good looking women among the people who came out from different houses to greet us.

We returned to Atzcapotzalco without any casualties, but quite a number of men were missing. They had faded away for some fun while returning through the outskirts of the city. We camped, therefore, at Popotla as an advance guard, and to pick up stragglers. These were the first rebel troops to camp in Mexico City.

When we returned to camp, a rumor told us that the provisional President Carbajal had resigned and left the country, and that General Velasco had taken charge. This day Obregon, it was reported, accepted the surrender of the Federal Army and government at Teoloyucan. It was also reported that General Huerta when he left on July 15 said, "I leave Mexico with a heavy heart," but we also discovered this burden of grief did not prevent him from carrying with him about two million gold pesos from the National Treasury.

In the forenoon of August 14, the cavalry division entered Mexico City in a demonstration of strength. As we did not have too many men available to show off with, I suggested to Blanco that we duplicate our display in Guadalajara, to which he agreed. Each regiment was to march separately, each taking a different street, and continue riding in and out of the city for several hours.

The regiments were separated; Acosta went off with the 1st his way, and I with the 2nd moved south, then east through the city. At Ixtacalco, Pedro came back and reported the presence of an advance-guard of a Zapata regiment not far away, and the sergeant in charge turned out to be our Guerrero Indian friend of two nights before, Juan Herrera. He greeted me with a salute and friendly smile, much to the surprise of my officers who knew nothing of the affair.

The close presence of the Zapatista regiment was disturbing in spite of the friendly greeting, as we knew Zapata had about 15,000 men south of us, but not of a full regiment at the very edge of the capital. Evidently our scouts and intelligence had either failed to penetrate this far, or had been taken prisoners, because no information of their presence had reached us.

As it was imperative to know more of the Zapatistas, I accepted Herrera's invitation to meet his colonel and followed him for about three miles, to near the foot of the hill at Ixtapalapa, where a dismounted Zapata regiment stood ready to move. The 2nd Regiment was halted and ready for action some distance away, and I went forward and met the commanding officer, Colonel Antonio Morales, who turned out to be a pleasant Guerrero Indian with the refined manners of a *cacique* (Indian nobleman) rather than a Zapatista. He knew of the scrap with the federals the other night, and warmly expressed his appreciation for the help.

He informed me that he had instructions to move south as soon as contact had been made with the Carranzistas, and to avoid a clash with them. Then he added, "Why don't you and your men come with us and join Zapata? We do not trust Carranza and will have nothing to do with him." When his friendly and well meaning invitation was declined with thanks, he added, "I understand quite well for there are many *cantinas* and lovely *señoritas* in the city," and with a friendly, *Adios amigo!*, he departed, moving fast eastward, and keeping fairly good formation.

On our way back over another street I noticed foreign flags on some of the houses. In a doorway of a house flying the Swedish flag two men stood looking at us as if surprised. I halted the regiment when one of the men called out in Swedish to someone inside the house, "Come out and see the rebels." They were somewhat startled when we halted, but calmed down when I addressed them in

their own language. The three of us, Carl Erik
Ostlund, Gosta Lundberg and I developed a close
friendship which has continued to their children and
grand-children after them.

Obregon enters the Capital

General Obregon and part of the Rebel Army,
including Lucio Blanco and his cavalry, moved into
billets in the capital on the afternoon after meeting
the Zapata regiment. Blanco, and his staff, occupied a spacious house on Paseo de la Reforma.

This move was not only for the purpose of occupying the Capital, but to keep order as looting here
and there had taken place. Some unfriendly soul
started ugly rumors that this was not to keep order,
but to give Obregon's men the first chance to
plunder the city. These malicious, and anti-revolu-
tionary rumors were created by the *cientificos* to
hamper the rebel cause.

During the morning of August 16, the day after
the occupation of the city, Blanco invited Acosta and
me to come with him and see the inside of the
National Palace, the home of the Presidents of
Mexico. A strong rebel guard under a captain was
sitting around inside the two heavy swinging doors,
and a sentry stood in the doorway, for the doors
were wide open. The guard which was made up
of Obregon's Yaquis recognized us, and we went
upstairs without interference. After walking through
several elaborately decorated rooms, we came to a
large salon where I observed a full size painting of
Kaiser William II in a field-marshal's uniform and

stopped to have a look. After that Blanco led me by the arm to a large and highly decorated chair, over which was hanging an enormous velvet canopy. The chair was exquisitely carved and impressive; the kind of throne-like chair one might expect Napoleon to have used in his heyday, it was obviously the Presidential Chair, used on State occasions.

Before I knew what had happened, Blanco and Acosta swung me around and pushed me into the chair, and bowed to me ceremoniously. When I told them the chair was not very comfortable to sit in, Blanco remarked, "Huerta did not find it very easy to sit in either," and we all had a good laugh. We continued our wandering, but in one corner of that stately salon I had to stop and look, as I could not believe my eyes — there stood two very large brass spittoons.

We went through one or two doors decorated in Moorish style, then came to a well decorated room which contained a large desk. On a table were several articles gathered together, it seemed, in a hurry for removal. On examining these things we found that all of them had the initials P.D. engraved on them, and must have belonged to Porfirio Diaz, presents, no doubt, given at one time or another.

I was especially attracted by a large heavy silver knife eighteen inches long with scabbard. The hilt was embossed on one side with an Eagle on a cactus with a snake in its beak, an old legend of the Aztecs. On the other side was embossed what could represent a feather head-dress or Montezuma's war helmet. The sturdy steel-blade was richly engraved with writing, but somewhat difficult to read due to constant polishing and some rust spots. However, one could read; "Porfirio Diaz, 15 September 1891". It seemed to have been a present to him from Oaxaca, his home state.

On the table was also a large silver replica of an old-fashioned and life-size hand-grenade, used as a cigar lighter with P.D. engraved on it. While admiring these things, Blanco picked up the knife and pushed it inside my sword-belt, and handed me the grenade with the remark; "Take these things as mementos from the revolution."

The British Legation

When we returned to headquarters from the palace, we found a committee of four lieutenant colonels waiting to see Blanco on a subject which startled me. Blanco was told that a group of officers in the garrison had met that afternoon to discuss the activities of all foreign representatives and their legations, especially the British. The meeting decided that the British government was against the Revolutionary Party, as it had lent several million pounds sterling to Huerta, and that the British Minister, Sir Lionel Carden, had worked constantly against us and given aid to Huerta whenever possible.

This committee proposed that, "the British Legation be closed forthwith; that Sir Lionel be declared *persona non grata* and sent home". When asked what they would do if the British refused to close and go home, their answer was prompt and to the point, "We will burn the legation to the ground, arrest the minister, and send him and his staff to the Americans in Veracruz".

These were drastic measures, and fearing Blanco's enthusiasm as a Mexican and his inexperience in international problems, I suggested that someone call on Sir Lionel and ask him to leave Mexico, before forcing him out without a hearing. The idea took root, but the word "ask" was replaced by "demand", and they suggested that I be the one to inform him. Knowing these men and their sudden and almost uncontrollable outbursts of patriotic fervor, I was on my way to Sir Lionel within minutes. I was received most courteously by Mr. Thomas Hohler, the First Secretary of the Legation, and found him an unusually broad-minded and understanding person for a diplomat, who in those days was often evasive, stodgy and buried under a needlessly stiff-shirted etiquette, which was dangerous in the middle of a revolution.

As I was told by Mr. Hohler that Sir Lionel was not at home, the matter of my mission was brought forcibly to Hohler's attention. It was most unpleasant, but I had to be blunt as well as abrupt. I requested Sir Lionel Carden's immediate departure from Mexico and gave the reason why. If he did not leave, the Legation would be burned, and the minister and staff sent to Veracruz by force.

My request made Hohler wince for it was tantamount to a demand. It jolted, it seemed, the very foundation and tradition of the service as well as his dignity, for it left him speechless. He collected himself after a few minutes, and said he would bring the matter to Sir Lionel's attention the following morning. At this answer, I startled Hohler a little further by telling him to convey the message tonight, as the rebels were restless and demanded action. While leaving the legation, I stopped and spoke to a British military guard inside the sand-bagged building, and from what he said, Sir Lionel Carden was actually at home then and probably heard our conversation.

About this time Mr. George G. de Parada Jr. came with his uncle to cavalry headquarters to see me. Parada, a very pleasant intellectual Mexican of the International set, invited me to move to his house, "Casa de la Condessa," in Tacubaya, and I found it one of the most beautiful homes in Mexico City. The place was a little too far from Blanco's headquarters, but I accepted the invitation and moved in.

XII

A mission to Zapata—Prisoner of Zapata—An old Aztec Priest—The ruins of Tepoztlan—Zapata pays a debt—Our escape from Morelos

The day after our visit to the Palace General Blanco, looking rather nervous and upset, called us into a conference of a most confidential nature. Without any preliminaries he said that Carranza, more stubborn than ever, refused to negotiate with General Emiliano Zapata unless that "Indian bandit" came to Carranza, with his hat in hand like a servant (*mozo*) and acknowledged him as the First Chief. "You know," he continued, "that Zapata is very independent with an army of his own, has never recognized Carranza, and it has annoyed the chief and hurt his dignity. Zapata knows he cannot come to the capital with his troops for it would mean war. He also knows he cannot come alone as he would be arrested, tried and shot within a few days, if not at once."

Blanco now disclosed that he and four other generals, all disappointed in Carranza's attitude toward

Zapata and Villa, had had a talk. He did not dare to speak to any one on the subject, but it was imperative that something be done at once, and he wanted the opinion of his *compañeros*—hence this conference.

Carranza was still outside the capital, and it was well known among the senior officers that Obregon was not happy inside the city as Villa had a large army poised in the north and almost ready to strike. Zapata in the south was much closer, in fact uncomfortably so. It was also known that Villa and Zapata had been plotting for some time to oust Carranza and Obregon from the capital and to eliminate them entirely from the Mexican political scene.

Acosta looked my way but said nothing. It was obviously up to me to express my views, and I asked if an emissary had been sent to Zapata for his opinion. Both of them seemed startled, but Blanco said, "An emissary from Carranza to Zapata! Why, he would be skinned alive at the whipping-post or buried alive in an ant-hill as soon as he had delivered his message. No! That couldn't be done, and Carranza will never agree, as he is too proud. Besides, such a move may appear as a recognition of Zapata's strength, and his own weak position — that would never do."

Then I made the suggestion that Acosta and I go to Morelos and have a talk with Zapata. Acosta seemed quite interested in the idea, but Blanco thought it imprudent for both of us to go at the same time, as difficult questions might arise; rumors and misunderstanding of our purpose could result. "Besides," he added, "it will be difficult for me to lose both my right and left hand at the same time."

Blanco had never been told of our trip into the capital on August 12, but I did so now; how we had run into a Zapata patrol, the fight and how we helped them against the federals. I also reminded my astounded chief how my troops had run into the Zapatista regiment in the capital under Colonel Morales the following day. Then I ventured to say that, in my opinion judging from the Zapatistas I had met, it would not be impossible to smooth matters over with Zapata.

While Blanco was pondering over this, I suggested that he bring the disgruntled generals before Carranza and recommend to the First Chief that a less dictatorial approach be adopted in his dealings with Zapata. On hearing this Blanco laughed for the first time that day and said, *"No, amigo!* That is impossible! You have no idea how stubborn, suspicious and resentful to advice the Chief really is."

Realizing Blanco's difficulties I then proposed to go alone to Morelos in an attempt to convince Zapata that Carranza's bark was worse than his bite, and that the Indians would no doubt get their land. Blanco agreed, but on condition that the mission be kept strictly confidential, that I try to avoid armed clashes with the Zapatistas except in self-defense. Should the errand appear impossible at any time, I would return to the capital without delay.

When volunteering to go to Morelos, I figured on traveling light and taking only my two scouts Pedro and Tekwe with me. However, Blanco insisted that at least one hundred men go along. He stressed the danger of the many bandit gangs roaming the hills who would think twice before attacking a well-equipped squadron of veteran Yaqui warriors.

It did not matter how much I objected to having a cumbrous squadron on my hands, he insisted and I knew he meant well. It was all settled in a few minutes, and as we were leaving Blanco handed me a very handsome 44 Colt Revolver, exquisitely chased with gold inlay. He asked me to give it to Zapata with two hundred rounds of ammunition as a token of friendship.

It had been decided that one hundred picked men and horses from the 1st and 2nd Regiment would form my escort, ten more would lead sixty spare horses, three of them with pack saddles for ammunition and extra food. Besides these Acosta gave me four special Indian scouts, all of them tried and trusted men, although born and brought up in Morelos, the State ruled completely by Zapata.

To prevent the real intention of the expedition leaking out, officers and men were told we were on an extended scouting-patrol south of, but beyond Toluca, in the southwest. We rode out from the capital about one o'clock the following morning taking a westerly direction as a blind. When we had Chapultepec on our left, we turned southward and passed through a portion of Tacubaya, a large thriving town of about 35,000 inhabitants, but really a suburb of Mexico City,

We passed east of San Angel, through Coyoacan, Tlalpam and reached Ajusco without meeting a scout or patrol of any kind. As Mexico City was obviously wide open for an attack, a trooper with a note to this effect was sent back to Blanco.

We off-saddled at Ajusco to rest the horses and for something to eat. The cavalry scouts were called in and three of the Morelos Indian guides sent forward in their place. They had instructions to lead us to Zapata's men, and to tell them that "a foreigner, a friend of Pancho Villa, wished to speak with Zapata."

Each guide was now on his own, but they were to try and contact one another whenever possible as well as the cavalry scouts following them, as this was a rough country full of sharp volcanic stones and large boulders, ideally suitable for an ambush at almost every point of the way.

Just before noon Tekwe told me he didn't like the looks of one of the guides and proposed not to send him out alone. As I had implicit faith in my trusted Yaqui friend, the guide was kept with the main body.

When we moved on, a formidable mountain could be seen some three or four miles to the west. It was the range and crater of the extinct Volcano Ajusco, which looked bluish in color and rose to an elevation of about 13,200 feet. When we reached El Guarda, a cold wind was blowing uncomfortably at an elevation of over 9,800 feet. There was a road-junction there, with one road winding southward to Cuernavaca and the other pointing eastward, but it looked in poor shape.

From a tactical standpoint this was anything but a good place to halt, but as the stony country had been hard on the horses of the scouts, we off-saddled for a rest, when several bales of hay were discovered seemingly placed there recently. Tekwe, always an excellent scout nosing around everywhere, brought to my attention that a large number of men and horses had camped quite close to us the night before.

Pedro, who had been instructed what to do, now changed his uniform for native garb. When ready he came to me, touched my shoulder with his left hand and said in his native tongue:

"Simi ne norawa, Onorugame kuira ba"
("I go my friend, Father Sun preserve you")

Then he started off at an ambling-trot typical of the Tarahumara long-distance runner. He stopped some distance away to adjust one of his sandals, raised his arm in a wave and was soon out of sight, for he had left the road and gone into the rocky ground of the mountain.

When I thought Pedro and the three guides had had ample time to overcome their difficult terrain, we began our march on the village of Zacapexco, located a few miles northeast of Huitzilac, which we had been told was held by quite a number of Zapatistas. We were advancing behind a double line of cavalry scouts, preceded by the remaining Morelos guide — the one not trusted by Tekwe.

As we moved along we could see now and again far to the east what appeared to be an uninterrupted range of mountains, culminating in the majestic snow-capped peak of Popocatepetl (Smoking Mountain) and some distance to the north was Ixtacihuatl (Sleeping Woman). Indian legends say that Smoking Mountain loved the Sleeping Woman, but killed her while in a jealous rage and even today is spewing fire, ashes and stones as a warning for everyone to keep away from her.

So as not to run into a large body of Zapatistas on the highway, which might be difficult to explain, we left the road south of El Guarda. It was tough going over the rocky ground. When we came to a pine-wood, we encountered the Zapatistas so recently our ally but now an enemy. Every precaution against surprise had been taken, a trusted Morelos guide was ahead, but I didn't know he was in cahoots with Zapata's men. Every one of my scouts was a seasoned Yaqui warrior, the best hunters and trackers in the land, and yet we were at a disadvantage as we had to trust the guide to some extent.

My desire was to negotiate with the first Zapatista commander, for an interview with Zapata, but the guide had led us into a trap instead, and as we were on the defensive, it was not an opportune time to ask for a chat. To avoid a head-on collision we turned south, which was luckily the side of least resistance, and forced our way through the trees, bushes, boulders and a few Zapatistas into a gap, between two steep cliffs which looked like a Mexican saddle.

When the non-com in charge of the rear-guard joined me, he brought a prisoner and reported that the Zapatistas had cut us off and were bringing up reinforcements behind us. This was bad enough, but the prisoner was also full of disturbing information. When he was told of my looking for Zapata, he became talkative and disclosed quite frankly how he belonged to a strong flank-guard of a large Zapata "army," now marching on Xochimilco (Place of Flowers), and then on to capture the City of Mexico.

As Xochimilco is only a few miles south of the capital, this was disconcerting news, because I knew there wasn't a patrol out to sound the alarm. He also said that our so-called trusted guide was a member of Zapata's body-guard, made up of Guerrero Indians who had been serving in the ranks of the Carranzistas for a long time to see what was going on. This guide had informed them of our presence, but there was no time for a real ambush due to the Yaqui scouts coming too fast behind them. This was the man Tekwe had warned me against, and he had also warned his scouts, which probably saved us from an untimely as well as unpleasant end.

To retreat toward Mexico City at this point was impossible and foolish to attempt, nor did I relish the idea of giving up the mission without a struggle because of a set-back. I did, however, wonder what had happened to Pedro and the other Morelos guides. Apparently we had no choice but to try to extricate ourselves from a nasty situation before even thinking of anything else.

After awhile the pressure by the Zapatistas, who apparently were of regimental or brigade strength, became so great that we were forced through the narrow gap which was full of boulders and easy to defend. Fearing encirclement, I left six Yaqui volunteers in the gap as a rear-guard with instructions to hold it for about half an hour, and "Try not to kill or wound any of the Zapatistas." This was not an easy task for six young Yaqui braves with guns in their hands, and being attacked by an overwhelming force of more than 100 to 1.

The rest of us, taking the horses of the rear-guard with us so as to give these men a better chance to escape in the night, started them down a very steep and horribly rugged stony mountain trail, which was more fit for baboons than horses. We walked for about two hours and there was not a sign of the rear-guard, who could easily have caught up with us on foot. Tekwe hoped they would eventually come, if they were not killed at the gap, and with this doubtful consolation we moved on. After awhile it became obvious that we had outdistanced our pursuers, and we halted in a sheltered spot for a well earned rest.

On checking over our losses, I found them comparatively slight for only two men and sixteen of the led horses were missing, due, no doubt, to the valiant and discreet behavior of the Yaquis assisted by the complete darkness which had fallen over us like a blanket. Our prisoner, who turned out to be a sergeant, was brought along, and he seemed to enjoy the company of my Yaquis and told us that Zapata had quite a number of them fighting for him. He was sure that Zapata would be glad to have all of us, but indicated it would be difficult to find him, as no one ever knew his whereabouts. He thought, however, that Zapata was not in Cuernavaca (Spanish: Cow's Horn), but in the southeast or on the way to Xochimilco with the first of the three contingents that were to emerge from Morelos to drive Carranza from Mexico City. This somewhat congenial sergeant also said that one of Zapata's most trusted friends should be near Tepoztlan with his regiment, and if anyone knew of Emiliano's whereabouts, he would.

Tekwe, always wary of a trap, did not seem to object to the man being sent with a message to this colonel. "Providing," he said with a grin, "that

I go with him." A scout returned at this moment and reported a path had been found leading to better ground in the south which the prisoner confirmed, and he offered to lead the way.

We moved on, after changing some lame horses for remounts, with the prisoner leading and Tekwe close behind him — in case. We crossed a railroad track and then another, which I found was a hairpin bend on the railway from Mexico City to Cuernavaca. The path became more passable after a while, and the prisoner informed me we were near Xaltitla, a small place north of but close to Santa Catarina, and only a few miles west of Tepoztlan.

A close guard was placed over the sergeant while we bivouacked for the rest of the night, but no fires were allowed. It had been a hard twenty-four hours, as we must have ridden and walked about forty miles under difficult conditions, to put it mildly. As I was afraid of being discovered by some stray enemy scout or patrol, the prisoner, under Tekwe, was sent to Tepoztlan with instructions what to say, and then it felt good to lie down for the hour remaining till dawn.

Prisoner of Zapata

Daylight came, and as it was cold, the men were allowed to make fires and cook whatever they had while waiting. At nine o'clock a scout reported that three men were approaching, and to my delight it was Pedro, Tekwe and the prisoner. Pedro's instructions had been to find Zapata. He had managed to slip through the Zapatista scouts, gone around their outposts, and eventually had found Colonel Morales, who happened to be the same man mentioned by our prisoner and the one I had met in Mexico City while on patrol. Pedro brought instructions from Morales for us to move to Tepoztlan without delay, and this we did with pleasure, for our horses needed food and water.

My second meeting with Colonel Morales was friendly, although his first act was to order the men to stack their firearms in a near-by building. The Yaquis hesitated for an anxious second but did as told. When I was depositing my two guns the colonel, gallantly as in the days of old, told me with a graceful and courtly gesture with his hand befitting any Grandee of the Middle Ages, to retain them.

That he was suspicious was only natural when finding a squadron of Carranzistas — their enemies — in his front yard, for no information of our skirmish of the day before had reached him. Within five minutes he was told of my wish to see Zapata, which coincided with what Pedro had requested. He answered me with a question, "Why did you come to Morelos on a peace mission with a strong armed force? You could have done better with one or two companions. I am puzzled how you escaped annihilation."

When I told Morales how we had left the road just south of El Guarda and went across country, his serious face broke into a smile of understanding, but he shook his head and said it was a foolish thing to come with so many men. When I told him of the six Yaquis left as a rear-guard in the gap, he promised to send a patrol into the hills to investigate.

Morales then told me that he might permit me to return to Mexico City since it was amost impossible to see Zapata at this time, as he was busy with most important matters. "However," he continued, "if you will tell me what Carranza is actually willing to give the Indians in land immediately, I will convey it to Emiliano, for he will not listen to any more double-tongued promises of Carranza."

I was in a difficult spot. I could hardly tell this man that Carranza had refused even to negotiate before Zapata came to the capital, hat in hand, and recognized Carranza as his First Chief. It would have been an insult. Instead I told him how several generals and colonels were disappointed in Carranza's stubborn refusal to do anything, but that Obregon, Blanco and most of the other leaders really meant to grant land to the people as soon as practical. Time, however, was needed to put the new government in motion to do the job, as neither Carranza nor Obregon could grant the land without the legislature. I also pointed out that should Zapata declare open war against Carranza, it might unify their own somewhat shaky loyalty and start another Civil War, which would kill the people's chance to obtain land for a long time to come.

Colonel Morales was a man of action, and yet thoughtful, for he gave food and water to my men and horses. When this was completed, he informed me he was leaving at once to try to convey to his chief what I had said, but he thought the gulf between Zapata and Carranza had become too wide and could not be bridged.

Before he departed I gave him the gun brought as a present to Zapata. Morales admired the gun but wasn't sure if he could contact Emiliano as he was busy with his troops. As this sounded a little ominous, I asked about Zapata's intended advance on Mexico City, mentioned by everyone we had met. The answer was evasive in the extreme, and he got up to go when I asked him for a favor: I requested permission to visit the pyramid-temple of Tepoztlan (Place of the Axe) in his absence. I did this without the slightest hope of the wish being granted, but it seemed to please him, for he looked up toward the summit of the rugged mountain and said, "It's quite a climb, but you can make it easy." He also gave me two guides, both of whom had been born and brought up in the shadow of the temple. My men were strictly confined to within the town, with the exception of Pedro, who was permitted to come with me and retain his guns.

When the guides were ready, we started out. Pedro came with me, but Tekwe was left in charge of the men. We started on foot for it was only a short distance to the foot of the mountain. The village of Tepoztlan is located more or less in the middle of a crater which forms part of the plain on which the town stands in the northern extremity of the valley of Cuernavaca. The inhabitants of the place seemed to be of almost pure Aztec descent and speak that language. Their isolated mountain homes lie a little aside from the main route running north and south, and in consequence they have preserved and clung with admirable tenacity to many of their ancient habits and charming customs.

Tepoztlan was first captured by the Aztecs under Emperor Montezuma I, about 1440 A.D., when he, also known by the name of Ilhuicamina (He who shoots at the Heavens), extended his power toward the south from the Aztec capital of Tenochtitlan— now Mexico City.

Tepoztecatl was an Aztec-Chichimec and probably a Toltec "God of Drunkenness; God of Alcohol" (being one of several Octli gods) to whom the temple of Tepoztlan was dedicated, or perhaps it was the other way around. It is hardly likely, however, that Tepoztecatl derived his name from the temple which was of comparatively recent origin, as has been suggested by some.

The guides had instructions to keep behind me, as I wanted to investigate everything at close range without interference. We came to a gorge and while gazing around, I was startled by a very old Indian standing suddenly quite close to me; he seemed to have sprung up from nowhere. The two guides came forward and undoubtedly paid him homage and greeted him with unmistakable reverence. Then I found him to be a pagan priest of a fine old type who carried himself with great dignity and as a worthy descendant of his famous ancestors. He had come from the mountain, and we exchanged the customary greetings. Grumblingly he added something about being too old to visit every day the temple so high up in the sierra. My interest was naturally aroused by his remarks as well as by the respect paid him by the local men. I sought further information, but my questions elicited mere grunts that indicated plainly his disinclination to talk. The man was starved, so I asked Pedro for my lunch and gave it to the old man who ravenously devoured everything; especially did he relish the last piece of white bread brought from the capital.

He sat silent for a moment but belched noisily a couple of times in contentment. Then he noticed my gun and asked to see it. I removed the shells, and he was quite happy holding the revolver as if it had been a sacred idol. As I knew Pedro carried two guns, I asked him for one of them and gave it to the priest as a present with twenty rounds of ammunition. The old man was stunned. He looked at it, then at me—words failed him. Then I gave him a good nip of *tequila* and his contentment was complete. Seeing the complete change of attitude in the man, I reopened the subject of the temple, and he, tired and old as he was, insisted on showing the place himself, and we were on our way up to the temple, which was located about 2,000 feet above us.

We started to ascend through a gorge at the foot of a somewhat precipitous mountain. Here and there we came upon long flights of steps, some of which were cut out of the solid rock, and some were built of or supported by masonry. Suddenly the path seemed to leave the gorge side, and came out more in the open; we seemed to have climbed the face of the cliff. This was the most difficult part as the steps, about a hundred in number, appeared to be almost perpendicular, making the ascent tiresome and tedious.

On reaching the top we found ourselves on what seemed to be two plateaus connected by a narrow

409

ridge. There was a trace of sadness, mingled with pride, in the old man's voice when, pointing to what appeared to be the western plateau he said: "There is what is left of the House of Tepoztecatl. I was taught from childhood not to fail to pay tribute there at a certain time of the year, as did my father and all our ancestors before him. It is a very ancient and sacred shrine, though the White man has desecrated it. And there," he continued, pointing to the other plateau, "where you see the ruins of what were once beautiful buildings, lived the priests and high functionaries who attended the God, and the holy fire within the temple itself. Farther back in among the cliffs and the trees you will find a spring of good water which very few people know about."

The east side of the temple appeared to be a three-terraced pyramidal structure on a rougher kind of sub-structure built as a foundation on the uneven rocky ground. It was made of volcanic rock and mortar. The Pyramid stood near a precipitous rock formation which dropped perpendicularly into the bush below.

The first terrace was reached by two stairways, one on the east and the other on the south side. Both were in bad condition and looked as if they had been deliberately destroyed. The terrace on the east is about thirty-five feet from the ground and forms in part the actual base of the temple proper which was made up of the two remaining terraces. The front of the pyramid seems to be on the west side where there is an open space on the first terrace, in the middle of which stands a slightly raised rectangular platform that may have been a sacrificial altar.

From the open space a stairway leads to the second terrace and continues to the gates of the temple which are on the third terrace. The walls here are about eight feet in height, over six feet in thickness, and constructed of volcanic rock with mortar of lime and sand. The roof, which had fallen in, was made of the same material with masses of mortar in thick layers added and looked as if it had been flat. At the entrance of the temple were the remains of two masonry columns, rectangular in shape, which had supported the roof. The interior consisted of two rooms, one inside the other, connected by an open doorway about six feet wide.

In the middle of the front room, said the old man, was the place, where in ancient days the sacred fire burned, from which coals were obtained for the incense-burners on the altar of the Brandy God. In the inner room against the wall and facing the entrance there was once a pedestal on which stood the image of the God. The old man stood gazing at the spot with reverential awe, and we had to force him to come along with us. There were also stone benches, covered with carvings in front, standing along the walls.

Two stone tablets are built into the lower terrace. One of these has been translated to be an Auitzotl (an odd looking little water animal mentioned in Aztec legends) from which the great Aztec fighting King Auitzotl got his name. This king expanded the empire to its zenith during his reign from 1486 to 1502 A.D. On the other slab is carved a rabbit within ten circles representing the date "10 Rabbit," being in our time of reckoning the year 1502, the date of the king's death.

For what particular purpose this pyramid-temple was built in such an inaccessible spot the old man knew not except to honor the Octli God, but to me it looked like a fortress—an outpost—as well as a temple, for it was strongly built in a hostile territory by a conquering Aztec army.

The visit to this remarkably interesting Aztec shrine would have culminated in disaster had it not been for the old man. During the visit I had out of curiosity kept an eye on the old fellow and noticed him constantly keeping a close watch on the adjoining mountains and, fearing foul play, I did the same but could not see a sign of life. Suddenly, however, he emitted a grunt and said we must leave at once as a party of Zapatistas was moving towards us.

We seemed in a fix, but I knew the enemy could not climb the precipitous sides of the mountain we were on; they could only come up on the side where the stone-steps had been cut. The place was, therefore, easily defended with rifles, but with revolvers short of ammunition and no food, defenders wouldn't last long.

I had a good look at the mountains. There wasn't a soul in my line of vision. Seeing nothing alarming I peeped into the sky and noticed the sun had long since passed its zenith and lovely white clouds were chasing each other merrily, but some were pink in color in the western sky. Pedro broke the silence by suggesting he run down to the village and alarm Tekwe and the men. He could do that, he thought, before the advancing Zapatistas had reached the valley, but in case he couldn't, "You better take this," he said, and tried to hand me his gun. When I reminded him that our fire-arms were under lock and key, we both realized it was time to go and rushed with the old man down the path leading to the uncertainty of the valley.

How we reached bottom I will never know, as we fell several times and could have dropped for hundreds of feet onto the rocks below. When we eventually got there, we were met by an officer with a message from Colonel Morales requesting my immediate return. When told of the advancing Zapatistas, the officer looked worried and urged us to hurry.

When I turned around a little later to look, the temple walls were visible. It was an imposing sight, but it gave me a feeling of the mystic, brought about no doubt by its obscure origin. It was late in the afternoon when I looked for the last time, and the pyramid seemed to form part of the mountain; one couldn't tell which was which, rising like a wall dark and grim. The shadows made it look fierce, unyielding, unmercifully wild and weird—and I thanked my lucky star for bringing me down from there.

When we parted from the old man, who bore the rather modern name of Pedro Prieto, I gave him a federal ten peso bill. As we walked away, Pedro, the priest, called out something in a strange tongue which one of the guides hitherto silent interpreted to be, "an appeal to the ancient God whom he had faithfully served all his life, to protect you."

It was late in the afternoon when we returned to the village, but there was no sign of the pursuing enemy. Pedro told me, though, he had seen what he thought was about a hundred men at the foot of the mountain, but they had halted when they saw us moving toward the town.

Colonel Morales met me in a room used as head-quarters. With him was a man of medium height dressed like an ordinary peon, wearing a large sombrero which remained on the head and pushed down over the face. He had a long dark mustache, the dark eyes were round and a little fishy perhaps. These eyes never seemed to leave my face, which gave me that queer feeling when one is too near a coiled rattler that is ready to strike. The eyes bored through me in an uncomfortable manner, as if seeking my innermost thoughts—like a cobra charming its prey. This man, to whom I was not introduced, kept in the back part of the dark room as if shy or not wishing to be noticed. There was something strange and mysterious about him, which was accentuated by Morales when he turned to him several times as if looking for approval of what had been said.

Morales now gave me some bad news; first I learned that the trusted guides sent with me by Acosta were Zapata's men who had led us into the trap, but it was much worse to hear that the six Yaquis left behind as rear-guard were all dead. They had refused to leave the gap as ordered, they had stayed instead and kept the Zapatistas at bay until the break of day when they were surrounded and killed, one by one, as they refused to surrender . The news grieved me because they were friends and part of my body-guard of Yaquis. We had served together all the way from the northwest and had enjoyed innumerable tilts with the federals and, like the proverbial Irishman, had always been ready for a scrap. These were real Yaquis, and I have no doubt they

414

reached their Happy Hunting Grounds. There are not many White men who would sacrifice themselves to save their comrades when there was an avenue to escape the responsibility. Each one of these Yaquis reminded me of the legendary "Sven Duva," a soldier of Finland, who was stationed on a bridge during the war against Russia, about 150 years ago, with orders "Let not one Devil over the bridge," and he died doing just that.

The colonel then placed the revolver, which I had brought for Zapata, on the table and said something to the effect that since his chief was not within reach at this time, he was returning it with thanks. When I pushed the gun back toward him and asked him to keep it for himself, he cast a fleeting glance to his peon-companion who seemed to nod, and he accepted, for it was an exquisitely engraved and gold-inlayed weapon.

Morales thanked me for the gun, and then he said, with another glance toward the peon stranger, that the presence of a Carranza squadron in Morelos had not yet been reported at headquarters. "Your presence," he continued, "can be pardoned due to your mission, but your Yaqui rear-guard accounted for sixteen of our men before the last one was killed, which cannot be so easily condoned." With another look at his companion Morales spoke once more, "I understand your position and will let you go because of the assistance you gave our men a few days ago against the federals in Mexico City. You must, however, leave before an hour has passed and hurry *compañero,* because you will be hunted to the very gates of the capital when the news leaks out, and I may get orders to join in the chase."

In return, I thanked Morales for his kindness. Then I told him a white lie when I asked him to tell Zapata to be careful when attacking Carranza, as he was well supplied with a large number of men and machine-guns; that he had over forty pieces of artillery with large quantities of ammunition taken from the federals. When finished I got up and called my men.

Morales had thoughtfully fed men and horses with what he had before I returned from the temple. There was nothing to hold us except the guns still impounded, but which this gallant soldier handed over without murmur after his companion had nodded his approval, for he could so easiy have taken us into custody and had us before a firing-squad.

When we were about to leave Colonel Morales made his last effort to win us over to Zapata. As he was not successful, he looked toward his friend standing in the dark doorway and when he gave a nod, we received a guide to show us the beginning of a path leading over the mountains in the north and we were off.

Our escape frm Moreles

When we had gone a bit on the road, Tekwe rode up alongside of me and asked, "How did you like Zapata?" He now informed me that the man with Morales was Emiliano Zapata himself, dressed as a peon for the occasion, as he wanted to see us for himself. The Zapatistas with whom our men had spoken during the day, told them our men had to join Zapata or get shot, and some of them didn't seem to mind doing so, Tekwe said. I had never seen a photo of Zapata, but the description given me fitted perfectly with this man, except for his clothes.

We had hardly gone half-a-mile and were about west of the temple, when a man halted the column. He turned out to be our friend the pagan-priest Pedro Prieto. In some way he knew of our trouble and volunteeed to guide us over the paths and short-cuts, but demanded that the Zapatista guide be sent back and asked for a horse to ride and urged us to speed up as we were in grave danger.

Somehow I felt a perfect trust in this old man and sent the Zapata guide back to Tepoztlan, after giving him a few pesos of Diaz's printed money. When the guide had departed, the pagan-priest told Tekwe to hurry as there were thousands of Zapatistas swarming in the mountains looking for us. He was given a horse belonging to one of the fallen Yaquis, and he sat in the saddle as if he had been a cowboy all his life.

Now began a strange ride of hide and seek, for we had been warned three times and realized we were hunted; therefore we proceeded with care. We were moving north toward San Juanico and could not have been far from this small place, when the old man decided we must leave the road, and we entered a very stony path leading in the direction of Santa Domingo which was in the opposite direction to which I wanted to go. When questioned, the old fox told me, "Should any one have followed us, and I think some one has, he will hurry back to whence he came and give the information of our new direction. We will remain here for a short while only, then return to the other road, cross it, and make for the sierra

417

and the place where the railroad runs toward the setting sun."

When I asked Tekwe if the rear-guard had seen or heard anyone, he answered in the affirmative, but whoever it was gave it up after we turned off the road. When the old man heard this, he swung around and led us over a rough country without any path, and then suddenly there was one, if it could be called a path.

After a while we reached some badly torn up railroad tracks and halted soon thereafter for a rest and information from the scout ahead. From what we learned it appeared as if we were in a tight corner because Zapatista pickets and scouts seemed to be everywhere in front of us. Don Pedro, as I affectionately called the old man, hearing the report, led us northwestward on a winding and, in the dark, invisible footpath. We were leading the horses higher and higher and halted on a stone ridge, in sheer amazement, for in front of us not a mile distant was a line of fires burning, and toward the west we could see new fires being kindled, one after the other.

The plan of the Zapatistas was plain enough. They were fencing us in by a line of fires through which we could not escape without being discovered. They had, however, not reckoned with Don Pedro, for when he saw the fires, he moved us eastward down a steep incline and told Tekwe there was only a small chance to escape, and that was over very rough country for horses. When quite a way down a ravine we turned northward up over a ridge and then followed another gully-like ravine running northward.

It was past midnight and dark as pitch when the Yaqui scout returned and reported that quite a large number of men were standing in extended order north and south, facing east, as if waiting for something. Many of them had made fires which were visible far and wide. This old Yaqui warrior had found not only the enemy, but also a deep gully between two of the fires which we might get through, he said, if we acted at once.

At this point Don Pedro joined me and said, "We must get into the mountains on the other side of these men or we are lost. We can go around them, but it is a long journey and cannot be completed before daylight. Besides, troops may be there also to dispute your right-of-way. This man is right; we must try the gully for it is deep, long and the darkness will help us."

It was three hours before dawn when we started, and I thanked my lucky star for leaving the sabers behind in Mexico City, for many of them rattled enough to wake the dead. We struggled along as fast as was physically possible, almost blindly in the dark ravine and in a black night. And this was done on the advice of an old pagan, whom I had never seen before, who might easily have led us into a trap. He had, on the contrary, inspired me with confidence and thanks to him and the excellent Yaquis, we got through. We were, no doubt, assisted by the fires that not only half-blinded the enemy but also made them huddle close to keep warm, and their constant chatter gave us the chance we so bady needed.

When we had gone through the deep ravine, we came into a long, steep but dry watershed leading to a high stony ridge, running north and south, and halted in the deep saucer-like hollow at the top as dawn broke in all its glory. There was a bitterly cold wind blowing that seemed to go through into the bone. The horses were off-saddled, and the men laid down for a rest. The bivouac must have been at an elevation of about 8,000 feet, as we had been climbing a great deal since leaving Tepoztlan.

For a time at least we had eluded the Zapatistas and hoped for a few hours rest. Don Pedro, Tekwe and I went up to a high point where I searched the mountains near and far with binoculars without seeing any life except the smoke from the fires we had passed between in the night.

While at the observation post, I pumped Don Pedro about Zapata and asked if he knew that he was in Tepoztlan the night before. He did and hinted it was the reason he was leading us over the sierra, as Zapata had been moody and restless for days and might have changed his mind about our leaving. Further, he said, "Had it not been for his friend Morales, you would probably not have seen another sunrise," and with these remarks he returned to the usual silence of an Indian.

The old man was sitting very intent behind a boulder looking westward. Suddenly he emitted his usual grunt and pointed. I looked with glasses but could not see anything unusual, which seemed to irritate him for he called sharply to hurry, the Zapatistas were moving in from the west.

What he actually saw I do not know to this day, but it disturbed him, and we rushed down to the camp where almost everyone was in deep slumber. The horses were saddled in no time, and we were on our way northward along the ridge but below it, which protected us from view from the east. As we marched off I couldn't help smiling to myself at the blind trust I had in this pagan priest.

We had been in camp not over two hours, but it had done wonders to both man and beast. There was no path and the going was rather tough, but the old man urged us on. He never seemed to tire. At about ten o'clock, a machine-gun opened up at long range, and then the rattle of musketry could be heard. Their aim was high, and only a few bullets came zipping close but doing no damage. The distance to the western ridge was about 1,000 yards, with a deep stony gully between, which evidently was difficult to cross, for the Zapatistas did not even try it or, perhaps, the stubborn defense of the six Yaquis two days before had made these men cautious.

We moved northward fast without flank or rear-guard except for one man in each direction, and even that was difficult. The advance-guard was extended as scouts, but even here they had to be drawn in as they impeded our advance, and it was reduced to one man—Tekwe himself. We were soon out of rifle range, which was a relief, as we made a large target, and wounded men would hamper us with every step. We climbed higher which helped us because the country became wilder with every yard.

At about four o'clock in the afternoon we had shaken off the pursuers by changing direction toward the formidable looking Mount Chichinautzin, and then doubling back over a difficult terrain westward. When on the ridge, Don Pedro pointed to a high range and said it was Mount Tres Marias, close to which was a trail to the west of El Guarda. Then he told me something we already knew, that Zapata's men were patrolling the main road as far as El

Guarda and beyond, and it was unhealthy to enter that road before reaching the junction at El Guarda. He now suggested a plan. He proposed that we make for the trail, but long before entering the highway we send out scouts to locate the Zapatista patrol. If it was north of us, or had moved south again, which was their habit, we could then decide what to do.

As we had no other choice, we moved on carefully but with all possible speed. Time was now an important factor; we must get out of Morelos before reinforcements had been rushed from Cuernavaca or Tepoztlan to outflank us, which was now our greatest danger, although I felt that Colonel Morales would hold back his men all he could.

When we reached the trail, the sun was near the horizon. Tekwe, who had been in the lead, reported that about 30 horsemen had gone north on it not many hours before, but we continued nevertheless. Farther on there was a fork in the path; one was the shortest way to El Guarda, the other turned eastward and eventually came to El Guarda by a long and roundabout way. Don Pedro wanted me to take the shorter trail, as he thought the Zapatistas ahead would take the other to ambush us, coming from the east to reach El Guarda on that road. As Pedro and Tekwe both agreed with the old man's logic, we took the shorter route. Before we continued, however, I gave Don Pedro all the federal money we had left, amounting to some eighty pesos, and made him a present of the horse and saddle he was riding, for his yeoman services, and told him to return to his eagle's-nest-like temple immediately with our warmest wishes and thanks. He refused to go

PLATE XV

Cuerpo de Ejército del Noroeste.

COMANDANCIA.

N° 929.-

   Esta Comandancia ha tenido a bien disponer cause
alta con esta fecha en el Primer Regimiento de Artillería que es a las ordenes del C° Mayor Juan Mérigo, con
el grado de Capitán 1°

     Sufragio Efectivo. No Reelección.

     Hermosillo, Diciembre 9 de 1913.

     El Gral en Jefe.

   Al C° Ivor Thord Gray, Capitán 1°

       presente.

Gen. Obregon's Order to join the Artillery.
Hermosillo, Dec. 1913.

PLATE XVI

COMANDANCIA MILITAR
DE LA PLAZA
10.

Por disposición del C. General
on Jefe de la División del Noroeste, comunicada á
esta Comandancia de mi cargo con fecha 3 de los co-
rrientes, causa Ud. baja en el 1er. Regimiento de
Artillería y alta en la Columna del C. General Lucio Blanco.

Lo que comunico á Ud. para su co-
nocimiento y fines consiguientes.

Reitero á Ud. mi consideración.

SUFRAGIO EFECTIVO-NO REELECCION.

HERMOSILLO Enero 5 de 1914.

El Tte. Corl. C. M. de la Plaza.

Al C.

Capitán 1/o. Ivor Thord Gray.   Presente.

My transfer to the Cavalry.
Hermosillo, Jan. 1914.

back at once as he wanted to see us safely to the highway which he said was quite close.

When we reached the highway to the capital, the sun had set. Taking advantage of the road we cantered off in good order in the fast falling darkness with Don Pedro still in the lead. It seemed but a moment after hitting the main road when from the left rear we heard the rattle of musketry. The spurs came into play and bending low over the horses we urged them into a gallop and dashed away, merging almost into a mob in confusion.

The Zapatistas had apparently been located off the road near the trail, which here branches off to Cima, and as they had not expected us so soon, they evidently off-saddled and could not pursue. When we were nearing the road junction of El Guarda, it was occupied by troops, but as we could hardly stop to investigate their strength, I decided to ride through them as the safest way out—and so we charged.

We were in among them before they realized we were the enemy, and as the road was now open before us, we continued on with heavy but rather spasmodic rifle fire from behind. It was all a matter of a minute or less, but when we halted a mile or so down the road to reform, four men were missing and three slightly wounded. Don Pedro, the tough old pagan, was not among us—may his God Tepoztecatl save his soul, for he was an unusual man—and I hope he escaped. He had saved us from an impossible situation, found water where it did not seem to exist, and led us over trail-less mountains in the middle of the night at the risk of his own life, to show his gratitude over a small gift or perhaps a few words of understanding and friendliness.

423

As we never left any wounded behind, I asked Tekwe to find what the men wanted to do. The answer was in the negative because they had seen them fall close to El Guarda, and it would be impossible to get there before they were shot by the Zapatistas. One of the men said he had seen the guide turn, and gallop to the right, when the shooting started, which I hoped was true. As it was impractical to remain so close to the enemy, although expedient perhaps for the sake of the horses, we continued slowly to Ajusco. Here we halted to attend the wounded and the horses, so badly cut on the sharp stones during our cross-country flight from Zapata's clutches.

The night was more or less peaceful although not a restful one, as a mysterious incident disturbed us. We, as always when in a tight corner, were sleeping close to our horses in a corral behind a house. I woke with the others when the horses began to snort and paw the ground. Then we could hear in the stillness of the night the ominous beat of several horses' hoofs on the road.

We remained still but ready. They passed our corral but couldn't see us and went on toward the capital and we, although disturbed, settled down for the rest of the night as there was no better place to go. Suddenly my horse raised his head, snorted restlessly, and soon thereafter we heard several shots and then silence. A minute or two later two men came galloping past us, riding for their lives toward Morelos and the Zapatistas.

The following morning we found that forty horses were too lame to ride, so we started out for Mexico City, on foot, those with good horses leading the lame ones. Before leaving, Pedro was sent with a note to Acosta asking for forty remounts to meet us at Tlalpam, a few miles from Ajusco. The horses came two hours after our arrival there, which gave everybody a chance to clean up which was so badly needed. By six o'clock in the evening the same day all hands were in their quarters, and our jaunt into Morelos to see Zapata was a thing of the past.

During dinner that night I gave Blanco and Acosta a verbal account of the expedition. Both of them expressed their surprise at our escape from Zapata after being disarmed and virtually prisoners. Acosta, who was an exemplification of honor and a stickler for the upkeep of old traditions, said, "It is pleasant to see Zapata's gallantry in return for a favor. It shows that chivalry has not entirely left our beloved land."

When I reported the loss of fourteen men, Blanco brushed it aside as a minor matter in comparison to what might have happened. Then he said, "Your entering into the very heart of his region with an armed force, might throw some doubt in Zapata's mind as to the invulnerability of his bragged about position." This remark by Blanco was proven correct later, as Zapata postponed his already protracted attack on the capital and remained in Morelos. Two months later, however, in November, he joined Pancho Villa, and they chased Carranza and Obregon out of the capital and occupied it themselves for a time.

XIII

Sir Lionel Carden in trouble—The police mutiny—
Carranza and Obregon—I leave for Veracruz and
Europe—A murderous attempt—With the Amer-
icans in Veracruz

The morning following our return from Morelos,
I received a note from Mr. Hohler, of the British
Legation, inviting me to lunch with Sir Lionel that
day. When I arrived, Sir Lionel, strangely enough,
appeared more congenial than at our former meeting, when he was overbearingly condescending and
arrogant of manner.

During lunch, however, the conversation was dominated by him in a series of nonsensical small-talk,
the kind one might expect from a bunch of old
women at a coffee-break. After a while I began to
wonder if he took me for a moron, but Hohler's
facial expression was almost that of disapproval of
his chief, and I realized that the old man was deliberately stringing me along.

Being a guest, I refrained while at lunch from
mentioning the subject of his leaving Mexico as de-

manded by the revolutionary committee of colonels, previously mentioned. The invitation extended to me for lunch was of course for a purpose, but Sir Lionel did not make a single peep indicating why he wanted me at the legation.

Eventually we moved to another room for coffee, and he became more buoyant of spirit but continued in the same manner—only worse. As I had been absent from headquarters for a week or more and could not afford to waste time, I stopped the absurd prattle by asking bluntly, "Sir Lionel, when do you intend leaving Mexico?" The question took him off his guard because it was unexpected and unwelcome as well as undiplomatic, but I had no other choice. He puffed and snorted like an old water-buffalo in embarrassment and anger, his face turned purple, and I was afraid he was going to have a stroke.

It took less than a minute for him to calm down when he admitted having received the message but added, with a great deal of ill-suppressed anger, "You and your bandit associates have no right to dictate to His Majesty's representative. Your demands are outrageous. Good day, Captain Gray!"

Sir Lionel's stand was commendable, but I noticed with some amusement that he called us "bandits" and gave me the British rank of captain instead of colonel, which was plainly shown on my shoulder-tabs. As he had literally kicked me out, I got up, bowed politely, and left without a word. Hohler, obviously alarmed at the turn of events, came with me outside and whispered, "I will call on you this afternoon at five. Please don't act before I come as I have a plan."

The committee of four came unexpectedly during the afternoon, grim and determined, and I did not dare to tell them what Sir Lionel's attitude had been, but did mention that the Secretary of the Legation was coming at five. Hohler came, met the committee and tried hard to postpone any action against the Legation. He was checked about half way by the spokesman, who told him to stop stalling, and demanded Sir Lionel's immediate removal from Mexico.

Hohler, now desperate, asked to be heard and told us that in extreme circumstances the Secretary of a Legation had on rare occasions in the past cabled London for advice when he thought the Minister to be in the wrong. This he offered to do, although it might cost him his career in the Diplomatic Corps. He thought it would probably take ten days to get a reply, due to the war in Europe.

The officers left after being invited to return the following morning for a chat with General Blanco. I suggested to Blanco that he do something to calm them down, as I was afraid of the United States intervening, if the British Legation was destroyed by our men. When the committe turned up, Blanco promoted two of them to colonels, and promised the other two promotion at the first vacancy, and told them not to push the idea of burning the legation.

A day or so later Hohler informed me he had wired London recommending the immediate transfer of Sir Lionel. When everything was done and impossible to undo, he had told his chief of his action. When asked how the minister took the news he said, "Sir Lionel was practically prostrated from the shock."

At noon about August 23, Hohler called and invited me to tea at the British Legation with Sir Lionel that afternoon. When I hesitated, he informed me that Sir Lionel had been relieved of his post by orders from London, following the cable sent, and was leaving for Veracruz the following day, and added, "He wants to see you." It was an unpleasant tea-party for the old man was obviously upset, and I felt very sorry for him. The only interesting point in the conversation was his admission of being in the wrong, and his regrets at not having heeded the warning.

We parted as friends, and he was kind enough to take a letter to my family to be posted in the U. S. Army Post Office in Veracruz. The following day, Hohler came to our headquarters and everything was straightened out with the self-appointed committee. Two of them seemed quite important, and strutted a little at being able to remove a British Minister from his post. Mr. Hohler was later appointed Minister to Mexico, knighted, and became Sir Thomas Hohler. We met many years later at the home of a C.M.R. friend, Major Frank K. Norman, at Sevenoaks, England, and we went over those difficult days.

The Police Mutiny

Mr. Hohler came to my quarters one afternoon and invited me to dinner at the Legation that night. When leaving Casa de la Condesa in an old landau Tekwe had found somewhere and which I am sure had been a hearse, I placed a mauser-carbine on the floor of the carriage as a matter of habit. Tekwe was driving the horse and Pedro sitting proudly and happily beside him. Everything seemed so peaceful.

We had not gone far, as we were still in Tacubaya, when the vehicle was halted by a large body of armed men. They closed in so quickly, and in such numbers, that it was foolish to try to get out the carbine, and then I noticed they were in the uniform of the Metropolitan Police. The officer in charge ordered me out abruptly and seemed astounded: first at my uniform which was of English cut and make, without insignia of rank, and then at my Australian double-brimmed felt hat. He then began a series of questions which came fast as if he was in a hurry. He soon realized that I was not a Mexican, and when he asked Tekwe, "Where are you driving to?", he truthfully answered, "The British Legation." The answer must have convinced the policeman that I was a member of the legation staff, as he cried out, "Ah! You are English. They are friends of ours!"

He then told me in all confidence that the Metropolitan Police, about 2,000 strong, had mutinied and that Obregon and the rest of the rebel leaders would be locked up in jail before midnight. He then urged me to drive direct to the legation and remain there, as some street fighting might take place. We did not need any urging, but when out of sight Tekwe egged the horse into a gallop, not to the British Legation but Cavalry Headquarters. Along the road I thanked my lucky star that I had removed the insignia of rank from my coat, and that the police did not look inside the carriage as the gun might have given me away.

General Blanco and Colonel Acosta were at home, and it did not take long to arouse the 1st and 2nd Regiments, while Acosta rushed to Obregon's Headquarters. When the mutineers in their over-confidence reached the center of the city, they were not prepared for the somewhat warm reception by some of Obregon's Yaquis on the one side and our cavalry on the other. The Police withdrew in confusion, but the fighting continued here and there throughout the night.

I never did know how many of them were killed in the ambush, but it was reported that over 180 bodies were picked up in the streets at daybreak. We lost seven killed, but how many of Obregon's Yaquis went down I never knew. A few days after the mutiny, the police, less some of the leaders, were on their beats as usual.

Carranza and Obregon

Venustiano Carranza was undoubtedly the key figure in the revolution of 1913-1914. His lack of military knowledge seems to have made him afraid of General Angeles, but it might have been because Angeles constantly reminded him of his promises to the Peon-Indian, which in some way interfered with Carranza's own ideas.

Angeles soon became convinced that Carranza, as well as Obregon, had ambitions which had to be satisfied before anything else. Deeply disappointed and feeling perhaps not too safe among these men, he went to Pancho Villa and offered his services. Villa had by this time begun to realize the necessity of trained men and received Angeles with open arms —they became close friends. When Villa and Carranza eventually had an open break, and there was war between them, Angeles, the hidalgo, decided to remain on peon-bandit Villa's side.

Before, as well as after, President Huerta's hurried exit from the capital on July 15, there was a period of uncertainty in which several rebel leaders began to scramble for the presidential chair. The Constitutionalist Army under Carranza, being the best organized, survived the crisis, with Villa and Zapata taking second and third place. There was some dissension within the Carranza group, but aided by Obregon, the First Chief weathered the storm fairly easily. However, had Obregon declared himself a candidate, Carranza, in spite of his experience and venerable looks, might have fallen by the wayside in defeat.

Carranza moved into the capital with his staff about August 22; General Gonzalez occupied Pachuca and General Alfred Robles went to Puebla. His journey through Mexico City was quite a triumphal march and a number of "Viva Carranza" could be heard, which pleased him immensely. On the same day or the next, Carranza gave out a proclamation to the effect that he had taken over the reins of the Mexican State as per his "Plan of Guadalupe" of March 1913. He also sent a request to the United States for the immediate withdrawal of the American troops from Veracruz.

Some one had to be appointed president sooner or later, and a conference of generals was called by Obregon. This meeting decided, although the decision was of a foregone conclusion, that Carranza was the most suitable man as provisional president. Villa and Zapata, two of the three leading commanders of large forces, were conspicuous by their absence at the meeting—they had, of course, not been invited.

Some time after Carranza's arrival, he maintained that the revolution was over, and that all revolution-any units not forming part of the New Army should send in their arms forthwith; then return home and go to work for a living. Under this edict the regular army would practically consist of only Carranza and Obregon men.

This was disturbing news for many of both large and small *cabecillas,* as most of their men had lost their homes and had no place to go. When the disarming order reached Zapata, he gave one of his sardonic sneers and refused to comply until the oft-promised land had been granted, and his own Plan of Ayala agreed upon. Pancho Villa, who actually did not receive the order, smiled at the very idea as he was about ready to march an army against Carranza, to oust him from the capital.

It was a difficult situation for every one. Villa, in the north, called for Carranza's removal from the political arena; if not, he demanded to run the State of Chihuahua and part of Durango in his own way, which was impossible without the country having another Civil War on its hands. Zapata, in the south, insisted on immediate partitionment of the land. Thus we had four forceful men, Carranza-Obregon on one side, Villa-Zapata on the other—each with an army. Carranza, aided by Obregon, holding the capital, was too stubborn to yield an inch, and the others were disinclined to lessen their demands.

To the outside world, as well as to many within Mexico, the revolution was over as the First Chief had said so, although it was far from over. The progress of peace was halted even before it started by the conflicting opinions of the prominent generals. The Carranza-Obregon combination opposed by the Villa-Zapata groups became deadlocked, and there could be no reconciliation or unity, as they had different methods of reasoning, and there had developed a revolution within the revolution. Chaos and anarchy were staring Mexico in the face.

Although there was an open fight for power in which jealousy and grasping for lucrative posts played a prominent part, some of the leaders did think that it would be a good thing for the representatives of the Carranzistas, Villistas and Zapatistas to meet and try to iron out their differences. It was a good idea, perhaps, but it was strongly opposed by Carranza and maybe by Obregon. Both these men did apparently not consider Villa or Zapata fit to rule, or to have any say in the future policy of Mexico as their views had impractical left-wing tendencies. Besides, Villa-Zapata demanded that Carranza step down and eliminate himself at once as the Head of State, which naturally blocked all further discussions on the subject.

General Alvaro Obregon was the most able commander in the revolution. He joined Madero against Diaz, but did not seem to have any particular personal interest or ambition to be a soldier at that time—it came later. He had a keen foresight, and a determination to learn everything on military strategy and tactical problems, and followed military history as keenly as any West Point or Sandhurst Cadet.

He was fearless, cautious and deliberate, with a natural genius in leadership; his talent was mingled with the sternness necessary, and he was calm and cool. His imperturbable nature was, nevertheless, aroused now and again at the wild outbursts of patriotism often displayed by the peons and Indians. Their insufferable strain of passion for land and freedom at first seemed to leave him unmoved. But a change took place within him later, because it was he who made Carranza issue edicts in favor of the Peon-Indian. The Yaquis and Mayos swore by him.

Strong and firm as he was, Obregon was, nevertheless, often swayed one way or another by doubtful influences, especially by Serrano, his chief-of-staff. But when his mind was made up, it was difficult to change it. His pride, which in the beginning might have been an inferiority complex or mere sensitiveness, seemed to increase with time and his rise in position and authority. His better nature and sense of fair play were often subdued by his indomitable will, and his ambition for power forced him to crush all those who refused to be subordinated, or take orders without question.

Obregon was respected but also feared by the upper class, especially the clergy, as they had worked against the freedom movement of the people and had hidden thousands of rifles with ammunition, under and behind altars, for use against us. The clergy also preached that he was an antichristian, which as far as I know, he was not, but he did believe that the power of the Church should be reduced as well as separated from the State, and that it should return and act as a religious institution, and not as rebel-rouser.

When Obregon took over the capital about August 14, he did so in the name of Carranza and the Revolutionary Party. Later, he was naturally forced to levy certain taxes for the upkeep of the city and feeding the starving population. This usual procedure in war was strongly opposed in certain quarters, and principally by the clergy, but their objections were brushed aside as a matter of course.

Whatever his enemies said about Obregon, he always maintained better order and discipline than any other general and he did not tolerate any looting. There were cases of theft, but these men were severely dealt with when caught. Reports came in from some civilians, but no substantial evidence was ever produced, that the Constitutionalist Army was looting the city. Some stores were broken into, of course, but this was done by the usual sneak thieves of the city and by hungry people looking for food.

There were, nevertheless, persistent rumors that some senior officers had obtained large sums from the well-to-do in the shape of protection money and in a kind of blackmail system of—pay or we confiscate everything. Other rumors mentioned mysterious visits in the middle of the night by masked men at the home of the wealthy. These visitors carried legal search-warrants, entered private homes and took with them everything of value. People did not report or even mention these night-raiders, as they thought it the work of some Secret Police and were afraid of reprisals. We believed it was the work of gangsters assisted by one or two officers of high rank, as there was evidently no doubt that some of these night-raids did take place.

There were also several ugly rumors that millions of pesos, intended for the National Treasury, were illegally channeled into private bank accounts by high officers, but these statements were not substantiated.

After my return to the capital from the Zapata region, I noticed with a certain amount of distress how carelessly our forces had been spread all over the city under the pretense of facilitating the feeding and billeting of the men, but in reality to make it comfortable for the various commanders. This had practically immobilized all regiments and made the defensive position of the army extremely shaky. Should Villa and Zapata attack suddenly, we would be scattered like chaff in the wind and probably lose most of our equipment. In fact, had Zapata carried out his intended three-pronged attack, we would probably have been forced to evacuate the city, as he controlled not only everything south of us, but also could cut the railroad to Veracruz whenever he chose to do so.

Our position as victors in the revolution was not an enviable one, as the revolutionary army had split into three parts under Carranza, Villa and Zapata. Each of these had his own army and different aims and ideas as to what should be done.

A great number of officers of all ranks believed the revolution was over because Mexico City was theirs, Utopia had been reached, and they must celebrate. The temptation to glorify the victory over the Huerta government was too great and many small *fiestas* were noticeable everywhere. As a result outposts, scouting, patrols and intelligence work had practically ceased to exist in several brigade units, and the roads into the capital, from every direction, were practically wide open.

The elements of surprise attack were therefore constantly with us and irritatingly disconcerting. This nervous tension was aggravated by the lackadaisical manner into which so many officers had drifted in carrying out their duties. Men were allowed to wander around, slovenly and aimlessly, which often led them into trouble. This was noticeable more among the newly raised units, and I feared the infiltration of a great number of men from both Zapata's and Villa's armies.

As we were too vulnerable for comfort, Acosta and I had a long talk with General Blanco and suggested that we move the cavalry division out of the capital to a more practical, as well as tactical position. Blanco agreed, but to our dismay he informed us that he was under suspicion of being in sympathy with Pancho Villa, and this we knew was not so. The real trouble behind this was Blanco's tremendous popularity among the troops, the fair sex, and civilians wherever we went. Several delegations had come to our headquarters and requested Blanco to declare himself a candidate for the presidency. It happened in Culiacan, Guadalajara and in Mexico City, but he always declined with thanks as he was loyal to Carranza. Obregon and Carranza had heard of these visits, misconstrued them, and were incensed at the very idea as they had arranged otherwise between themselves long ago and tolerated no antithesis.

Blanco, although in favor of moving to a more advantageous position, said, "If I gave orders for the cavalry to move out of the city, Obregon might think we were deserting him to join Villa. We would be arrested, tried and probably shot within twenty-four hours." Then he looked my way with his friendly, but serious smile and added, "Colonel Serrano wanted to know yesterday why I retain you, a *gringo* who served with Villa in 1913."

The significance of Serrano's remark was obvious. I was still under suspicion of being an American, and friendly with Villa, but the direction from which it came made it more serious for Blanco and myself. Serrano, more formidable than ever, was trying to implicate Blanco with Villa through me as an excuse to get rid of Blanco. To be accused by this man, at this time, was tantamount to conviction and a firing squad.

One of the several international problems that struck me as downright peculiar in Mexico City was the clannishness, which amounted to a strain between the Americans and the British. They invited me into their clubs out of curiosity, perhaps, but they gave me a pleasant time. They could not, however, hide the unpleasant under-cover feud. This seemingly unnatural situation may have been due to their different political affiliations in Mexico or to the Americans chumming with the rebels, or perhaps the European war. The exclusive Jockey Club also invited me, and to my surprise, its atmosphere was cleaner and the milieu more pleasing because it seemed free of the intricacies of political intrigue.

The clannishness of the Americans on the one side, and the British on the other, was analogous to the interesting, queer but thoroughly understandable social change which took place among the revolutionary leaders. These men had, unconsciously or otherwise, become divided into two racial and social groups. The educated creoles and Spanish mestizos on the one side, against the illiterate Indian and peon on the other. Thus we had Carranza, Obregon, Blanco, Calles, Gonzalez, Acosta and many others working together, all of them creoles or mestizos, against Villa and his generals, all Peon-Indians, and Zapata with his leaders, all Indians. Angeles was an Indian who supported Carranza and Obregon at first, but was eventually forced to go to Villa, the half-breed Indian peon.

I leave for Veracruz and Europe

Ever since Sir Lionel informed me of the war in Europe, I had tried unsuccessfully time and again to resign from the Mexican Army. General Blanco was quite willing to let me go, as he realized my desire to rejoin the British, but our G.H.Q. seemed to have a different concept as to my reasons for leaving. Blanco was told by Colonel Serrano, "Colonel Thord-Gray cannot possibly intend to join the British Army as it is in retreat. It is better for him to remain here for awhile yet."

As Blanco, evidently still under a cloud of suspicion, could make no headway at headquarters, I called on General Francisco Urguizo, a member of Carranza's staff. We had become friends during the early part of the campaign in Sonora and Sinaloa, and he promised to intercede with the First Chief on my behalf.

A day later Urguizo informed General Blanco that Carranza was disinclined to go against Obregon's headquarters, but hinted that Blanco could grant me "leave of absence" without referring the matter to the C-in-C. Upon this information Blanco granted me "unlimited leave" from the Mexican Army in a letter dated September 3, 1914. (SEE PLATE XVII.)

As I wished to place Pedro and Tekwe in a position of financial security for some time at least, arrangement was made with Blanco and Acosta to allow these men to return to their native land at once, and that each be allowed to keep his horse, saddle, and equipment which included their guns. To be quite sure of this I gave each an official letter stating that they were traveling to Sonora in the revolutionary cause and that the horses and saddles belonged to them. They also received twelve hundred pesos each in Carranza money as a small token for their splendid and unselfish services. The money was the last of my wad of Carranza money kept for emergency along the line of march, and I regretted deeply there wasn't more to give these fine men who had, time and again, risked so much in their loyalty.

In the afternoon of September 7, 1914, everything was in readiness for my departure from Mexico City to Veracruz, the first leg of the journey to England. Unknown to me, General Blanco in a gesture of good-will had asked Obregon's headquarters to give me a private car, which was granted, although it was usually only given to senior generals.

This favor of a private railroad car from Colonel Serrano seemed unnatural to me, as he had hinted to Blanco and others only a day or two before that I was in cahoots with Pancho Villa which, even as a rumor, was equivalent to guilt. It had also come to my attention through my Tarahumara friends and Tekwe that the many attacks on my person in the past by hired assassins had been instigated from the same direction. When I told Blanco of my fears, he told me he had requested the car. He also said something about Serrano's change of heart, and how he had praised the work I had done in the past, and added, "You can hardly refuse the car now."

When there was nothing left for me to do except to bid my friends good-bye, Blanco and Acosta brought me outside into the street and there to my surprise came into view the 1st Cavalry Brigade, all veterans from Sonora and Sinaloa. They lined up in front of the building, then swung smartly into columns of troops and trotted past in review with colors flying. It moved me deeply. I advised Blanco and Acosta not to come to the train, as rumors, now openly discussed, stated that I was on my way to join Villa, which would be detrimental to any one seeing me off.

A Murderous Attempt

Pedro and Tekwe had been sent ahead to the station with my few belongings, and I followed in an old Victoria. When about two hundred yards from the depot, these two Indians surprised me by stopping the carriage and asking me to get out. Each, dressed as a *mozo,* was acting very servile and gestured to me mysteriously to one side. Here these two friends, tested in hundreds of skirmishes, informed me that I was in a bad fix, almost too preposterous to believe, except that this was Mexico in time of revolution.

Pedro now divulged how he and Tekwe, when hearing of the special car granted by Colonel Serrano, had gone to investigate among their friends at headquarters staff and discovered that this car by order of someone high in authority was to be lost while going down the steep grade into the lowlands, because it contained a *gringo* spy.

Pedro, God bless his soul, continued, "We three are blood-brothers and have been through much together. You have listened to our advice sometimes, and now as a last favor, we request that you do not go on this train, but as you cannot remain in the city, we have a plan." He then said in effect, "On the other side of the passenger train is a freight train which will leave a little before the other as it carries supplies for our troops facing the Americans in Veracruz. We will carry your things into the car designated for your use and you follow us, but as there might be someone watching you, take out some money and pay us off like *mozos,* and don't say good-by to us. We will soon return from the other side and take your bags across the tracks and place them in the last boxcar of the freight train. Watch me carefully, for when I come out from the boxcar, you must rush toward it and jump in. Don't dally, as the train will be moving slowly before you get there."

There wasn't much time to decide one way or another, because what these men told me was too fantastic to believe, so I agreed. While watching them carrying my things across the tracks out of the corner of my eye, a major and a captain walked into the car, saluted and asked if they could get a seat as there was not a vacant place elsewhere. When they walked in, I was sure it was part of the plot mentioned by Pedro, not derailment but plain murder. Who would ever know?

Under the circumstances I could hardly refuse the request. They both rushed out for their things, and then I remembered Pedro; there he was, already on the ground and running my way. Evidently some time had been lost in talking to the officers, and I rushed out bending down so that no one could see me from the platform. Without the aid of my two friends I could never have gotten on that train now picking up speed.

I turned and heard Pedro call out somewhat wistfully, *We ari bache norawa* (Good-by friend). I cast a glance toward my so-called private car and saw two men getting in. The last I saw was Pedro and Tekwe standing there, each with one arm stretched out toward me, and I felt a great loss within me. I was also ashamed of leaving these faithful friends and warriors behind as I could, perhaps, have taken them along with me—a crazy idea, maybe, but it was there.

Everything went well, but the train stopped at a station east of Paso del Mocho and remained there for several hours. I had been informed that the passenger train would pass us at this point, and that I had to change into it as the freight train was not going any further. The passenger train came, and I discovered there had been a delay due to an accident. The last car had broken its coupling, run

445

amuck and tumbled down the mountain side. Pedro was right again, and once more had saved me from an unpleasant end. The one high in authority, as Pedro called him, had made his final murderous attack but failed, thanks to the vigilance of my two *compañeros*.

With the Americans in Veracruz

Eventually my train arrived at Veracruz Station at 11 P.M., September 8. My presence created quite a commotion as I was dressed in Mexican field service uniform, having no other clothes. There was a distinct flurry of activities among the American officers as they had not been advised of any military mission and could not make out how I got through the cordon of American troops. The intelligence department had said nothing — someone had fumbled the ball. However, they treated me in a most friendly manner, and I was escorted to the hotel, but noticed, with some amusement, that I was under strict surveillance.

The following morning an officious looking shavetail came to the hotel quite early to inform me that Captain Burnside of the U. S. Army Intelligence would call on me at 10 A.M. for questioning, and I must remain in my room. Captain Burnside came, and it was a surprise for both as we were old friends from Manila in 1908.

Captain Eames of the 28th Infantry and Lieutenant van Nostrand of the Marine Corps came and paid their respects, but it was pretty obvious they had been sent to pump me, check on my activities or to see if I was pucka or not. Eames took me everywhere I wanted to go although the city was quarantined because of yellow-fever. He drove me around to find some civilian clothes, and I managed to purchase a ready made suit, which was exchanged for the Mexican uniform.

A courtesy call was made, by request, on General Frederick Funston, the G.O.C. American troops in Veracruz the morning of September 10, and I took a great liking to him. Nevertheless, he gave me a regular going over as to the strength, disposition and efficiency of the Mexican forces as well as my opinion of the prominent generals, guerrilla leaders and politicians. The information he received was in no way detrimental to Mexico. The American newspapermen in the capital had already published what I had said.

During my visit to the American Headquarters I bumped into an old friend from Manila, Lieutenant Jacob Wuest of the 30th Infantry. He, Lieutenant G. Maurice Kelly, also of the 30th and I used to play around a good deal in Manila just before I left to join the French in Tonkin, 1909. Near General Funston's quarters I met another old friend from the Philippines, Major La Mot, who was with the 14th Infantry in Cebu, 1908.

Lieutenant King of the U. S. Navy called in the morning of the 11th, and invited me to lunch aboard The Virginia, Admiral Nettey's flagship, in the harbor. King was my host in the ward-room, but the admiral took me into his quarters, and like Funston, questioned me unmercifully on the efficiency of the Mexican Army and the general attitude of the Mexican upper class toward the United States.

The admiral was a wonderful host and his officers were overwhelmingly friendly. They asked me, it seemed, a thousand questions about Mexico, the revolution and, of course, what were the girls like. I enjoyed my visit immensely because they were real fellows, and the American food was something out of this world after the somewhat tiresome cornmeal-and-water consumed for so long.

That afternoon Jake Wuest and von Nostrand obtained a Navy launch and we went over to the old fort San Juan de Ulua to visit the famous dungeons where for centuries so many Mexican political and military prisoners have died from slow starvation.

There was a special dungeon excavated out of the solid rock, so deep that when the tide came in, it filled the cell with water and the prisoner had to stand on a ledge or drown. When standing on this ledge a man of average height must rise on his toes and even so the water came up to his chin. This went on for weeks, month after month, year after year, until when almost starved to death the man could not stand up any more and so drowned.

These dungeons had obviously not been cleaned since the fort was built several hundred years ago, because human remains, bones, skulls and excrement littered the floor two feet deep. It took one back to the middle ages and the awful tortures used during the Inquisition. These dungeons had been in constant use by the Mexicans up to the time of the American occupation in 1914.

I left Veracruz during the morning of September 13, 1914, on the S/S City of Mexico bound for Texas City. Many of the American officers came to see me off, but I was never quite sure if it was from friendship, curiosity or to make certain this strange Mexican colonel had really gone. Thus ended my Mexican military career, and my first trip to that lovely country.

In front of me was another war which everybody thought might be over long before I ever reached England. The war, later known as World War I, which President Wilson called, "A war to end all wars," was not over for me until 1920, when I, as a wounded prisoner of the Bolsheviks, got out of Siberia by the Grace of God and a very decent, as well as considerate, Red Commander.

APPENDIX A.

The Cause of the Revolution

The reason for the revolution goes back into the period of the Conquest. The three hundred years of Spanish Colonial History, and the hundred years that followed the War of Independence, are so full of persecution of the Indians and Peons that it would fill a large volume to scratch only a small part of the surface of these centuries.

The Conquest was a brilliant achievement by the Spanish forces. It was, nevertheless, reduced to a sordid enterprise by the greed for gold. The shameless murder of Emperor Montezuma and the torture of the gallant Guatemozin and his companion by burning their feet over a fire to force from them the whereabouts of the hidden treasure of the Aztecs, was a disgrace.

The "Painted Books," the priceless literature of the Aztecs which gave the records of their astronomy and sciences and, perhaps, their origin, were put to the torch because the stupidity of superstition proclaimed them heathen and hence work of the Devil.

The period mentioned is characterized by a tyrannical domination by the upper class, religious intolerance, slavery, inquisition and brutality toward the Indians. What was done in the name of Christianity during these four centuries seems to put Genghis Khan and Attila into the shade as second raters.

When the Indians did not willingly accept Christianity the bull-whip came into play and was freely used. They were also robbed of their land, their temples and civilization destroyed, and they themselves were enslaved by the hundreds of thousands. The Indians were made to obey a God whose teachings, as well as language, were beyond their understanding, except, perhaps, that this new God was obviously more savage in his demands than their own deities had been.

As time progressed the peonage system was established. The peon received a meager salary from the *hacendado* but the man was forced to purchase everything he needed from the hacienda store. His wages were not enough to cover expenses and he ran into debt. Month after month, year after year, the debt increased — that was the system. Not only must he work but his wife and children were pressed into the peonage service "to pay off the debt" which, due to the system, was impossible.

The peons wanted to rid themselves of these oppressors, but they were powerless because they had only bows, arrows, knives and slings with which to fight. From these conditions there was no escape, not even hope. Not yet. There was, however, ill-will and deep resentment brewing in every Indian pot throughout the land.

When the Indians were in the depth of despair, their ancient gods seemed to have taken compassion on them as there appeared two signs that gave them hope. In 1909, there was an eruption of the Colima Volcano and the sky became dark and threatening. The descendants of the priests before the Conquest came out of hiding and predicted that the war of deliverance was near.

In 1910, there was a sign in the heavens — Halley's Comet. Some Indians thought it was a good omen, but when the cattle and goats became restless, and the people couldn't sleep, it was a bad omen — it meant war, pestilence — death. Some of the shamans predicted war, but who was going to lead them?

Then like a miracle, a strange voice was calling them to rebel against their oppressors and promising "Land and liberty" to all. It was Francisco Madero urging them to rise against the *cientificos,* the indolent short-sighted oligarchy under whose tyrannic rule temper and patience of the masses had reached the breaking point. The insolence and stupidity of the *mayordome* became unbearable and, driven to desperation, the peons, urged by their pagan priests, retaliated by joining the revolutionaries in a happy mood.

The angry uprisings of the multitude to whom peonage slavery and the whipping-post could no longer be made tolerable did not inspire the upperclass with compassion or understanding. Instead they forbade the peons to take part in the freedom movement and threats of excommunication were hurled at them if they disobeyed.

The betrayal of the confessional trapped thousands into federal hands who shot them. Thousands of others were banned into purgatory, their children refused baptism and burial, land and domestic animals confiscated. Slavery was not permitted by law but the Indians, especially the Yaquis, were sold by the thousands at so much per head into tropical labor camps. The sun was, however, setting fast on the power of this tyrant caste — the air was pregnant with revolution.

The birth of a new life for the Peon and Indian was at hand, as the cup of bitterness was running over. The people got beyond control and swarmed to the revolutionary standards of *tierra y libertad* (land and liberty), all more or less indifferent to the anathema.

The diabolical wrongs forced upon the natives made these decent people into canaille brimming over with passion for revenge, and caused the mighty river of blood which overwhelmed Mexico.

However, in spite of the opposition by the ruling class, the Peon-Indians, the pariah-caste in the Mexican social scale, pulled themselves up by their own bootstraps to a much better station in life.

With this dawn of the Indian awakening, there rose political and military leaders of great ability from the ranks of schoolteachers, cowboys, ranchers, storekeepers, peons, full-blooded Indians, and bandits, but they returned usually, if not always, whence they came, by the assassin's bullet.

The first rebellion against Diaz was a success. Their chosen man, Francisco Madero, was unanimously elected president in November 1911. His election should have been the beginning of a new and peaceful era for the Indians and Peons as peonage, whipping-posts and hacienda debts lay behind them. The land, the corn-fields (*milpas*), stolen from them was

454

PLATE XVII

COMANDANCIA.

Número 790.

De acuerdo con su petición,este Cuartel General concede a usted licencia ilimitada para sepa-
rarse del Ejército Constitucionalista y marchar a Eu-
ropa al arreglo de sus asuntos particulares.

Es la oportunidad de darle las gracias por
sus magníficos servicios que prestó a nuestra causa,
estando al frente del Regimiento que confié a su dig-
no mando.

Hágole presente mi atenta consideración y -
aprecio.

Constitución y Reformas.

México,septiembre 3 de 1914.

El General,Jefe de la División de Caballe-
ria.

Al C

Coronel I.Thord Grey   Presente.

My leave from the Mexican Army.
Mexico City, September 3, 1914.

to be returned. The Big Chief, Madero, in Mexico City had promised and he would not fail them. But during 1912-1913, there was a period of setbacks caused by broken promises, treachery, treason, counter revolution, and a series of assassinations.

These unfortunate and deplorable happenings are, it seems, predestined in revolts that are national in scope as they crop up in the history of all nations. In Mexico, however, they acted more as a pause before the real Dawn of Freedom, as an interval of uncertainty and doubt between the die-hards of the Old Era and the Birth of the New.

When Madero promised land to the Indians he was, no doubt, inspired by well-meaning philosophical ideas, but he lacked experience and common sense. He was also guided by unwise impulses, and depended on spiritual inspirations derived, it seems, from advisors plotting for his downfall.

Madero retained the Diaz army intact with all of the generals and colonels. Taking advantage of the situation, they advised Madero to disarm and demobilize his own irregular rebel troops — by force if need be. These men who had carried Madero triumphant into the capital were now to be hunted down like vermin, by the very army they had defeated.

Rumors of plotting among the higher officers against him soon reached the president. Rumors, false or true, state that Madero turned to astrologers and the ouija-board for advice, and did nothing. While Madero was walking around in his fallacious political vision, oblivious of his surroundings, General Huerta decided the time was ripe to act.

On February 19, 1913, he had Gustavo Madero murdered; then he placed President Madero and Vice

President Suarez under close arrest in the National Palace. During the evening of February 22, Huerta ordered the President and Vice President to be transferred from the Palace to the city jail "to protect them against harm." When the soldiers reached the back of the penitentiary the two men were forced out of their autos and assassinated by shooting.

General Victoriano Huerta had now reached his objective, the presidency, but the murder of Madero was the spark that ignited into flame the passion for freedom and the hatred for the *cientificos.*. It started the bloody Civil War of 1913, which lasted several years in which tens of thousands of Peons and Indians bit the dust so that their children could be free.

APPENDIX B.

The aftermath—The end of Carranza, Pancho Villa, Zapata, Obregon, Lucio Blanco, Serrano and Calles.

The reader might be interested in the eventual fate of some of the Mexican leaders as they were eliminated by their opponents, one by one, by the persuasive method of assassination — call it military or political expedience if you like — but it was still murder.

When Carranza entered the Capital in August 1914, he took over the government and demanded the immediate withdrawal of American troops from Mexican soil, and they pulled out from Veracruz in November. Carranza now claimed that the revolution had come to an end, but resisted vigorously making good his, and Madero's, many promises to the Peon-Indian.

Obregon and others considered the revolution far from over, as there were numerous guerrilla bands roaming the country, besides the two armies of Villa, in the north, and Zapata in the south, both defying Carranza and his government.

457

The general condition in Mexico wasn't good, and so it was rather asinine to say the revolution was over, when in reality there was a serious revolution within the revolution. Confusion and disorder reigned in many parts of the land, often due to inconsiderate but ambitious generals reaching out amateurishly for the guilded-chair in the National Palace. But the real trouble came from the *cientificos,* because they complained in the United States with grossly exaggerated half-truths and fabricated rumors which grew into tremendous proportions each time they were passed along. The American Press, not knowing the truth, called for intervention, and the Hearst papers practically demanded, "Plant the American Flag all the way to the Panama Canal."

The revolution against Huerta was won, but the struggle for power between the revolutionary leaders continued, and the ugly rhythm of jealousy and hate increased daily. This struggle for the control of Mexico did, however, soon simmer down to four men, Carranza-Obregon on the one side, Villa-Zapata on the other, who chased one another in and out of the capital at least twice.

About the time when Pancho Villa's lucky star was in the zenith, but showing a tendency to descend, Obregon thought it expedient for Carranza to strengthen his somewhat shaky political fences by making good some of the promises to labor.

Carranza had undoubtedly been an astute politician, but he had become somewhat obstinate and unyielding. This inflexibility made him struggle against Obregon's suggestions, as advice, which differed with his own ideas, were apparently unacceptable. Besides, he thought the time immature.

As a result more unrest came to the land, and commercial labor went on strike for better wages and shorter hours. The agrarians, the Peons and Indians, were rapidly verging toward a revolution against Carranza if not granted the often promised land, for which they had been fighting for years.

Someone had to do something to save the country from another Civil War and probable anarchy under Zapata or Villa. There was only one man in sight for this difficult task, Alvaro Obregon. Taking the bull by the horns, Obregon forced Carranza to legislate certain social reform laws beneficial to the working class. Outstanding among these were perhaps the manifesto from Veracruz, December 12, 1914, and the Agrarian Bill of January 6, 1915. These Bills started a rift between Carranza and Obregon, which came into the open later, and was never bridged.

The End of Carranza

As mentioned, General Obregon and his associates did not approve of Carranza's method of government and started to resist vigorously his rather one-sided system after the revolution. This movement might have been brought to a head by the New Constitution, which was written entirely by Carranza men without due consideration, it was claimed, for the country as a whole. The move against Carranza might also have been aggravated by Obregon's followers who requested him constantly to be a candidate for the presidency.

About this time, Germany was apparently not so cock-sure of winning the war in Europe. This is evident when Mr. Zimmerman, the German Foreign Minister, sent a note to Carranza proposing an alliance between Mexico, Japan and Germany against the U.S.A. In this correspondence, which became famous as the "Zimmerman Note," Germany offered Carranza the return of most of the vast territory Mexico had lost to the United States in 1847, if she joined in the war against America. The offer might well be called a tempting one because it involved the whole of Texas, New Mexico, Arizona and California, an area of over 661,000 square miles and a population of millions of people.

The differences of opinion in home affairs was increased by the international nature of the Zimmerman Note, and the unavoidable open break came. Carranza believed Obregon stood in his way, and being badly advised or overestimating his own popularity, he issued an order for Obregon's arrest. To save himself, or being tired of Carranza's stubborness, Obregon joined up with Adolfo de la Huerta and General Plutarco Calles in Sonora, and marched on the capital. When this became known, many of Carranza's friends and supporters flocked to Obregon and so did a vast number of agrarians.

When Obregon was approaching the capital, Carranza left by train for Veracruz where his friend General Sanchez was in command. Sanchez is supposed to have promised aid to his chief, but when Obregon entered the capital and appointed Adolfo de la Huerta president interim, he went over to Obregon's side. He also sabotaged the president's train which forced Carranza to move into the adjoining hill country for safety. However, three days later his enemies caught up with him and Carranza was murdered while asleep on the mud-floor of a hut at Tlaxcalantongo May 21, 1920.

Pancho Villa in Defeat

When Obregon received orders from Carranza in 1915, to move out and crush Pancho Villa, it seemed a two to one chance that he would not succeed. Few people knew, and among them certainly not Carranza, that Obregon had from the very beginning taken great interest in military strategy and tactics and had studied hard the different phases of defense and attack. While in Culiacan, Obregon became almost obsessed with the idea of common field trenches protected by barbed-wire entanglement and realized fully the fundamental principles of reserves and artillery support in both defensive and offensive action.

On the eve of leaving on the campaign against Villa, he recognized the fact that more field-guns were necessary, and as he could not obtain them any other way, Obregon took them from Carranza. It is doubtful indeed if Carranza knew of the transfer of several field-batteries and machine-gun units from his own to that of Obregon's army, as it was done secretly and in the middle of the night. Obregon's cavalry was good as it was the remnants of the 1st Cavalry Division trained in Sonora. His most reliable infantry was the Yaqui and Mayo Indians from Sonora — the best in Mexico.

Obregon, taking no chances, moved cautiously on to Celaya in Guanajuato, and took up position of

461

his own choosing, entrenched himself, and made liberal use of the barbed-wire he had brought along. Well supplied with food, artillery, ammunition and knowing the impetuousness of Pancho Villa he sat down, but had not long to wait.

Villa advanced early in April from his base in Aguascalientes and occupied Irapuato. Then he moved east with undue haste, pushing Obregon's advance-guard back to Celaya without any trouble. This easy operation should have made Villa cautious, but instead it increased his contempt for his enemy. He even neglected to use his usually good intelligence service. He advanced recklessly without scouts and knew nothing of Obregon's barbed-wire, which was entirely new to Villa.

Not knowing what he was up against Villa sent his hitherto unbeaten cavalry in a charge against barbed-wire, trenches, and masked machine-gun nests, without making use of his artillery. His famous cavalry met a terrific concentration of fire. Again and again they charged but were forced back, leaving about a thousand dead and wounded on the field, some hanging like scarecrows on the barbed-wire.

Villa returned the following morning and after a brief shelling, he sent his cavalry against Obregon's defenses to their certain death. It was another massacre. Villa retreated after several desperate but foolish charges and left some three thousand dead and wounded behind.

Badly mauled, Villa moved away for a rest and reinforcement. He had never suffered a major defeat before, but should have known better than to return against Obregon, short of ammunition as he was. On or about April 13 he made another frontal attack and, as before, his men were slaughtered — only worse. In his ignorance of military tactics Villa did not even imagine that Obregon would dare to counter-attack. But while Villa's men were trying to extricate themselves and the plunging horses from the barbed-wire, Obregon sent in his cavalry on both of Villa's flanks. This ended the fight. Villa lost all of his artillery, some 5,000 rifles, over 6,000 prisoners, and thousands of killed and wounded were spread over the battlefield.

Soon after this disaster, Villa was joined by General Angeles with quite a large force and several batteries of good artillery. Instead of turning against Obregon's tired troops, now short of ammunition, Villa sat down and refused to move. He seemed to have lost his former self and desire to act. He lost his chance, but Villa was not himself and his indecision was, no doubt, his undoing. To the surprise of his men, Villa began to retreat from place to place apparently without an objective. Taking advantage of the situation, Obregon, who had sat tight until now, left his almost impregnable position and captured many important points from Villa.

About this time Adolfo de la Huerta, located in Sonora, had rebelled against Carranza. He also made overtures to Villa, promising him all possible assistance if he would continue his fight against the Carranza regime. Villa, in a defeatist mood, avoided Obregon and decided to cross the sierra into Sonora to join De la Huerta and make that state his own base.

Far in the northwest and close to the American Border was a Carranza force at Agua Prieta under

General Calles. This place became suddenly important in Villa's distorted mind, and he began to cross the Sierra Madre with men fresh from a temperate clime and dressed accordingly. His force suffered much from the cold winds in the high mountains, but they went on without a murmur as their faith in Villa was still great.

Obregon had a good intelligence service. On hearing of Villa's intentions, he requested permission from the American government to transport a Mexican force over United States soil from Piedras Negras to reinforce Calles at Agua Prieta. The request was granted and the troops were sent, of course without Villa's knowledge.

It must be said that Villa had expected aid from De la Huerta and Maytorena, but no help came. Restless, and no doubt out of sorts, he made a frontal attack at night without any reconnaissance. He may have had a bold plan because Mexicans do not like night-fighting, but if so, it went astray, for a large and strong search-light blinded Villa's attacking force, and it was cut to pieces almost to a man, while trying to get through the barbed-wire.

To escape capture Villa retreated with the remnants of his corps reduced to about two thousand strong. He abandoned his now useless artillery and all other superfluous impedimenta and began his march over the snow-clad mountains in the middle of winter with his men dressed in tropical clothing. He arrived at his destination in western Chihuahua but with only about five hundred men. The rest were frozen corpses lying where they fell, scattered all over the sierra, giving the coyotes a good feast.

His mind full of bitterness against the United States for aiding Calles with transportation and the search-light, Villa began to brood revenge. His men did the same and often did him harm by their actions. Villa was accused of certain attacks in which he really had no part, such as the Santa Isabel incident in January 1916, when some American mining men were killed. It was a revenge raid, however, by some of his men who had survived the Agua Prieta massacre.

Then in March 1916 came the Mexican raid on Columbus, New Mexico, U.S.A. in which some eighteen Americans were killed, among them several U. S. soldiers. This also was charged against Villa and may possibly have been his doing. It brought on the American Expedition under General Pershing. There were, however, persistent rumors at the time that the raid was engineered by some German international plotters to keep the United States from joining the British and French against Germany.

Pancho Villa suddenly snapped back to his former self and managed in some miraculous way to raise another army. He attacked Carranza's troops and drove them out of Chihuahua City, then captured Toreon and many other places, but this time he was under General Felipe Angeles' guidance. Villa was, however, not quite in the mood and did not wish to hold the places captured, so abandoned them. About April 1919, Villa's troops took Hidalgo de Parral and almost destroyed the entire Carranza garrison.

Villa looked up to Angeles as one would to a demi-god, but Angeles, finding Villa tiresome to handle, retired for a rest in the backwoods of Durango. When he tried to rejoin Villa, he was captured by some Carranza troops and rushed to Chihuahua City. He was tried for treason by a military court and executed by a firing-squad September 26, 1919. In the eyes of many, this was considered plain murder. With Angeles' death Villa was a completely changed man. He disbanded all his men except for about a regiment of cavalry, and with these men he kept on embarrassing the government, but it was not the same as before.

The End of Pancho Villa

With Angeles dead and Carranza out of the picture, Villa, tired of his turbulent existence, wished to retire and contacted his friend De la Huerta in the National Palace. The president granted Villa the sum of 500,000 pesos in gold and a large hacienda in Durango for his services in the revolution and an absolute immunity by the government. When Villa took up his new life in Durango some of his men came to work for him and he helped many to obtain land not far from his own.

The only three peaceful years in Villa's life went by, and then one day he was asked to be a god-father to a child of one of his old comrades. On his return home from the *fiesta* on July 18, 1923, an assassin with several accomplices ambushed Villa, and he was riddled with some fifty bullets. Thus ended the life of the most colorful peon-bandit general in the revolution. A rumor went around for a long time that the assassin collected only part of the blood-money, as those connected with the sordid affair did not dare, for fear of exposure, to pay the balance.

The End of Zapata

As Emiliano Zapata could not be conquered by force of arms, threats, or bribery, the government being desperate, perhaps, arranged for his downfall by a dishonorable stratagem. General Gonzalez had been sent to Morelos to remove Zapata from the political and military scene by fair or foul means. He did all he could. He looted villages in sympathy with Zapata and even destroyed villages and shot some of the people for refusing to give information of their hero.

Gonzalez had a Yaqui-mestizo colonel in his command who had served with Villa, but joined Carranza with some men after Villa's defeat by Obregon. Early in April this colonel, in cahoots with the commanding general, and with a promise of blood-money of some 100,000 pesos in gold, took with him about a regiment and entered the Zapata region under the White Flag. He told Zapata's agents how he had deserted from Gonzalez and wished to join the Great Zapata with his regiment fully armed.

Zapata was slow in accepting the renegade colonel, but decided to meet him after he had attacked and captured a Carranza garrison and incidentally killed a number of his own comrades, to show the Zapatistas he had come over to their side. Emiliano probably felt safe within his own domain and arranged to receive the man, although he met strong opposition from his cronies.

The story goes that Zapata and the colonel arranged to meet but that each should bring ten men only. Zapata left his troops in Cuautla, under the command of his brother Eufemio, and went to the meeting as arranged. The renegade colonel had treacherously sneaked up a hundred men and, with them well hidden around the meeting place, he advanced with his ten men.

The hidden men began to move forward as only Indians can and by the time the conference was about half over, they rushed in shooting. Zapata, armed with a machete, rushed at the colonel, but the officer's sword went clean through the general. This happened about April 1917.

Zapata's body was exposed to public view in his home town, but his followers said it was not he as Zapata could not die. He was decapitated and the head exhibited on an iron hook at some barracks in the capital. The large reward for the murder was not paid at once, as some influential people objected to such a large sum being paid for the head only and wanted the body too, especially as the Indians said it was not Zapata. But, as Zapata's body had disappeared in the meanwhile, the claimer of the blood-money found an Indian whose body was similar to that of the general. The man was murdered, beheaded, and his body forwarded to Mexico City. The colonel was not only paid but also made a brigadier. He did not last long, however, for he was executed a few months later for plotting against the government, they said. It was rumored that the Yaqui-mestizo had tried to blackmail those who had promoted Zapata's assassination and had to pay for his perfidiousness. There is another story about Zapata's death. On or about April 17, 1917, Zapata was shot while entering as a guest at the hacienda of another recreant.

With Zapata gone, the Zapata movement, also called *Zapatismo,* came practically to a halt as his brother could not handle it. The Zapatistas broke up gradually into small bands but continued to harass the government with petty banditry.

Tales of Zapata's adventures against the White Man are handed down from father to son and the crimes he committed have become great deeds of valor. These legends proved fatal to many a man who dared to venture too far into the region so full of his memories. Their bodies were found, and it puzzled the police, for they were usually shot by silver bullets, which Zapata in his heyday sported in his guns.

Many Indians, scattered far and wide in southern Mexico, declared they had seen Zapata years after his death riding alone through the hills and mountains at night. These men also show silver pesos which he had thrown to them in the passing, but he never spoke. Some Indians placed out food and drink here and there for Zapata, to help him along in his loneliness; others kept certain patios swept clean for his use, and huts were at his disposal in the mountains for many years after his death, and might still be. His name is often mentioned in whispers because he had become almost a divine creature, a living spirit of the people, that might never die. He is a demi-god-hero who some day might take his place in that mystic empyreal sphere, the abode of the Indian gods of Morelos.

The End of Serrano

General Francisco Serrano, so often mentioned in this book when a colonel, became Minister of War under President Obregon, although he had a most unsavory reputation. When Calles took over the presidency he made him governor of the Federal District, although he had gambled away large sums of government money at some public Casino. Later Serrano and General Arnulfo Gomez were both candidates for the presidency. When they found themselves sitting alone, far out on the limb of the political tree, and without financial support, they revolted against the government. Calles, however, soon defeated them, and both these renegades, who wished to be president, were shot.

The End of Calles

General Plutarco Elias Calles took part in the revolution from the beginning. He had been a school-teacher, but some of his enemies said he was a bartender. Be this as it may he was, nevertheless a capable man. When Obregon's presidential term was running out, many believed that General Benjamin Hill would succeed him, but Hill died suddenly, and there were rumors that he had been poisoned. General Calles, a close friend of Obregon, was nominated instead and inaugurated December 1, 1924. He retired to his home in Cuernavaca in 1928, but he found it difficult to keep out of politics and was suddenly exiled to the United States and died there in 1945.

*Murdered and exiled presidents and vice-presidents
between 1911 and 1929.*

President Diaz, exiled 1911; Vice President Corral, exiled 1911; Provisional President de la Barra, exiled 1911; President Madero, murdered 1913; Vice-President Suarez, murdered 1913; President Huerta, exiled 1914; President interim Carbajal, exiled 1914; President Carranza, murdered 1920; President interim de la Huerta, exiled 1924; President Obregon, murdered 1928; President Calles, exiled 1929. (Four murdered and seven exiled in eighteen years.)

The End of Obregon

General Alvaro Obregon was elected president in 1920, and General Calles succeeded him in 1924. Toward the end of Calles' four years as president the Revolutionary Party realized that another strong man must be nominated and picked Obregon. But as the law did not permit the re-election of a president, a special Act was passed permitting him to run for a second term.

About ten days before his inauguration a banquet was given in Obregon's honor near the capital on July 17, 1928. During the festivities a member of the *Cristidos* assassinated Obregon with a bullet from behind, while he sat at the table in front of all those present.

The End of Lucio Blanco

General Blanco, who commanded Obregon's best cavalry, was a very popular man with troops and civilians alike. Obregon seemed hampered in his judgment of Blanco because of the jealousy created over this popularity. Both Carranza and Obregon in their attempt to side-track their best general, in the same manner as they had previously dealt with General Felipe Angeles, forced Blanco to break away for them. Lucio Blanco was eventually shot while swimming across a river on horse-back and thus another candidate for the presidency was eliminated.

The Rebels in Power

The pernicious abuse by the upper class through centuries, equally vehemently displayed during the revolution, boomeranged and hit the arrogant ruling caste with full force in their weakest spot—their land. Rebel leaders, some with their backs covered with welts and deep scars made at the hacienda whipping-post, came to power and enacted Land Reforms which made the hair of the opulent landlords stand on end.

When the Constitution of 1917 was written, it reiterated practically the Reform Laws of Benito Juarez, with bitter memories of the past manifesting themselves because it declared among other things that, "All land taken from the Peons and Indians is to be returned."

The clergy, not all but many of them, ignored the New Constitution and fought all agrarian movements beneficial to the Peon-Indian. They also accused the government schools of teaching atheism, socialism and worst of all, Protestantism.

472

The New Land Reform program hit the *cientificos* very hard as they owned vast regions of the best land. They cried out loud for aid in the United States which they had no right to do. But nothing was mentioned about how the land was obtained; how the millions of free men and women had lost their land; how untold thousands had been flogged and executed because they objected to this treatment, nor was there a mention how the Indians had been sold, and herded like cattle, into the slave-pens by force.

BIBLIOGRAPHY

Gruening, Ernest. *Mexico and its Heritage.*
(The Century Co., New York, 1930.)

Herring, Hubert. *History of Latin America.*
(Alfred A. Knopf, Inc., New York, 1955.)

Prescott, William H. *History of the Conquest of Mexico.* (Phillips, Sampson & Co., Boston, Mass., 1858.)

Thord-Gray, I. *Tarahumara-English, English-Tarahumara Dictionary.* (University of Miami Press, Coral Gables, Florida, 1955.)

—*Strategy and Tactics.* (For the 9th Coast Defense Command, New York, 1926.)

—*Attack and Defense in Trench Warfare.* McGraw-Hill Book Co., New York, 1917.)

—*Från Mexicos Forntid.* (From Ancient Mexico) (A. B. Gunnar Tisells Tekniska Forlag. Stockholm, Sweden, 1923.)

INDEX

Legend: (D.F.) Federal District; (f) federal; (L) lake; (M) mountain; (R) river; (rebel) rebel; (T) town; (V) village.

Acaponeta (T) Nayarit 13, 115, 127, 219, 220, 222, 225, 228-9, 235-6, 240, 244, 246-7, 249, 277, 358

Acaponeta (R) Nayarit 224, 226

Acatan (V) Durango 125

Acosta, Col. Miguel (rebel; mentioned constantly)

Adios (good-bye, adieu)

Agrarian Bill of 1915 459

Aguapan (V) Nayarit 278

Agua Prieta (T) Sonora 463-465

Aguascaliente (T & State) 462

Aguilar, Gen. Candido (rebel) 99

Ahuacatlan (T) Nayarit 315

Ahualulco (T) Jalisco 315, 318, 330

Ahuizculco (V) Jalisco 318, 319, 322

Ajusco (V & Volcano) D.F. 398-9, 424-5

Alamillo, Capt. (rebel) 252

Alica (V) Nayarit 278

Altata (T) Sinaloa 110, 197

Alvarado, Gen. (rebel) 92, 99

Ameca (T) Jalisco 330, 331

Angeles, Gen. Felipe (rebel) 78, 79, 99, 263-4, 268, 432-3, 463, 465-6, 472

Apaches (of northern Chihuahua) 33, 42, 44, 69, 91, 210, 235

Arms embargo 108

Arriero (burro-driver, muleteer)

Arroyo (dry or almost dry gully; narrow ravine) 177

478

San Sebastian (V) northern Jalisco 289-291, 295, 297-8, 305

San Sebastian (V) southern Jalisco 346

Sanchez, Capt. (rebel) 236, 252, 254, 277

Sanchez, Gen. (rebel) 460

Sanguanuey Volcano Nayarit 278

Santa Catarina (V) Morelos 404

Santa Catarina (V) northern Jalisco 296

Santa Cruz (V) Jalisco 330-1

Santa Rosa (V) Sonora 92

Santiago (R) Nayarit 117, 121, 125, 248, 278, 312

Santo Domingo (V) Morelos 417

Sapelio (V) Chihuahua 52

Sayelota (V) Nayarit 237

Sayula (T) Jalisco 346

Sayula (L) Jalisco 343-4

Seri Indians Sonora 90-1

Serrano, Col. Francisco (rebel; often mentioned)

Showers (an American in Sinaloa) 207

Sierra Cordorniges (Guanajuato 362

Sierra Guanajuato 357

Sierra Huicholes, in northern Jalisco (part of Sierra Madre)

Sierra Nayarit (part of Sierra Madre) 248, 309

Sierra del Tigre, southern Jalisco 345

Sinaloa, State of

Smallpox 103, 105, 109

Smith Brothers (rebel fliers) 74

Solares, Gen. Juan (f) 230, 232

Sonora, State of

Soto, Col. (rebel) 252

Spaniards (See gachupines and peninsulares)

Suárez. José Mario P. (rebel) 128, 214, 456, 471

Sukuruame (Tarahumara: wizards, witches) 170

Tahonitas (V) Chihuahua 145

Tacuba (V) D.F. 381

Tacubaya (T) D.F. 393, 398

Tala (V) Jalisco 316-318

Talamantes, Col. (Villa rebel) 52

Temaxcatio (V) Guanajuato 362

Tampico (T) Tamaulipas 99, 208, 214, 216

Tanhuato (V) Michoacan 349, 352, 363

Taquitzata (V) Jalisco 286

Tarahumara Indians in western Chihuahua (rebels; often mentioned, especially in Chapter IV)

Tasajera (V) Sinaloa 137-8

Tecamachalco (V) D.F. 383

ATLANTIC PRINTERS